W9-DJA-071

THE WOMEN OF COLONIAL LATIN AMERICA

SUSAN MIGDEN SOCOLOW

Emory University

CAMBRIDGE
UNIVERSITY PRESS

PUBLISHED BY THE PRESS SYNDICATE OF THE UNIVERSITY OF CAMBRIDGE
The Pitt Building, Trumpington Street, Cambridge, United Kingdom

CAMBRIDGE UNIVERSITY PRESS
The Edinburgh Building, Cambridge CB2 2RU, UK   http://www.cup.cam.ac.uk
40 West 20th Street, New York, NY 10011-4211, USA   http://www.cup.org
10 Stamford Road, Oakleigh, Melbourne 3166, Australia
Ruiz de Alarcón 13, 28014 Madrid, Spain

First published 2000

Printed in the United States of America

Typeface Goudy Regular 10.5/13 pt.   *System* QuarkXPress [BTS]

A catalog record for this book is available from the British Library.

Library of Congress Cataloging in Publication data
Socolow, Susan Migden, 1941–
The women of colonial Latin America / Susan Migden Socolow.
p.   cm. – (New approaches to the Americas)
ISBN 0-521-47052-8 (hb). – ISBN 0-521-47642-9 (pb)
1. Women – Latin America – History.   2. Women – Latin America – Social
conditions.   3. Sex role – Latin America – History.   I. Title.   II. Series.
HQ1460.5.S64   2000
305.4′ 098 – dc21   99-29134
                                                            CIP

ISBN   0 521 47052 8   hardback
ISBN   0 521 47642 9   paperback

To the memory of my two mothers:
    Edith Ginsberg Migden
    Edith Gutman Socolow

    Y la de mi quasi madre:
    Ora Waisman Diamond

Contents

ILLUSTRATIONS

Following Page 114

ACKNOWLEDGMENTS

In writing this book I have drawn widely and deeply from the published research of other scholars. Although I have chosen to keep footnotes and other scholarly apparatus to a minimum, I wish to acknowledge the contribution of all those listed in the "Suggested Further Readings" section. While not always in agreement with their conclusions, this book would not have been possible without their scholarship.

I also want to express my special thanks to Stuart Schwartz and Ann Twinam, both of whom gave me most useful suggestions. Students and colleagues at Emory, at the Ecole des Hautes Etudes, at various universities in Argentina, and at the Universidad Nacional de Montevideo have also added immeasurably to this work. The staff of the Emory University Library has also been most helpful.

My greatest gratitude, as always, goes to my husband, Daniel Socolow, who continues to provide endless support, love, and an anything-but-boring life after all these years.

WHY WOMEN?

Gender is crucial to individual identity and, in all societies, to the roles individuals will play and the experiences they will have. The position of men and women in any society is a social construct, not a natural state. Each society and every social group has a culture that defines the roles and rules of masculinity and femininity; by conforming to these definitions an individual becomes a "legitimate" man or woman.

The goal of this book is to examine these roles and rules and thus understand the variety and limitations of the female experience in colonial Latin America. One overarching limitation in both Spanish and Portuguese America was the existence of a patriarchal social organization. In the New World as in the Old, a clear sexual hierarchy placed women below men. By law and by tradition, men held the lion's share of power in government, religion, and society. Furthermore, a man, particularly a father, was supreme within his family. Legally, all those living within the household were required to obey him.

In this society women were defined first and foremost by their sex and only secondarily by their race or social class. In many colonial documents the lack of attention to women's race and class suggests that these attributes were malleable. Sex was not. Indeed it can be argued that sex was the most important factor in determining a person's status in society. Nonetheless gender alone does not explain the various experiences of women in colonial Latin America. We must also keep in mind the importance of race, class, demography, life course, spatial variations, local economy, norm and reality, and change over time.

Latin America was a unique region. Here, beginning in the sixteenth century, three peoples and their cultures were brought in close proximity with one another. Indigenous Americans, Africans, and European

Iberians were not on an equal footing, for by conquering America and importing African slaves, Europeans represented the dominant culture, the culture of the conquerors. Nonetheless, in Latin American colonial societies the histories of three major groups of people were intertwined. But race in colonial Latin America was even more complex than these three major racial groups. Over time, new and socially distinct racial categories were created – mestizo, mulatto, zambo, and their multiple variants – each with its individual social role and societal expectations. These expectations or stereotypes would at times provide women with both differing opportunities and limitations.

Colonial Latin America was also a society of clearly delimited social hierarchies. These hierarchies constantly affected the lives women led, whether at the top, middle, or bottom of the social scale. Acceptable behavior for a poor woman, daughter of a lamplighter or a weaver, was quite different from that for the daughter of a titled nobleman or a powerful miner.

Gender, race, and class functioned together. These overlapping categories produced situations in which a person's position in society could be both complex and contradictory. Because several elements determined what a woman could or could not do, one cannot simply consider one of these variables alone without keeping in mind other important factors. Perhaps foremost among these additional variables was demography. The number of females and males living at any one time and place was of primary importance. The ratio of men to women (differential sex ratio) could enhance or limit women's choices. In societies with a surplus of men, for example, women were a relatively scarce commodity and tended to have a greater field from which to select marriage partners. The relative number of males to females also varied by age and was usually the result of death rates and patterns of immigration. Regions that supplied migrants to developing zones often had an acute shortage of young men of marriageable age.

Life course also affected women, for their experiences changed as they moved through childhood, courtship, marriage or spinsterhood, motherhood, widowhood, and old age. Moreover a woman's responsibilities and power might vary greatly depending on her position within a household or family. For example, the wife of the head of a household probably had a far greater role in the running of her home than did a spinster aunt or an orphaned niece who lived under the same roof. A woman's role also changed when she became the head of a household or family.

Although all of the regions under study belonged to either the Spanish or Portuguese crown, important spatial variations also affected women's experiences. Regions differed in importance: Mexico and Peru from the earliest days of Spanish settlement were the centers of the empire, whereas Chile and the Río de la Plata tended to be more isolated. With respect to racial composition, some areas, such as the Andean highlands, maintained a relatively large indigenous population throughout the colonial period, whereas other zones, often along the coast, developed a large African American population. Women's lives were also influenced by the type of space they inhabited – whether they lived in cities, in rural zones, or along the fringes of the empire.

The local economy also had an impact on women's roles and women's relative power. The overall prosperity or poverty of a region could make a difference in women's lives. Elite women in seventeenth-century Mexico City, for example, lived lives of far greater opulence and diversion than did elite women in poorer regions, such as Santo Domingo. The nature of the local economy – agricultural, mining, or proto-industrial – as well as the specific goods produced often affected women, especially those forced to work for a living.

In these societies, there was often a gap between the social ideal, the model to which the society theoretically aspired, and the female-lived reality. To some degree, all women were subject to an ideal standard for female behavior. While this standard reflected social and racial variations, it was always clearly different from the standard for male behavior. But although both the law and cultural norms set standards, the experience of any one woman or group of women might vary significantly from the stated ideal. We can also ask how and when women were able to violate these standards and examine to what degree, and under what conditions, women challenged these culture ideals.

Women's experiences in colonial Latin America changed over time. As the region moved from a society of conquest to one of stable institutions and Counter-Reformation Catholicism, and then to a society of modest enlightened reforms, both the female ideal and the female reality shifted.

My goal is not to present colonial women as either empowered or victimized by their culture. All people live in their culture and usually act in accord with the prevailing values of their time. Most women, and men, do not think of themselves as victims of those values or as rebels defying social norms. Instead of seeking heroines or victims, this book hopes to understand women in their time and their society, without judging them by the standards of our political or social agendas. Only thus can we penetrate colonial society while illuminating questions of gender, power, and race.

This book begins by examining the role of women in the three societies that later would be joined by the Iberian voyages of discovery – European, African, and American. Chapter 1 reviews the legal and religious gender ideologies as well as the social realities that shaped the lives of women in the Iberian Peninsula. The position of women in the indigenous societies that would eventually come under the political domination of Spain and Portugal, as well as the role of women in traditional African societies, is reviewed in Chapter 2. Chapter 3 analyzes the experiences of indigenous women within the New World through conquest and colonization. In Chapter 4 we follow the migration of European women to America, examining their experience and the effect of their arrival. Chapter 5 concentrates on the role of women within marriage and the family. An analysis of the position and power of elite women within colonial society follows in Chapter 6. Chapter 7 examines the religious roles of colonial women and considers those who were tied to the church, both formally and informally. Next Chapter 8 considers the economic roles of women, concentrating especially on the female presence in the colonial work force. Slave women, an involuntary labor force, are the focus of Chapter 9. The book then considers women who deviated from socially acceptable patterns in Chapter 10 and concludes by examining the gradual changes produced by the eighteenth-century Enlightenment reforms in Chapter 11.

CHAPTER 1

Iberian Women in the Old
World and the New

There are very few noble women who are beautiful, wise, soft, cap-
tivating, rational, and clean in all things that pertain to women
and who are not covetous and envious of that which other women
have. There are few women who are sincere and who do not con-
tradict everything a man may say, do, or dictate, but rather are
happy to accommodate his desires. But even though noble women
with good attributes are difficult to find, men cannot live without
them. Therefore, men must learn the ways to acquire their love.[1]

At the time of the discovery of the New World, a queen sat on the
throne of Spain. Isabel I was a strong, even dominant woman, as some
have argued. A fanatical defender of the Holy Roman Catholic faith,
she was instrumental in imposing religious unity on both her own
country and neighboring Portugal. At the same time, she fiercely maintained the juridical independence of Castile and established the laws
of her kingdom as the foundation of Latin American jurisprudence. But
Spain itself was the product of several traditions as well as the con-
flicting experiences of warrior and mercantile societies. Church, law,
and tradition all affected the role of women in the Iberian Peninsula
and by extension in the American colonies.

Because both Spain and Portugal had experienced years of Moslem
conquest followed by years of Christian reconquest, the position of
women in the Iberian Peninsula was quite different from that throughout the rest of Europe. The role of women in these societies reflected

---

[1] An anonymous fifteenth-century author, in Michael Solomon, trans. and ed., *The
Mirror of Coitus* (Madison, Wis.: Hispanic Seminary of Medieval Studies, 1990),
30.

the combined effect of Islam and Roman Catholicism. On the one hand, the Islamic ideal of the cloistered, sheltered woman, the woman protected in the home or the harem, continued to resonate in Iberian society, as did the strong link between female virginity and honor. On the other hand, the gap between the idealized conduct of women and their real behavior was sizable. Women in Christian society, for example, especially the rural peasants, enjoyed a good degree of independence. Furthermore, women in Iberian societies benefited from legal rights that went far beyond those accorded to other European women at the time.

Spanish thinkers and writers such as Fray Martín de Córdoba, Juan Luis Vives, Fray Luis de León, and Juan de la Cerda influenced the gender ideology that conditioned the official fifteenth- and sixteenth-century view of women. All opined on the nature of women and all agreed that women were less intelligent, rational, and wise than men, a result of a nature governed by flesh rather than spirit. Intellectually inferior and possessing only limited understanding, women were constitutionally incapable of treating matters of substance. Because of their natural foolishness, women were admonished to keep silent. Furthermore their lack of mental acuity made it unnecessary to teach them to write, although reading instruction sufficient to manage devotional literature was acceptable.

Not only mentally inferior, women were also morally fragile and prone to error. Their fleshly nature meant that women tended to have uncontrollable carnal appetites and could little resist temptation. They were particularly susceptible to evil and easily swayed by the devil. Unable to govern their own passions and behavior, women were dangerous to themselves, their families, and society at large if uncontrolled or uncloistered. Popular culture and literature not only accepted this vision of women; it also stressed that women were inconsistent, gossipy, overly emotional, irrational, changeable, weak, prone to error, deceitful, and profligate.

Although some sixteenth- and seventeenth-century Spanish and Portuguese writers emphasized the role of women within the family, the ideal of Counter-Reformation society was to keep women under control through enclosure. Only by remaining in their homes, convents, orphanages, *recogimientos*, prisons, or other institutions could women be protected from their "natural weaknesses." Only when placed under male religious guidance could women's unbridled sexuality be prevented from wreaking havoc on society. The growing strictures placed on women was for their own good, the good of men, and the survival of Christian society.

Central to this gender ideology was paternalism, a belief in the dominant position of the father over his wife and children. Just as paternalism ordered the relationship between the monarch and his subjects or between the pope and his flock, it shaped that between men and women. Men were by definition morally superior to women, whereas women, because of their natural fragility, needed restrictive regulations defining their conduct. A man's role was to guide and control, a woman's to obey, whether within the context of kinship, marriage, or the church. As a result, a woman's place in society was defined primarily by her relationship to a man or a religious institution. Her most important social attribute was that she was the wife of a particular man, the daughter of so-and-so, or a nun.

The teachings of the Roman Catholic Church regarding premarital purity, marriage, and the concepts of male and female honor also greatly influenced gender ideology. The church decided what constituted acceptable sexuality, with whom and how. Believing that marriage should be the norm for all but the most pious, the church stressed the importance of female virginity before marriage and chastity after. Although there was no room for female sexual pleasure outside of marriage, sexual relations between husband and wife were a vital part within marriage. In theory women had the right to demand that their husbands have sexual relations with them. Indeed both marriage partners were encouraged to perform their *debito matrimonial* (conjugal duty) in order to accomplish the biblical injunction to "be fruitful and multiply."

Furthermore, the church's concept of sin stressed the sins of the flesh. Sexual abstinence was a virtue and too much pleasure in sexual acts, even within marriage, was by definition sinful. This view was further enhanced in the mid-sixteenth century by the Counter-Reformation, which stressed the link between sex and sin. Ideas about female virtue were strengthened by an Iberian Christian culture that emphasized one female figure, the Virgin Mary, an idealized female distanced from any sexual contact or experience. Paradoxically, although her condition as a mother "without blemish" made her impossible to emulate, she was the model for all female behavior, combining sexual purity, perfect motherhood, stoic suffering, and sacrifice.

The church, in conjunction with a woman's male kinsfolk, was charged with the important task of inculcating socially acceptable behavior. Men, both clerical and lay, defined a woman's conduct and enforced their definition, and the misconduct of women was often seen as the private business of men. At the same time, the church worked to protect women's virtue and to control female sexuality by the use of the confessional, ecclesiastical visits, enclosure, and the Inquisition. A good woman was to be virtuous, pure, resigned to her lot in life, passively obeying her father, brother, husband, and confessor.

In addition to religion and gender ideology, Iberian society embraced a set of social codes in which honor figured prominently. For women, honor was tied to private chastity and public conduct. A woman's chastity was to be reflected in both her appearance and behavior, for "good" women dressed modestly and were not erotic in their bearing. Instead, being meek in behavior, they avoided all and any situations that could lead them astray and sought semi-seclusion or at least the company of female family members of high repute. Honorable women were those who displayed *vergüenza* by going to church frequently, living with a respected family or in a convent, and generally leading an "honest and sheltered life."

A man could earn honor by conforming to the social ideals of his status group while a woman could jeopardize it through the frailties of her flesh. According to prevailing ideas, women were divided into the "virtuous" and the "shamed," with the dividing line between these two groups closely linked to female sexuality. In theory there were no gray areas in this moral code, and any woman who sought sexual pleasure outside of marriage was the same as a prostitute.

Because the honor of the entire family depended on the sexual purity of its females, women's sexuality was subjected to severe control. But because not all families were equal, some had more honor to defend than others. Control of women's sexuality therefore differed according to social group. In Spain and in America there was little direct control over the sexuality of lower-class women, for they and their families were viewed as having no honor to protect.

From the late fifteenth century on, another attribute of honor was "purity of blood" (*limpieza de sangre*), the proven absence of Jewish or Moorish ancestry. In America, people of African descent would soon be added to the list of those with impure blood. In both the Old World and the New, male and female lineages would be scrutinized for impurities, but female virtue was of paramount concern in assuring that no impure blood entered a family's veins. Control of female sexuality, along with racial endogamy and an insistence on legitimacy, became the socially accepted method of guaranteeing that one's children enjoyed purity of blood.

Despite these values and stereotypes that placed women in a clearly subordinate position, the women of Castile – and, by extension, those of Spanish America – had comparatively greater legal rights that other European women. Although their legal condition was far from equal to that of men, Castilian and Portuguese laws were exceptionally fair to women. This was especially true for laws of inheritance: a complex formula stipulated which males and females were legal heirs. Indeed, inheritance depended on legitimacy and the degree of relationship to the deceased, not gender; if a woman was a closer blood relative, she was preferred over a man. Furthermore it was impossible to disinherit one's legitimate progeny, and all women regardless of their marital status could inherit and own property.

Iberian law also called for equal inheritance for all heirs of the same degree. This meant that heirs inherited irrespective of their sex, age, or order of birth. In other words, inheritance was gender blind. This principle of equality was highly beneficial to women. But paradoxically women from the wealthiest families in the Iberian Peninsula and America were at a disadvantage if their forebears had created entails (*mayorazgos*), which reserved the estate for the eldest male. In matters of mayorazgo, women could inherit titles and properties only when there was no surviving male heir.

With the exception of mayorazgo, women inheriting, owning, buying, selling, exchanging, and donating property had the same basic legal rights as men. Women not only inherited property; they could also bequeath it, thus transferring property to their heirs. Moreover, on the death of their husbands, widows were entitled to half of the property belonging to the couple. Widows also inherited the right of *patria potestad*, the legal control over the lives and property of their minor children. Even in marriage a woman's property remained hypothetically distinct from that of her husband, and as a result children inherited separately from their mother and father. If a married woman died without children, her parents, siblings, and cousins, not her husband, had first claim on her estate. Tied to the concept of separate maternal and paternal property inheritance was that of separate maternal and paternal lineage; in Spain and Spanish America children took the last names of both their father and mother.

The granting of a dowry at the time of marriage was another way to transfer property to women. Dowries, given to help support the expenses of marriage, were legally an advance payment of a daughter's eventual inheritance. The grant, usually made in the form of goods and cash, theoretically belonged to the woman, although the actual control of the property usually fell to her husband. But he could not alienate any part of the dowry and was responsible for preserving it as best he could. In Spain as in America, a woman who believed her husband guilty of malfeasance could bring him to court, demanding that her dowry be returned to her or administered by someone else. As early as 1693, for example, a Michoacán woman sued to reclaim her dowry, removing it from the hands of her spendthrift husband. Upon the death of her husband, repayment of the dowry to this widow took precedence over all other obligations. If a bride died childless, the dowry was returned to her parents.

The rights of single women were especially marked in Castilian society, and, like single men, unmarried women reached the legal age of majority at twenty-five. Paradoxically social pressures worked to encourage marriage, an institution that limited a woman's legal independence. Unlike men, women's legal rights were affected by their marital status, for marriage deprived women of a separate juridical personality, transforming them into the legal wards of their husbands. Married women needed their husband's permission to do what single women were free to do – buy, sell, give away their property, and draw up a will. Nonetheless, because both church and state were determined to safeguard the institution of wedlock, marriage also bestowed social status and limited power on women.

Marriage in the Iberian Peninsula was a legal, ritual, liturgical, and sacramental matter, governed by the rules of canon and civil law, which in turn were based on Roman law. Holy wedlock was also a legal contract that joined a man and woman in a household for purposes of sexual intercourse, procreation, and general cooperation. Marriage was a necessary condition to bear legitimate children – that is, children who were acknowledged by both parents, entitled to support from both parents, and legally able to inherit from both parents.

Because marriage was a religious sacrament, it was governed by the Roman Catholic Church. The church not only performed the marriage; it set the requirements for a marriage to be legally binding. Canon or church law established that a man or woman could have only one spouse at a time (monogamy) and defined eligible marriage partners. One could not marry one's father, godfather, or brother; first cousins could wed only if granted a special dispensation. Marriage of women below the age of twelve and men younger than fourteen was also forbidden, as was marriage to anyone who had taken a prior vow of chastity. Furthermore, a marriage was valid only if both husband and wife had freely chosen to take the sacrament. In theory Roman Catholic doctrine provided a strong bulwark against forcing women into marriages they opposed.

Matrimony was in fact a two-step process, beginning with engagement, a legally binding agreement in which the couple gave its "word of marriage in the future." Customarily this mutual promise was symbolized by an exchange of gifts. Within months (or sometimes years), engagement was followed by the marriage ceremony itself in which husband and wife gave their "word of marriage in the present." Until the mid-sixteenth-century reforms of the Council of Trent, both engagement and marriage ceremonies could be performed by the couple themselves as long as two witnesses were present. It is clear that for many there was little distinction between these two ceremonies. A promise to marry was as binding as a marriage itself, and many couples began sexual relations as soon as they had formally become engaged.

In the mid-sixteenth-century the Council of Trent drew up new, more stringent rules of betrothal and marriage. From then on, the church examined prospective newlyweds to determine whether they were not already related, whether they were entering freely into marriage, whether they were physically able to consummate the union, and whether they were already married to another. To end the practice of clandestine marriage, the council mandated that there be a public reading of the banns, that the couple be joined in Holy Matrimony by a priest, and that the ceremony be witnessed by at least two adults.

Iberian Catholic traditions such as choosing godparents for the newlywed couple continued to be observed. If the marriage was the bride's first, an additional veiling ceremony (velación), underlining the woman's virginity, was also performed by the priest. The liturgy of marriage also reinforced the notion of bridal purity and the woman's position within the new family. According to the marriage liturgy a wife was subservient to her husband and duty bound to obey him.

To be valid a marriage also had to be consummated. Marriage gave a man exclusive sexual rights over his wife. So clear was this conjugal right that only adultery by a wife or betrothed woman justified a man's abandoning a woman. Because the Catholic Church was highly favorable to marriage, even after the Council of Trent canon law made it relatively easy to marry but fairly difficult to unmarry. Instead of the easy divorce and remarriage of Roman law, Roman Catholic marriage allowed for only annulment or separation.

Theological treatises and confessional manuals both wrestled with the question of how men and women were to behave within the bounds of holy matrimony. Some authors saw marriage as a contract between two parties in which justice and reason was of central importance, while others viewed marriage as a mystical union, stressing the bonds of love. All underlined that marriage was a reciprocal, although unequal, arrangement between a man and a woman. Within the union a man's obligation was to honor, love, protect, and provide for his wife; a woman's obligation was to obey her husband. A man had right to punish his wife when she went astray, although the punishment was to be moderate. Thus marriage linked subordination with love, for marriage was a contract in which women were promised material support in return for their near total obedience. Marriage relationships were hierarchical; good wives were submissive and followed their husbands lead in furthering his and their family interests. This was the social ideal that both church and state hoped would be accepted by both men and women.

Marriage was also viewed as a partnership as reflected in Iberian "conjugal economics." The assets of marriage consisted of three parts: the property of the wife brought into marriage in the form of a dowry, that of the husband, and all property earned by the couple during the marriage. This last asset, the *financiales*, belonged equally to both husband and wife for it was assumed that the wife joined fully in the couple's economic fortune whether or not she owned property herself. The wife was thereby recognized as a full partner in supporting the couple and in making a useful and productive contribution to the marriage.

After the death of her spouse, a widow of any age was considered independent and free to remarry, but a widow who remarried too quickly (within less than one year) was looked upon askance. Fast remarriage raised suspicions as to her first husband's death, her comportment during marriage and widowhood, and the possible paternity of her children. Although widows had full legal power to act in their late husband's stead, they often entrusted this power to close male kin. It was also common for a widow to return to her family home.

Both crown and church encouraged marriage, but less formal sexual relations were common. In medieval Spain concubinage (*barragania*) between single or widowed people was extremely common and widely tolerated. By definition concubines were to be single people (*solteros*) who could have married had they so desired, but several cases of barragania involving priests suggests that this was not always so. Concubinage was a regular and recognized relationship, formalized by a notarized contract that laid out mutual obligations and responsibilities. These contracts stipulated the existence of a monogamous relationship and usually spelled out economic responsibilities for and protection of the woman as well as the inheritance rights of future children. It is not clear whether women enjoyed equal rights under barragania or, as suggested by some, that they were completely and legally under the control of their lovers. One major difference between barragania and marriage was the temporal nature of the former, for barragania contracts could be annulled by another notarized contract mutually declaring the relationship null and void. The widespread acceptance of concubinage was reflected in the ease with which the children of most of these unions could be legitimized.

Medieval Spanish laws did not consider barragania to be a crime, but the Catholic Church did believe it to be a sin. In addition to occurring without the blessing of the church, the church railed against barragania because it was a dissolvable relationship, motivated they believed by a search for pleasure and not intent upon procreation. The church increasingly grew more militant in its opposition to concubinage. By the late fifteenth century couples frequently dissolved their unions toward the end of their lives, thus hoping to remove a sin from their souls. The Council of Trent formally ended barragania, but, in the popular imagination and the behavior of the masses, concubinage continued to be a viable alternative to marriage. In spite of the reforming zeal of the Counter-Reformation church, in the Iberian Peninsula the medieval custom of barrangania continued to exist.

There were, of course, other types of nonmarital relationships including adultery and prostitution. Because Iberian law distinguished the degree of illegitimacy of children born of each kind of nonmarital union, it assigned a sliding social stigma to these children and to the women who had borne them. In addition to the "natural children" born of concubinage, there were children born of adultery, children born of prostitutes, children born of a concubine who had a relationship with another man, children born of an incestuous relationship, children of bigamists, and children fathered by priests.

The church worked to ban these "irregular" sexual relations, with somewhat mixed results. Inquisition records suggest that for at least fifty years after the reforms of the Council of Trent, women as well as men interpreted the relationship between sex and sin in far lustier ways than the church. Over and over again, common people claimed that it was not a sin, and certainly not a mortal sin, to make love. Some went as far as to give theological justifications for their unbridled sexuality. A widow who had had several children with a married man pointed out that "God had ordered people to multiple and have children, and thus it was no sin."[2] Some women justified their extramarital exploits by explaining that copulation was not a sin if you were married, while Bárbola Péres, an innkeeper from the Córdoba region, argued that "if her husband were here it would be a mortal sin to betray him, but as he was absent and the other man a bachelor, it was not a mortal sin to make love to him."[3] Still others argued that sex between the unwed was quite acceptable.

As a result, illegitimacy rates in Spain were among the highest in Europe. In at least one district of late-sixteenth-century Seville, one-quarter of all reported births were to unmarried women. During the seventeenth century, the illegitimacy rate in Valladolid ranged from one-fifth to one-fourth of all births. In addition, growing numbers of infants, many of them illegitimate, were deposited in institutions created to harbor abandoned children.

The social reality faced by women who transgressed the accepted social mores varied greatly by the nature of the sexual relationship and social class. While an easy acceptance of sexuality endured in the popular mind, the church, the state, and the Inquisition worked to root out what they viewed as sexually objectionable behavior. Female adultery was especially unacceptable, for although both spouses were duty-bound to be faithful, a wife's adultery constituted a basic transgression of the social and moral order. Adultery was a sin and an insult to the honor of the husband and his family, and it was punished harshly. Often the choice of punishment – a fine, public humiliation, or death – was left to the husband, as was his decision to absolve his adulterous wife. The woman was usually sent to a convent. There she was both pro-

[2] Archivo Histórico Nacional (Madrid), Inquisición, Córdoba, Legajo 1856, Documento 3, 1569–1570, quoted in Alain Saint-Saëns, "'It is not a Sin!': Making Love according to the Spaniards in Early Modern Spain," in Alain Saint-Saëns, ed., Sex and Love in Golden Age Spain (New Orleans: University Press of the South, 1996), 15.

[3] Archivo Histórico Nacional (Madrid), Inquisición, Córdoba, Legajo 1856, Documento 8, 1571–1572, quoted in Saint-Saëns, "'It is not a Sin!,'" 17.

tected from further sin and given ample opportunity to repent. Because adultery was also believed to be the first step toward female prostitution, women whose adultery resulted in a stable relationship with their lovers were usually punished less harshly than those who had more fleeting liaisons.

Increasingly in seventeenth-century Spain and Portugal, the church was more and more successful in its campaign of sexual repression. Using the confessional, a growing missionary movement, preachers, and the Inquisition, the church rooted "unnatural" sex out of Iberian life and culture. The official culture became one fixated on sexual taboos, and sexuality was repressed in life, art, and literature. At the same time religious moralists extolled female celibacy and glorified religious women who demonstrated self-loathing of the human body by practicing sadistic forms of penitence. For example, Mariana de Jesus, a member of the Third Order of Franciscans, was praised for hitting her breasts with stones "so many times that they became swollen and gushed blood," and for frequently scourging her naked body so that her blood splattered the wall of her bedroom.[4]

We do not know the end result of these campaigns against sexuality on the female psyche. We do know that in Spain and Portugal women continued to be housewives, mothers, stepmothers, nuns or beatas, mistresses, unwed mothers, and prostitutes. This multiplicity of women's roles continued in Latin American after the creation of a colonial society, as did a legal system that benefited women and a gender ideology that saw them as weak. Also imported into the colonial world was the Iberian dichotomy between good and evil women. But unlike Spain and Portugal the colonial world would be far more ethnically diverse, and the division between good and evil tended to be superimposed over ethnoracial categories. Since at least the mid-thirteenth century, enslaved women (and men) of African, Moorish, and Morisco descent as well as free people of color had been present in the Iberian Peninsula; however, in America Europeans would be greatly outnumbered by people of color. It was also in America where European or white women would be perceived as capable of upholding high moral standards, whereas women of color would be presumed to have evil habits.

[4] Archivo Histórico Nacional (Madrid), Inquisición, Sevilla, Legajo 2075, Documento 31, 1623.

CHAPTER 2

Before Columbus: Women in Indigenous America and Africa

Aztec birth ritual: "Thou wilt be in the heart of the home, thou wilt go nowhere, thou wilt nowhere become a wanderer, thou becomest the banked fire, the hearth stones. Here our lord planteth thee, burieth thee. And thou wilt become fatigued, thou wilt become tired; thou art to provide water, to grind maize, to drudge; thou art of sweat by the ashes, by the hearth."[1]

Andean burial ritual: "The women have their spindles and skeins of spun cottons, the men their tacllas or hoes to work the fields, or the weapons they used in war."[2]

[Among the Bijago] the women build the houses and work in the fields, and they fish and gather shellfish, doing all that men do elsewhere.[3]

The Iberian experience in the New World put the Spanish and Portuguese into immediate and intimate contact with peoples from two very different cultures: the indigenous inhabitants of America and Africans transported to the region as slaves. Although historians have examined the dynamics and results of the meeting of these three groups,

[1] From the Florentine Codex, in Bernardino de Sahagún, *General History of the Things of New Spain* (Santa Fé: School of American Research, 1950–1982), 6:33:172–173.

[2] Pablo José de Arriaga, *Extirpación de la idolatria del Piru* (1621) (Madrid: Ediciones Atlas, 1968), 27–28.

[3] Andre Alvarez d'Alamada, *Brief Treatise on the Rivers of Guinea* (c. 1594), trans. and ed. P. E. H. Hair (Liverpool: University of Liverpool, 1984).

few have considered the role of women in the Americas or Africa before these peoples were subjected to Iberian control.

Although Indians had inhabited America for thousands of years before the arrival of the Spaniards and Portuguese, we know very little about women in those earlier Indian societies. A multitude of Indian cultures had risen and fallen before 1492, ranging from hunting-and-gathering peoples to builders of sophisticated city-states. Because of the geographical proximity of some of these peoples, it was not unusual for one culture to borrow, adapt, or be subjected to the cultural and religious practices of a nearby people.

The information we do have is not only fragmentary but also heavily skewed toward elite women. Anthropologists, reviewing physical evidence and in the case of Mexico and Central America, codices and stela, suggest that among the Early Classic Zapotecs (200 B.C.–A.D. 600), the Late Classic Mayas (A.D. 600–900), and the Postclassic Mixtecs (A.D. 900–1200), elite women enjoyed high status and were sometimes rulers of city-states. Among a handful of female rulers of Mayan city-states were Lady Ahpo-Katun of Piedras Negras and Lady Apho-Hel of Palenque. One Mixtec codex tells the story of a female ruler who was insulted by a male ruler of another town while on a religious pilgrimage. Returning home, she changed into warrior garb, attacked the offender's town, captured him, and cut his heart out. Although female rulers and warriors were rare, elite women were important in establishing lineages of rulership and in creating dynastic alliances. Maya glyph data, for example, include many scenes with a female participating in various public activities, and genealogies trace male rulers' right to power through female members of their family.

Some recent research on Classic Teotihuacán in Central Mexico (A.D. 250–700) sheds some light on nonelite women by suggesting that when clay figurines were produced by hand, approximately 70 percent of these objects were made by women. As figurines began to be mass-produced using molds, 70 percent were made by men. Perhaps as the output of figurines became more industrialized and more economically important, women came to play a lesser role in their production.

The archaeological evidence for South American cultures is even more sketchy than for Meso-America because of the lack of indigenous literary sources. Pottery that displays elaborate scenes of Moche life, for example, rarely depicts women. When women are shown, they are either weaving or engaged in sexual activities with a man, a possible reflection of their principal activities within this Andean culture. Excavations of burial mounds in the Cochabamba area reveal that men were buried with much richer, more exotic, and more numerous goods than women, suggesting their greater social importance. Interestingly women's teeth were more worn and had more caries than did men's, reflecting perhaps women's role in producing the alcoholic drink *chicha*.

Because of a comparative richness of written sources, we know much more about those native societies which the Iberian conquerors actually observed. There are problems in using European sources for our picture of pre-Columbian societies, for we are forced to look through European eyes and can see only what and whom they chose to see. Sixteenth-century Spaniards and Portuguese were hardly disinterested observers; they were the product of a late medieval European society with specific ideas of what was "fitting" for men and for women. In the case of the Aztecs, we also have codices produced by Europeans working with Indian informants. Although these documents described Indian life, they were also produced after the conquest and probably failed to reflect local variations.

Nonetheless, gender and social status both played powerful roles in determining the position of women in all pre-Columbian cultures. A clear distinction in all societies between a privileged elite and the masses affected the role and power of women belonging to each group. Some anthropologists have theorized that the coming to power of the Incas eroded the local power held by women in earlier cultures, whereas others argue that, as the Aztecs were transformed from a wandering band of tribes to a powerful imperial nation, women were gradually but systematically excluded from political power. These interesting hypotheses, however, find little support in our knowledge of early indigenous societies.

Occasionally elite women could and did hold political power over designated regions, although they often held this power as a result of pleasing a powerful male. Although all of the major Inca political figures were men, Contarhuacho, one of the secondary wives of the Inca Huayna Capac, was named *curaca* (chief) of the Tocas and Huaylas. Her husband not only gave her control of four thousand to six thousand households but also granted her numerous household servants, including three hundred women.

Women of rank also played a role in the political and courtly life of the indigenous realms. In at least three cases, the *coya*, principal wife of the Inca ruler, advised her husband and sons in affairs of state. In

Mayan stela, the wife of a king was depicted as sitting next to him, suggesting at the very least that she was present in the governing of the
kingdom. Mayan stela also show the wife of the king participating in
bloodletting rituals believed to sustain the gods and associated with the
accession of a king or the birth of a royal child.

Although a few elite women held direct or indirect political
power, the marriage choice of the majority of noble women was a
matter of state policy and thus outside of their control. Daughters
of the Inca were routinely married to important military men or
political leaders, thus creating kinship ties and cementing alliances.
The same was true for Aztec and Maya noblewomen who were married
to the rulers of neighboring kingdoms, thus creating dynastic alliances.
Although the majority of these women probably did not have political
responsibilities, they were vital to the creation of the political fabric
of the state.

Women outside the nobility had no greater choice of marital partner
than those of the ruling elite. All pre-Columbian societies had carefully articulated rules governing the relationship between the sexes,
although these rules varied widely from one culture to another. These
rules governed who could marry whom. The Mayas, for example, prohibited marriage between a man and woman from the same kin group.
Aztecs, on the other hand, were given wives from inside or outside their
kin group, practicing both endogamous and exogamous marriage.
Among Aztec commoners, the groom's family was instrumental in
deciding on his choice of a wife, although old women called *cinhuat-
lanque* acted as go-betweens during the negotiations preceding the
actual ceremony. The marriage ceremony itself was performed at the
groom's house, symbolic of the fact that the bride was now joining
the groom's family.

Ideas about female premarital sexuality differed widely from one
culture to another. Some pre-Columbian societies controlled female
sexuality in ways strikingly similar to the Spanish. This was especially
true among the Aztecs, who expected unmarried girls to be virgins;
they were closely chaperoned to make sure that their condition did
not change before marriage. The female loss of virginity was considered to be a social and moral catastrophe leading to future marital
unhappiness. Concubinage was also severely punished among the
Aztecs, who banished both the guilty man and woman. The Incas, on
the other hand condoned and indeed, according to some sources,
encouraged premarital sexual relations for all women except the Virgins

of the Sun. Only through cohabitation before marriage could a couple judge the strength of its relationship and the probability that it would last.

All indigenous societies believed that marriage was the ideal state for women beyond the age of puberty. Among the Aztecs, for example, approximately 95 percent of all females married, an exceedingly high figure. Although historians differ as to the average age of women at the time of marriage, there is growing evidence of early marriage. Some girls were married as early as age ten, and most women were probably married before their sixteenth birthday. The average woman probably bore several children during her lifetime. Although permanent unions were the norm, Aztec society did recognize divorce.

The Aztecs and Incas allowed rulers and noblemen to have more than one wife, whereas the Maya allowed the king to have several wives and elite men to have one wife and many concubines. Thus, regardless of the specific rules, elite men were assured sexual access to multiple partners. An Aztec noble often took the highest-ranking woman as his first wife, and this woman's retinue of other noblewomen and servants as secondary wives and concubines. While it could be argued that polygamy helped to maintain population numbers in these warrior societies, it also created a dual standard of sexual conduct. Whereas men could take more than one sexual partner, women, regardless of their social status, were to be monogamous. Furthermore, female transgressors were often treated more harshly than men similarly accused. The Aztecs, for example, punished all female adultery with death, but married men were not considered to be adulterers if their relationship was with a single woman.

Among the Aztecs sexual moderation was encouraged for both men and women. Although there is little information on female sexual pleasure within marriage in Aztec documents, women were believed capable of having active sex lives into old age. The Aztecs had well-developed notions of human biology and female physiology and recognized that women had wombs where, after being impregnated by male sperm, they carried their children during pregnancy. According to Aztec belief, a woman became pregnant when, as a result of various sexual encounters, she had accumulated sufficient sperm within her womb to form a child. But pregnancy was linked to corruption, for insufficient sperm made a woman wormy. Once a child had been born, Aztec couples were counseled to avoid sexual relations during the lactation period for fear that a new pregnancy would harm the already born infant. Sexual abstinence was also required at certain times during the year because of religious rites.

All indigenous societies recognized the bodily contribution of the mother to the life of the child, but male kinship ties were paramount. Although the Aztecs acknowledged the importance of mother's kin, family names and their associated offices usually passed from fathers to sons. Only in the Andes was kinship calculated by parallel descent: male children followed their father's lineage and belonged to their father's kin group, whereas female children identified with their mother's kin group.

Gender also determined one's rights to own or inherit property, although the rules differed greatly from one culture to another. Generally land was held only by men, and passed from one generation to another through the male line. Among the Mayas, women could not possess or inherit land. They owned only what we might call "feminine goods": household objects, domestic animals, beehives, and their own clothing. Maya women could bequeath and inherit this property, but it was gender-specific and usually of less value than male holdings. In the Andes access to land was tied to gender parallelism, and women could claim a right to use community land if their mothers had had the same right.

The Aztecs allowed land, houses, and movable property to be inherited by either male or female children. Nonetheless, so closely were domestic goods identified with women that all general movable property in a house, including household objects and weaving equipment, was considered to be "woman property" (*cinhuatlatquitl*). A married woman's inherited property was considered to be separate from that of her husband, but her oldest brother usually acted as guardian of her inheritance. In addition, noble Aztec women could bring land in the form of dowry into a marriage, although the dowry was automatically passed to her husband. Because women exercised little to no direct control of their property, it is doubtful that its ownership allowed them to operate autonomously from their husbands.

Housing of the couple in most preconquest societies was also usually linked to the male kin group. In general, the newly married couple went to live with the groom's extended family, although in some societies there was a brief period, early in the marriage, during which the couple lived with the bride's family. Often this period was seen as a way for the groom to work for the bride's family, thereby repaying her people for her. We can only imagine what a young married woman's life was like, whether she went to live with her husband's family or stayed with her own kin. While these arrangements provided female companionship to young wives, initially they were at the bottom of a multigenerational pecking order. In polygamous households a woman's experience would be greatly affected by her relationship to other wives.

In all pre-Columbian societies, women were believed to have a great capacity for hard work. A wife's duties centered around her productive tasks within the household. As a woman, she was charged with childrearing, caring for the household (including cleaning and fulfilling household religious rituals), putting food on the family's table (marketing and cooking), spinning, and weaving. The latter two were especially important female activities. A promise to weave the garments that would clothe her family, for example, was part of every Aztec woman's marriage vows. Women's weaving was also used to pay the tribute that was due the Aztec state, a tribute that has been estimated to total three million pieces of cotton cloth per year. In Aztec society, female laborers (tlacohtin) wove to pay off debts or to atone for crimes. Throughout America, many of the religious adornments, such as mantles for priests, ceremonial wraps for idols, and tapestries for temple walls were the work of women's hands. The majority of women wove in their own households using backstrap looms to produce cloth, but some women were also employed as weavers in the households of lords. Regardless of the conditions of the labor, cloth produced by women was widely distributed throughout pre-Columbian societies.

The primacy of female household roles was symbolized in ceremony and reflected in the formal and informal training that girls received. At the time of birth, each Aztec girl was given small spindles and shuttles to symbolize her future role in household production; her umbilical cord was buried near the fireplace of her house in the hope that she would be a good housewife. A boy, on the other hand, was presented with a shield and four arrows to indicate his future role as a warrior; his umbilical cord was taken to a battlefield to be interred, thus insuring that he would be a fierce fighter. Aztec girls were given some formal schooling, but they received a very different education than boys. Studying in all-girl schools, they were taught only the arts that would prepare them for marriage and motherhood.

Sexual division of labor – the idea that certain work was exclusively for women and other work exclusively for men – was a hallmark of all pre-Columbian societies. It was the cardinal organizing principle, although the same tasks were not necessarily assigned to women in every culture. Agricultural roles of women, for example, varied from culture to culture. Mayan women did not take part in agriculture even when extra labor was required for tasks such as weeding and harvesting. Inca women, on the other hand, helped to prepare the fields, planted, harvested, weeded, and hoed, although they never plowed the ground. In general women's work was viewed as being of less importance, and therefore carried fewer social rewards than the tasks done by men. Moreover, because men lost social position by doing woman's work, the sexual division of labor was strictly enforced.

In some societies women were not only producers of goods; they also had a limited role in the market. Aztec women were especially active as market traders, usually dealing in cloth goods. In addition, these market women were under the scrutiny of female market administrators who oversaw price, production, and payment of tribute. It was not uncommon for Aztec women to commission apprentices for long-distance trading, but, unlike men, women never participated in actual travel. Indeed, in all pre-Columbian cultures women generally had more sedentary occupations than men.

Midwifery was another occupation available to women in all Indian societies. Aztec midwives also took an active role in the religious ceremonies surrounding birth, conducting some of the rituals themselves. In Andean societies midwives were considered to be "blessed" because of their links to fertility. Perhaps because of their knowledge of birth, women also tended to be healers, using a panoply of medicinal herbs and other compounds to ward off illness and restore good health. Women were also employed as prostitutes, working for themselves or employed by male and female procurers. Some Aztec women were small animal hunters, while others had sex-specified tasks in artisanal manufacture. Nonetheless, in general, any woman who worked outside the control of male kin was viewed with suspicion.

Women who survived the dangerous years of childbirth probably lived longer than men. In spite of women's active work roles, men were usually engaged in more physically taxing labor. In addition, men were warriors or long-distance travelers, two occupations fraught with danger. Higher male mortality rates (the average life expectancy was about thirty-four years) and polygamy meant that there was always a fair number of widows in pre-Columbian societies. Some societies such as the Inca provided for widows by assuring them minimum means of subsistence. But in general only married males could be heads of household. The net result was that widows were always found in the houses of male kin, be it a father, father-in-law, brother, brother-in-law, uncle, cousin, or son.

Furthermore, older women, those beyond menopause, were often believed to have special powers and, at least according to the Spaniards, were described as witches to be feared because they could speak to the devil. Some sources suggest that the Aztecs believed old women especially prone to being sexually insatiable and referred to them as *viejas locas de miel*.

While women were not excluded from the world of work, they were systematically limited in their participation in religion, political administration, and warfare. The degree of participation allowed women varied from culture to culture, but compared to men their power was always limited. A small number of Aztec and Inca women participated in temple service, for example, but these women usually played a secondary role. The most famous religious women were the Virgins of the Sun (*aclla huasi*) housed in the Inca state-run convents. Girls were chosen for these convents between the ages of eight and ten, and were assigned to different fates according to their social origin and physical beauty. The most beautiful noblewomen were reserved as lesser wives of the Inca, while others of high birth were slated to become gift wives used to cement alliances between the Inca Empire and other peoples. Additional noblewomen were chosen to devote their lives to the religious cult as virgin wives of the Sun. Women of more humble social background, especially those deemed less attractive, became either sacrificial victims or servants within the convent. Although it was a great honor for women to be called to temple service, men, not women, determined who would enter the religious life. Once dedicated to the gods, these women were strictly controlled. All *aclla* had to remain virgins while within the convent and were punished with death for defying this mandate.

Throughout America we can find female deities – almost universally associated with fertility, procreation, regeneration, and gender-specific occupations – in the pantheon of pre-Columbian peoples. Chief among these goddesses was some form of earth mother, a figure who linked motherhood with the earth's fertility and the production of food. The major Aztec deities of sustenance, tied to maize, salt, and maguey, were female, as were the deities linked to water, earth, and fire. The Mayan moon-goddess, Ixchel, was associated with spinning and weaving. In their religious mythology, Andean people conceived of all women being descendant from a female deity. Local Andean sacred beings (*huacas*) included several female figures. Some female deities were also linked to eroticism and sexuality. In highland Ecuador, the female *huaca* Chaupi Ñamca was renowned for her lusty sexual appetite, a trait honored by a fertility dance performed by naked men and women.[4] In Meso-America a Mayan goddess was depicted as a courtesan and associated with erotic sexual behavior.

Although the major female deities, often linked to male gods, were important to both men and women, some goddesses were held in special esteem by women. The Andean goddess of procreation and nurture, Pachamama, was believed to be especially protective of women in childbirth. The Inca moon-goddess was the deity of everything concerning women. At times, female deities were associated with less than flattering characteristics. The Aztecs, for example, portrayed the earth-goddess, Toci, as the deity of discord. Many local pre-Columbian myths often pointed to a female fall from grace, while several myths blamed women for sexually ensnaring men and causing them harm. Female goddesses usually preferred women as sacrificial victims. Toci and the goddess of tender maize, Xilonen, as well as Xochiquétzal, goddess of the mountains and special protector of prostitutes, were all honored with female victims. Only in being chosen, along with men, as human sacrifices did women gain religious equality.

There are occasionally references in European reports to female priestesses who were devoted to female deities and to the existence of religious cults that linked women together. In the Andes, the central figure of these cults was often the Corn Mother. Among the Aztecs, women were particularly active in ceremonies involving female deities, but female religious roles were typically an extension of female household chores. According to Spanish sources, these women "dedicated to the prompt service of the temples" were charged with "offering incense to the idols, watching the sacred fire, sweeping the courtyard,

---

[4] According to religious texts, Chaupi Ñamca, a rather demanding lover, "used to travel around in human form and . . . [have sex] with the other huacas. But she never used to praise any male by saying, 'He's good!'" This changed when she met Rucana Coto who with his large sexual organ "satisfied Chaupi Ñamca deliciously." Frank Salomon and George L. Urioste, trans., *The Huarochirí Manuscript: A Testament of Ancient and Colonial Andean Religion* (Austin: University of Texas Press, 1991), 78.

preparing the offering of food . . . and presenting it . . . to the idols, but . . . were excluded from the ministry of sacrifice and the pre-eminent dignities of the priesthood."

Just as women had limited religious roles, some pre-Columbian societies allowed them limited political and administrative roles. We have already spoken of Inca female curacas who held local office because of their ties to male political figures. Occasionally an Aztec woman held an office or title, but it was usually only to transfer it to her husband or male children. There were exclusively female Aztec religiopolitical offices that included *cihuatepixqui* (female person in charge of people), who oversaw women in neighborhood organizations; *cihuatetiachcahuan* (mistresses of women), who judged women accused of concubinage; and *ichpochtlayacanqui* (directors of young women), who oversaw female education. On the other hand, Mayan women were denied access to all civil and religious offices. Even among the Aztecs, women had no power of governance over men and there were no women in the higher levels of administration. Important governing positions were always held by men.

Warfare was an important and highly regarded activity for most pre-Columbian societies. In general, warlike cultures tended to glorify attributes such as bravery and ferocity and closely identify them with men. Women were peripheral to this most exalted human activity, but they were often included in the booty claimed by the victorious warriors. Archaeologists believe that some pre-Columbian societies cemented their conquest by capturing and marrying local women, whereas others created political alliances by distributing conquered women to their allies. (A mercenary group of Indians who allied with the Spaniards against the Incas would later complain that the Spaniards had failed to give them chicha and women, as the Inca had done.) All used the exchange of women to signal the supremacy of the conqueror and the vassalage of the conquered. Conquest also produced slaves – men and women – sold in the central markets of major pre-Columbian cities.

All pre-Columbian societies had strong conceptions of the ideal attributes of each sex, resulting in powerful sexual stereotypes. Both women and men were especially prized if they were hardworking, but women were also frequently identified with what society viewed as less admirable traits. The Aztecs, for example, believed that by nature women were fearful, fretful, and mercurial. Men, on the other hand, tended to embody those traits deemed most positive; they were courageous, generous, stoic, and self-controlled. Positive values such as virility and triumphant action were associated with men, whereas women were deemed to be cowardly, weak, lacking in spirit, and irresolute.

Pre-Columbian societies also tended to incorporate a degree of "gender parallelism," a belief in separate social structures and cultural configurations for men and women. Men and women were perceived to be different kinds of beings with separate responsibilities and fates. Male and female roles were seen as necessary for the survival of society, for they complemented each other. Nonetheless neither gender parallelism nor gender complementarity translated into equality between men and women. Men clearly held a superior position in the gender hierarchy. Indeed, although rarely defined in terms of patriarchy, women in pre-Columbian America were, like those in Spain, in a clearly secondary position in terms of social, economic, and political power.

Our knowledge of the role of women in the many tribal lowland cultures that also existed at the time of the Spanish and Portuguese conquest of America is even more spotty than for the better-documented major cultures. Anthropological data on some of these groups suggest a strict gender division of labor; men made war and hunted while women were chiefly responsible for planting and harvesting foodstuffs. Men were considered to be superior to women and were generally allowed to have more than one wife. Only men could initiate sexual relations, and it was a husband's right to exercise authority over all his wives. Women of all ages were prohibited from having an active role in the ceremonial life of the community. Only in old age, after menopause, were women in lowland cultures permitted to have limited power over younger women and to express their opinion.

Although we have only a partial understanding of women in pre-conquest societies, understanding the role of women in precolonial Africa is even more difficult because of the great diversity of African societies, the paucity of written sources, and the cultural biases of European observers. African societies ran the gamut from tribal to merchant to class-based aristocratic or dynastic societies. Furthermore, much of North Africa was influenced by Islam and Islamic ideas of women's roles.

Although descent from a common ancestor was of great importance to most African groups, some groups traced an individual's kin through his or her mother (matrilineal descent) whereas others followed the father in matters of kinship and inheritance (patrilineal descent).

Descent also determined marriage patterns. Some African groups, such as the Igbo of the Bight of Biafra region, prohibited marriage between people of the same lineage, particularly first and second cousins, whereas other societies encouraged marriage between close relatives.

Some African societies allowed men to have only one spouse, but others permitted men to take several wives. In some polygamous cultures all men were permitted to have more than one wife; in others just the chief and select others were so honored. European travelers reported tribes in which men routinely had twenty to thirty wives. The living arrangements of these women differed from tribe to tribe, with some tribes housing all a man's wives together and others having each wife in her own house. As in pre-Columbian America, women were always limited to one husband. In addition, wives were generally subordinated to their husbands.

Marriage was an important social institution, although in many societies marriage took place only after the groom paid bridewealth to the bride's family. In certain regions women could also avail themselves of the bridewealth system, purchasing other women for themselves and thus becoming fictitious men. Their brides bore children fathered by a male recruited by the female husband, but these children were deemed to belong to the female husband. At times this system was used by an infertile woman to perpetuate her husband's lineage; it also allowed her to gain control of other women.

Many African societies practiced female circumcision, a surgical procedure usually seen as a requirement for marriage. Elderly women performed genital excision on adolescent girls using a sharp instrument to remove the clitoris and vaginal lips. The aim of this surgery was to remove a woman's possible sexual pleasure, thus insuring that she would remain faithful to her husband. In addition to permanent disfigurement, hemorrhaging, infection, sterility, or death could result from these genital wounds.

Common to almost all African societies, like those in preconquest America, was a belief in the sexual division of labor. All groups divided work into men's tasks and women's tasks. Along the Gold Coast of West Africa, for example, men fished while women were charged with drying their catch. In general the pursuits assigned to women were generally more labor-intensive, had lower status, and were less desirable. In several societies, women did a wide range of the productive labor, including agricultural field work, trading, building, mining, certain crafts, childrearing, and domestic labor. Indeed, women were the predominant agricultural laborers in the major African societies. Men, on the other hand, hunted, fished, and reared livestock, although a Portuguese resident of Bissagos Islands reported that "despite all this work [in the fields, the women] still go down to the sea each day to catch shellfish." Although women usually grew cotton, spun thread, grew indigo, made dye, and dyed cloth, weaving, unlike in America, was generally reserved for men. Nonetheless, one seventeenth-century European observer reported that the ruler of the Warri used his large harem of wives to weave cloth, which was subsequently sold.

In virtually every African society women worked longer and harder than men. As in most societies with strict sexual division of labor, it was considered humiliating for any man to do women's work. In the more complex societies class distinctions also governed what certain groups of women did or did not do. In the Muslim areas of Africa, because upper-class women were secluded and did not work, female slaves were used to do women's work.

Slavery was a universal institution throughout Africa, with new recruits usually provided through warfare. Male captives were usually killed, but women and children were enslaved and set to work for male and female owners. Indeed, the majority of slaves owned by women tended to be other women. Female slaves did all types of women's work, including farming, winnowing grains, collecting firewood, making soap, producing pottery, and preparing food and dried fish for both home consumption and sale in the market. Enslaved women also cared for infants and the aged and were probably also used to enhance their owner's prestige. Men frequently used female slaves as prostitutes. Every village along the Gold Coast, for example, had three or four prostitutes drawn from among the enslaved population. Women taken as booty in war were also used to reward soldiers or as political pawns.

It has been suggested that the coming of European slavers in the fifteenth and sixteenth centuries and the resulting increased raiding for male slaves not only changed the slave trade in Africa but also altered women's situation. Persistent raids may have altered the male:female ratio, decreasing the number of men present and thereby increasing the labor burden on women. A surplus of women might also have lowered the total bridewealth a woman's family could demand, increased the use of polygamy, or produced greater reliance on female slaves as a work force.

Many African societies allowed women to own and control their own property, keeping their possessions separate from men's property.

Several regions in West Africa also had a strong tradition of market women. In the seventeenth century, powerful female traders who served as intermediaries and commercial entrepreneurs emerged in West Africa. Women of wealth and influence, they were often closely tied to European men and acted both as cultural mediators and slave traders. In some regions, such as the Senegambia, these women were agents of male family members, but in the Guinea-Bissau region they were independent, at times founding their own trading settlements.

The more warlike African societies usually had male initiation societies that prepared young men for warrior status and adulthood. Women were usually prohibited from taking part in any of these ceremonies, and thus did not join in the rites that linked members of society together. One of the more notable exceptions to this rule was found among the peoples of the Sierra Leone coast, where women, although barred from male religious activities, played a special part in preparing potions used for warriors and also participated in female secret societies. Among their other functions, these societies were involved in female puberty rites. The Portuguese, mistaking female initiation with convents, described how girls were kept in an isolated house for a year before joining a secret society. Some individual "medicine women" wielded special power and might have even been members of male secret societies.

Political power was generally in the hands of men, but among some peoples the queen mother seems to have had a revered position. Paradoxically one of the more warlike African societies, the Mbundu or Ndongo nation, was ruled by a woman, Queen Nzinga Mbande, from 1624 to 1663. Queen Nzinga, who probably killed her nephew to gain the throne, was a shrewd politician who manipulated the Dutch against the Portuguese for her own economic and political benefit. She was also a major slave dealer who continually raided neighboring tribes for slaves, which she sold to her Dutch allies.

Queen Nzinga was not the only African female ruler. There were occasional women chiefs, such as Madiamuteba, who ruled over the tombs of the Lunda emperors. Other African societies were ruled by both a king and queen. The queen of Kongo had her own household within the royal compound and her own entourage of ladies-in-waiting. Still other societies believed that women related to the king enjoyed power because of their lineage. King Mulohwe of the Luba Empire made a practice of marrying his own sisters and nieces, thus assuring that succession would be carried through both the male and female lines.

Regardless of these female rulers, the prevailing gender ideology assumed female inferiority. This inferiority was believed to be the result of women's basic nature and biological attributes. Women were viewed as both weak and dangerous because of their biology. Women in child-bearing years were feared because of their mysterious ability both to menstruate and to bear children. Several societies had strict ritual pro-scriptions against menstruating women. Only older women – that is, those who menses had ceased – were seen as benign.

Thus, cultures as distinct as those of pre-Columbian America, Africa, and the Iberian Peninsula had certain universal ideas about women. Virtually all societies believed in the sexual division of labor, structuring the workplace into male and female tasks. In general, women not only worked but worked at tasks at least as difficult, time-consuming, and laborious as those performed by men. Furthermore, almost universally these female occupations were socially undervalued and underrewarded. In most of these societies men controlled female sexuality, enforcing female virginity and monogamy while not requir-ing the same conduct from men. To a greater or lesser degree all these societies were patriarchies, giving men special powers over the women and within the family.

Although we have mentioned a few exceptional cases, in general men had the ascendant role in all these societies and monopolized political and religious power. Even where female lineages were recog-nized, male lineage tended to take precedence in determining a couple's living arrangements and matters of inheritance. Virtually all these societies imposed a dichotomy between the public and the private arenas, limiting women to the private sector, the home. Although many of these cultures worshiped one or more female deities, these goddesses were almost universally linked to fertility, thus echoing women's primary social role, reproduction. And although a goddess of fertility was present in all cultures, men almost always controlled female sexuality, imposing the rules about who could and could not marry and dictating female monogamy. Many of these cultures also displayed a deep-seated fear of women, viewing them at best as inferior and at worst dangerous and unmanageable. Even those peoples who respected women's roles believed men to be far more vital to their society's survival.

CHAPTER 3

CONQUEST AND COLONIZATION

a Chinese wide shawl
another wide shawl, from the Quixos region, embroidered
a woolen wrap-around skirt and a woolen wide shawl
a large Chinese porcelain
two large stickpins with their bells
one small chain with two other stickpins of marked silver
one woven belt or girdle of purple silk, in the Roman style, with
    an ornamental border
a scarlet satin wide shawl with its silver brooch [?]
a new wide shawl of light silk or linen, with Castilian
    needlework
a wide shawl of green Castilian damask with golden edging
a choker of pearls and purple beads
some filigreed earrings with small pearl pendants
some earrings with three pendants edged with pearls
a choker of pearls and blue and red beads
more chokers of baroque pearls, silver, and bells
another choker of pearls and little golden bells and coral . . .
two bracelets of coral and pearls.[1]

The early years of European discovery and conquest of America was
a period of violence, dramatic social change, and profound transformation in the lives of indigenous peoples. The Indian world was conquered, dismantled, and restructured according to the conqueror's

[1] From the estate inventory of María de Amores Quito, 1596, in Archivo Nacional
de la Historia, Quito, Primera Notaria, tomo 3, folios 504r–505r, cited in Frank
Salomon, "Indian Women of Early Colonial Quito as Seen through Their
Testaments," *The Americas*, 44:3 (January 1988), 334–336.

vision. The conquest probably had a more varied effect on Indian women than any other single group. But not all Indian women were equally affected by the conquest. The aftermath of conquest severed the lives of some women and reduced others to slavery; still others managed to integrate themselves into European society, in many cases more successfully than the Indian men. Thus, the conquest could be a traumatic experience or a new opportunity. In addition, the effects of conquest varied over time, with those who witnessed the destruction of their world and the imposition of European cultural, religious, and social values being far more affected than succeeding generations, who were born into a world already changed.

European women were for the most part absent from the initial ranks of conquistadors who extended Spanish dominion over the islands of the Caribbean, Aztec Mexico, and Inca Peru, but this did not cause Spanish men to undertake lives of voluntary celibacy. Instead they turned to the available Indian women for immediate sexual pleasure. Many native women were accosted, abused, beaten, and raped. As early as two months into his first voyage to America (1492), Columbus, who had repeatedly remarked upon the beauty and fine figures of the native women, mentioned that Indian women were now being systematically hidden from the Spaniards.[2] Rodrigo Rangel, a member of the De Soto expedition to Florida and the Mississippi Valley (1539–1543), reported that the Spaniards took Indian women "who were not old nor the most ugly" and that "they wanted the women in order to make use of them [as servants] and for their lewdness and lust and that they baptized them more for their carnal intercourse than to instruct them in the faith."[3]

Other women, from tribes allied to the Spanish or those conquered by them, were persuaded to become lovers and concubines of Spanish soldiers. Indeed, chiefs offered their sisters and daughters to Spanish conquistadors, continuing the pre-Columbian pattern of using women to appease the powerful and ally with them. Indian women probably

[2] According to the Admiral, "[Indian] men make their women hide from the Christians out of jealousy." One can question both whether the women hide on their own volition, and what was the root of the supposed jealousy. Oliver Dunn and James E. Kelley Jr., eds., *The Diario of Christopher Columbus's First Voyage to America, 1492–1493* (Norman: University of Oklahoma Press, 1989), entry of Friday, 21 December 1492, 255–256.

[3] Rodrigo Rangel, "Account of the Northern Conquest and Discovery of Hernando de Soto," in Lawrence A. Clayton et al., eds., *The De Soto Chronicles: The Expedition of Hernando de Soto to North America in 1539–1543* (Tuscaloosa: University of Alabama Press, 1993), 1:289.

willingly accepted these relationships, for this behavior formed part of their culture. The native rulers of Tlaxcala (Mexico) gave their women to the Spaniards in the hope that the children of these unions, perceived by the Indians to be of a high social rank, would remain within the Indian community. Quetzalmamalitzin, lord of Teotihuacán, married his daughter to a Spaniard to strengthen his family's power. If no women were offered, the Iberian conquerors simply helped themselves to any women they wanted. During the conquest of Spanish America, Indian women were routinely taken captives and distributed as booty among the victorious conquistadors. Jiménez de Quesada in Colombia, for example, gave three hundred Indian women to his minions.

As the European conquest was extended to the more remote regions of America, the same patterns continued into the seventeenth century. In Central America, for example, Indian caciques continued to give women to Spaniards as a way of ingratiating themselves with their new rulers. In Brazil, Indian men routinely offered unmarried girls to Europeans as a gesture of hospitality or in return for a bauble or two. The kidnapping of Indian women along the frontier also continued throughout the colonial period. As late as 1772 the marques de Rubí suggested that Spaniards along the war-torn northern border of New Spain take Indian women prisoners, thereby limiting the ability of hostile Indian tribes to reproduce themselves. During the last decade of the eighteenth century it was common to ship Apache prisoners of war, primarily women and children, from New Spain to Havana, making it impossible for them to return to their tribe.

Some European men brutally violated and abandoned Indian women, but others began long-lasting relationships with the conquered women. We should remember that it was not unusual for men in sixteenth-century Spanish society to have stable unions with women of lesser social rank either before or outside of marriage. In addition, Indian women who had grown up in societies that accepted polygamy may have found concubinage with Spaniards to be not all that different from the sexual relations that they had previously known.

Although we have no notion of how the Indian women viewed their new situation, these Spanish-Indian unions at times resulted in enduring romantic attachments or even lifelong companionship. The most famous of these romantic liaisons was that of Hernán Cortés, conqueror of Mexico, and Malintzin, an Indian woman he met in 1519, shortly after arriving in Veracruz. Probably of noble Mayan birth, Malintzin (called "doña Marina" by the Spaniards, and also known disrespectfully as "La Malinche" in present-day Mexico) had been captured and enslaved by Tabascan Indians and then given to the Spaniards, along with nineteen other female captives, as a welcoming gift. She showed her gratitude to her new masters by becoming their principal interpreter and go-between as they made their way to the Aztec capital of Tenochitlán. She also became Cortés's concubine (his wife had remained in Cuba), his trusted adviser, and the mother of his illegitimate son, Martín, born in 1522. In 1524, seeking to improve her situation, Cortés arranged a legitimate marriage for her to Juan Jaramillo de Salvatierra, a Spanish soldier in his army and holder of the *encomienda* (royal grant of Indian labor) of Xilotepec.

Cortés and Marina are far from a unique example. Pedro de Alvarado, conquistador of Central America, took as his mistress doña Luisa, the daughter of a powerful Tlaxcalan cacique; during a long and affectionate relationship, she bore Alvarado several children. Francisco Pizarro, conqueror of Peru, had an intimate friendship with Inés Yupanqui, daughter of the Inca Huayna Capac who had been given to the Spaniard by her half brother, the Inca Atahualpa. Inés, far younger than her Spanish lover, bore him two children and was referred to by him with great tenderness. Shortly after the birth of her second child, she married Francisco de Ampuero, a page in the Pizarro brothers' retinue who was rewarded with an encomienda. Pizarro's next lover was another noble Inca woman, doña Angelina (Cuxirimay Ocllo), who also bore him two children. After Pizarro's death, she married the Spaniard Juan Díaz de Betanzos.

As these examples show, high-ranking conquistadors did not usually marry their Indian lovers, but the longevity of some of these relations leads us to believe they combined mutual endearment with mutual opportunity for both man and woman. Because of these intimate ties, Indian concubines probably received better treatment that Indian men. Indeed during the conquest, Indian women – lovers, wives, concubines, prostitutes, and/or servants – had greater and more intimate contact with Spanish men than did their menfolk. Whether given to the Spaniards by Indian caciques, taken by force, or attracted to European men of their own volition, these women often accompanied the Spaniards in the conquest, preparing food, carrying baggage, nursing the sick, providing companionship and information, serving as cultural interpreters, and bearing children. Many of these women went on to become agents of cultural miscegenation (*mestisaje*) once the period of Spanish conquest ended.

Perhaps the most famous Indian woman of her time was Isabel

Moctezuma (originally named Techichopotzin), whose dramatic life provides an extraordinary example of the complex role of elite Indian women in the years of the conquest and early settlement of America. Born in 1509 or 1510, she was one of perhaps 150 children sired by Montezuma II, the Aztec emperor. At age eleven, the Aztec princess was married to her uncle, Cuitláhuac. Widowed within two months of marriage, she was quickly remarried to her cousin, Cuauhtémoc, the last Aztec emperor. Cuauhtémoc's defeat and torture by the conquering Spaniards, and subsequent death, left his bride again a widow at age sixteen. Quickly baptized and christened Isabel, the young woman became a symbol of the Hispanization and Christianization of Mexico. She was also granted a major encomienda, that of Tacuba. Combining the necessary attributes of Indian princess and wealthy *encomendera*, Isabel was married to her third husband, a Spaniard. Only nineteen at the time of his death, Isabel joined the Cortés household and briefly became the conquistador's lover. Indeed she was pregnant with Cortés's child when she married for the fourth time. After bearing Cortés's daughter and a son to her legitimate husband, doña Isabel was again widowed by age twenty-one, but within a year she married her fifth husband, a Spanish conquistador. This marriage produced five more children and lasted until Isabel's death in 1550. Isabel was buried in the Church of San Agustín, her favorite religious institution. All of her children, with the exception of two daughters who became nuns, married well and became part of the Mexican colonial nobility.

These examples also show that Spanish men of both middling and modest social and economic background could and did marry Indian women, especially women who belonged to the preconquest indigenous nobility. Although some Indian women refused to be used in these Spanish power games, these women were desirable marriage candidates for lesser conquistadors and others seeking to improve their social position in America, for they knowingly brought a degree of prestige, important social ties, Indian lands or other dowry property, and pre-Hispanic legitimacy to their European husbands. Nearly one-fourth of first-generation Spanish settlers in sixteenth-century Puebla de los Angeles married Indian brides. Indian wives were the most privileged of all conquered people, and it has been suggested that, until the arrival of large numbers of Spanish women, these Indian wives were considered to be honorary Spanish women and were treated as such. Indian women who lacked noble Indian blood, while still desirable as concubines, were less in demand as formal marriage partners.

The female offspring of these first Spanish-Indian unions, especially those mestizas who inherited from their conquistador fathers, were also attractive marital partners. In general their wealth and perceived social status overcame any possible problems associated with legitimacy and race. Francisca Pizarro, the illegitimate mestiza daughter of Francisco Pizarro and Inés Yupanqui, inherited an enormous fortune from her father and had several eager Spanish suitors. Educated in Peru, she was eventually sent to Spain where she married her paternal uncle, Hernando Pizarro, a man approximately thirty years her senior. Widowed seventeen years later, Francisca soon remarried a young Spanish nobleman, son of a Spanish grandee and brother of her own daughter-in-law. Ana García de Loyola, legitimate mestiza daughter of Martin García de Loyola and Beatriz Clara Coya, and granddaughter of the Inca prince Sairi Tupac, also returned to Spain as a young adult. She was named Marquesa de Oropesa and later married the son of the Marques de Alcañises. Other mestizas were married off by their Spanish fathers to create political alliances. The most famous case is that of Governor Irala of Paraguay who forced his defeated political enemies to marry his mestiza daughters.

Conquistadors were followed by merchants, artisans, and others seeking to make their fortunes in America. Among the many married men who arrived in the New World, the general pattern was to leave their wives and children in Spain until they were economically established. In the interim, an interim that could last for several years if not indefinitely, nonnoble Indian women and poor mestizas served as lovers and concubines. But in the marriage market Spanish men preferred Spanish women, who were arriving in America in increasing numbers after 1560, followed by Europeanized mestizas of noble lineage.

As the years of conquest gave way to a more settled society, a new colonial world emerged, determining the parameters of the possible for Indian women for the next two hundred years. One of the hallmarks of the more mature colonial society was the growing importance of race as a social marker. While the numbers of mestiza women remained relatively small, some of them had easily integrated into Spanish society. Of course, we have no idea how many were absorbed into Indian society. With the passing of time, and the continued numerical growth of the mestizo community, these people of mixed race came to constitute a separate racial category. Paradoxically, because in the eyes of the Spaniards mestizos were increasingly identified with negative values, mestiza women found their acceptance into Spanish society increasingly difficult.

Throughout America, Indian peoples suffered a dramatic demographic decline. The arrival of Europeans and European pathogens combined with the violence of conquest to produce a demographic disaster of massive proportions. In parts of Latin America approximately 90 percent of the Indian population disappeared. Indian women probably experienced lower mortality than men, who were actively engaged in warfare. As the balance between European women, born either on the Iberian Peninsula or in the New World, and Indian women gradually changed, the options available to the latter group continued to diminish. Nonetheless, the lives of Indian women varied greatly.

The end of conquest did not stop sexual contacts between Spanish men and Indian women. Spanish acceptance of concubinage, the position of power that these men enjoyed because of their gender and race, and the availability of native women often allowed a Spaniard to have an Indian concubine in his house. In some isolated rural areas, government officials and others routinely kept two, three, or four Indian women as their mistresses. These liaisons were hardly discreet. Francisco de Aguirre, noted Indian fighter in Chile and Tucumán, boasted of fathering fifty illegitimate children by Indian women.

Concubines were not limited to the lay population. Clergymen also took Indian lovers, although they tended to be a bit more circumspect. Nonetheless, these relationships were so widespread that the church encouraged priests to employ only old women as cooks and servants in their homes. The level of well-being provided Indian mistresses and conversely the level of physical abuse in the relationship varied from case to case, but in general priests and friars seemed to have treated their concubines better than did other men. Often when these relationships ended, the Indian woman returned to her community of origin to raise her mestizo children.

Other sexual contacts between Spaniards and Indians were more ephemeral, and often more violent. Some Spanish officials, as well as encomenderos and their mestizo, black, and mulatto foremen, believed that they had unlimited access to all Indian women, both single and married. Indian women were whipped, raped, physically abused, tortured, and killed for resisting unwanted sexual advances as well as other minor infractions. In some regions, regardless of laws that theoretically protected them, Indian women were enslaved, bartered, sold into prostitution or concubinage, and even used as stakes in card games.

Indian women were also at risk of being abused by blacks and mulattos. Priests and civil authorities worked to separate slave and Indian populations and were especially concerned with preventing black men from taking Indian concubines. Nonetheless, by the mid-sixteenth century blacks in Peru were reported to be forcing Indian women to weave large quantities of cloth for them; sexual abuse, rape, and forced concubinage were also reported. Strict ordinances tried to curb this type of abuse; in theory a black man who sexually abused an Indian women was to be castrated; other abuse would be punished with one hundred lashes. Black women who abused Indians were to receive one hundred lashes for their first offense and have their ears cut off for repeat offenses.

Neither the crown nor the church condoned what it viewed as widespread immorality in the Americas. In the eyes of the church immorality was the result of both loose Indian moral practices and the lust of unattached Spanish men. Priests, for example, complained that Indians "got drunk and fathers became involved with the daughters or brothers with sisters with no restraint of any kind." But Spanish laymen believed that fornication with Indian women was at most a minor sin. In 1547, for example, the bishop of Honduras reported that there were not ten Spaniards in the province who did not have at least one Indian mistress. The situation was aggravated by the rootlessness of the Spanish population, easy access to Indian women, and the relative absence of Spanish women. Over and over the authorities suggested the same solution: limit Spanish immigration to married men whose wives accompanied them to America. Beginning in the sixteenth century and continuing until the end of the colonial period, the Spanish crown repeatedly issued edicts and laws requiring married Spaniards who came to the Indies to send for their wives within two years. But the crown was unable to effect such a policy, and concubinage continued throughout the colonial period.

In certain regions of colonial Latin America, Spanish men continued to marry Indian women, especially when marriage gave them rights to Indian land or power within indigenous communities. In 1582, for example, the viceroy of Mexico sought information about one Diego García Villavicencio, married to an Indian women whose kin held positions in the Indian Cabildo of Cholula. García Villavicencio was suspected of using his relationship with several Indians to intervene in the community's government. At times these marriages were mutually beneficial, as when the Indian woman, doña Maria de la Cruz, descendant of the principal Indian noble families of Tepeaca, married the Spaniard Alvaro Pérez de Navia so as to defend more effectively the land and other property she had inherited.

Other Indian women proved to be more than able to defend their property and their interests without the help of European husbands or lovers. During the sixteenth century more than one Andean Indian woman, often the daughters of local caciques, successfully challenged Spaniards who were attempting to encroach on their lands. Doña Mencia Nuncati, daughter of an Indian cacique in the Chillo region of Ecuador, blocked a Spaniard from claiming six *caballerías* (approximately 630 acres) of rich land by presenting a formal complaint against him in the high court of Quito. Mencia presented several witnesses who testified that her family had owned the land since "time immemorial," convincing the judges of the validity of her case.

In the years following the Spanish conquest, large numbers of Indian women were drawn to towns and cities. Probably there was a combination of "push" and "pull" factors that influenced this female migration. In addition to a severe demographic decline, which in turn affected the productive capacities of the indigenous world, the conquest no doubt disturbed gender relations within the Indian community, thus encouraging women to seek their livelihood elsewhere. Other Indian women were coerced by their Spanish encomenderos to move to the city, where they became either domestic servants or concubines. Indian women had traditionally been active in the marketplace, and new opportunities in the provisioning of Spanish towns also drew women to these urban centers. Lastly, late-sixteenth-century changes in the laws of the Viceroyalty of Peru allowed Indian women who had borne children to Spaniards to accompany these men anywhere in the empire, thus encouraging these women to leave their communities.

The end result was that Indian women migrants learned the European's language and his ways and served as cultural interpreters between the conquerors and the conquered. Working as servants, cooks, nursemaids, and laundresses, these women played a crucial role within the households of Spaniards. In many homes they found themselves doing familiar tasks, often surrounded by other Indian women domestics. But some of these "domestic" tasks could be very physically demanding. While in theory Spanish laws such as the Laws of Burgos (1512–1513) protected pregnant women, nursing mothers, and single girls, this humane legislation was never enforced.

In cities, towns, haciendas, farms, and ranches, Indian women working within Spanish households were often the first sexual partners, and sometimes longtime companions, of Spanish men, as well as the mothers of their illegitimate children. We can only wonder about the psychological effects on both Indian women and Spanish men. Furthermore, these women were frequently at risk of being sexually molested by Spanish, black, mestizo, mulatto, and nonkin Indian men. The Indian servant Juana, for example, was raped by her master because he wanted "to determine if she was a virgin." When she attempted to resist, she was hung from the roofbeam and beaten.

While Spanish men clearly held the upper hand in these sexual liaisons, some Indian and mestiza women profited from their proximity to power. Inés González, a Peruvian Indian servant of the cleric Rodrigo González Marmolejo, enjoyed such a close relationship with her master that she adopted his name and accompanied him to Santiago when he was named first bishop of the fledging city. Shortly thereafter he presented her with a *chacara* (farm) on the outskirts of the city. Less than eight years later, Inés owned this farm, two houses in the city, horses, goats, sheep, and swine.

For some Indian women migration to the cities of colonial Latin America created economic opportunities. The emergence of a market economy created new positions for Indian women as small independent sellers, market women, peddlers, producers of foodstuffs or goods, and even long-distance traders. Among these women were those who were able to amass enough capital to invest in real property. Many prospered by participating actively in the real-estate market, using Spanish inheritance laws to will their land on to female kin, although there was no clear, universal pattern. Other women became small-scale entrepreneurs, owning taverns that catered to the urban Indian population, functioning as pawnbrokers, investing their cash, and owning slaves.

The records these women left make it clear that they understood and skillfully used the rules of Spanish commercial law. In addition, urban Indian women probably benefited from European laws of property and inheritance and Spanish tolerance of pre-conquest social structures. The result was that Indian women were allowed to own property and enjoy considerable leeway in passing it to their chosen heirs. Wills drawn up by Indian women detailed the property, goods, and ornaments they had amassed during their lifetimes, and frequently favored other women and/or Indian, rather than mestizo, descendants. Their possessions might range from modest goods to rather impressive lists of holdings.

City life produced a slow process of acculturation to Spanish ways. Throughout the sixteenth and seventeenth centuries, women reflecting various stages of this process could be found in any large town. Newly arrived women or those who married Indian men from the same linguistic group continued to speak their native languages and hold an essentially pre-Columbian world view. Others not only began to speak Spanish but also gradually became acculturated to Spanish ways at the same time as they modified Spanish culture. The end result might be seen in the last will and testament of Maria de Amores, drawn up in Quito in 1596. (See the document quoted at the beginning of this chapter.) The listing of her personal prosperity reflects a degree of acculturation and the emergence of a new cultural mix. Reviewing her wardrobe, we can see that Maria Amores dressed herself in luxurious native clothing and jewelry, while mixing garments from several indigenous cultures with Spanish and Oriental pieces. Maria's wardrobe was not specific to any one Indian group but rather the clothing of a new "universal" Indian, with recognizable non-Indian elements. Nonetheless, the vast majority of Indian women did not live in Europeanized cities but rather in Indian towns. Many continued to live within rural indigenous societies, albeit societies deeply transformed by Spanish economic, political, social, and religious structures.

A sexual division of labor had been a hallmark of preconquest societies. Now a new sexual division was imposed by the Europeans. This allocation of specific tasks by gender could be very different from that in preconquest societies, as Iberians transferred their own ideas of female and male tasks to Amerindian societies. For example, in coastal Brazil the missionaries transferred farming, which had been a feminine role in Tupí society, to men. In a similar fashion priests working among the Pueblo Indians decided that building construction, heretofore considered women's work, was a male occupation. In general, European-imposed occupations were less onerous to women than those they had exercised before, but the loss of traditional roles might also have translated into a corresponding loss of social position and prestige. In other regions, there was little change in the sex-specific tasks performed by women. Mexican Indian women, for example, continued to be weavers, producing cloth for both their own use, the use of their family, and tribute payment.

The Spanish conquest also produced important modifications of pre-Columbian tribute systems. Those Indians who had "voluntarily" accepted Spanish rule were first divided into encomiendas and put under the "care" of Spanish settlers; later the Indian population was subject to *repartimiento* (a form of labor tribute) under the aegis of government authorities. Who among the Indian population was subject to pay tribute, as well as the form of this tribute (labor or payment in goods or coin), was continually revised during the entire colonial period; there were also local variations in tribute payments.

Ideally, only a household composed of a man and wife was a tribute payer. In some regions female labor probably freed men to undertake tribute obligations; in other regions female labor supplied the tribute. Throughout the colonial period, for example, Mayan women bore the brunt of product-tribute demands. This tribute was paid in cotton cloth, hens, honey, and beeswax, all goods produced by women within the household. The same was true in Indian communities to the north of the Audiencia of Quito, where women cleaned, carded, and wove cotton cloaks. In the words of a Spanish observer, "the tribute that the Indian men are supposed to pay is paid by the women through their weaving. They have no time to care for their children and serve their husband and make their clothing because in addition they have to fill their encomenderos's demands for garments. Even though the women are free from paying tribute everywhere, it is the women who really pay the tribute."[4]

In Mexico, the type and quality of the cloth demanded for tribute changed, with large pieces of plain cloth increasingly replacing finer, more ornate weaving. Encomenderos took Indian girls from their villages to a house where they were forced to spin and weave cotton cloth used to pay tribute. In areas of Mexico and Central America, encomenderos and clergy demanded that women supply goods such as *huipiles*, petticoats or blankets, to be used in trade. As the Indian population shrank because of the postconquest "demographic disaster," and as the demand for cotton cloth grew with ever increasing Spanish, black, mulatto, and mestizo populations, Indian women were forced to produce this more monotonous weaving in greater quantity, thereby balancing out the relative task simplification.

The form of tribute payment also varied widely. In some regions, such as Yucatan, tribute continued to be paid directly in woven goods until the eighteenth century. In other regions, such as central Mexico,

---

[4] Archivo General de Indias, Seville, Justicia 683, 1566, folio 761v, as quoted in Chantal Caillavet, "La artesanía textil en la época colonial: El rol de la producción doméstica en el norte de la Audiencia de Quito," *Cultura* (Quito), 8 (January–April 1986), 527.

monetary tribute replaced tribute in goods by the middle of the sixteenth century. Although women continued to weave, they now also entered into the local market to sell their goods for cash, some of which they used to help fulfill their family's tribute quota. In southern Mexico and Peru, Indian women received token wages as they wove for the local *corregidor*, a royal official who distributed raw cotton and collected finished piece goods.

The onerous system of personal service to the encomendero ended early in some parts of Latin America, but it continued to be exacted in more distant regions throughout the colonial period. In late-sixteenth-century Nicaragua, Indian women were forced to work in the *obrajes de tinta*, cultivating and processing indigo, and many were reported to have died in these plantations because of the exhausting labor. Up to the second half of the same century, Indian women in Bolivia were compelled to spin thread and weave cloth as part of their tribute payment.

In parts of America, Indian women also supplied forced labor tribute (*servicio personal*), often exacted by the encomendero in the form of domestic service. In Chile, Indian women were subjected to personal service well into the seventeenth century in spite of repeated efforts on the part of government administrators to limit the abuses of the system. Young adolescent girls who worked as domestics or nursemaids were in especially high demand. Indian women working and living in the homes of Spaniards, especially those forced into personal service in rural settings, could be abused physically, emotionally, and sexually with little effective recourse to justice.

Even where Indian women ceased to pay labor tribute by the end of the sixteenth century, women continued to shoulder the burden of commodity and monetary exactions. Eventually the power of the encomendero was limited as government officials were charged with rationing Indian labor. For young Indian women this substitution of unscrupulous bureaucrats for licentious encomenderos probably made little difference.

Continual modifications of the tribute system went hand in hand with the continuing demographic collapse of indigenous populations. In rural districts the destruction of native societies and the demographic upheaval produced a large number of Indian widows and orphans. Young orphan girls, with no one to protect them, were particularly vulnerable to exploitation. Indian widows were also unprotected and in the years following the conquest more likely to be drafted for heavy labor than other women.

The effect of heavy labor on Indian women, especially work that required the lifting and carrying of heavy loads, probably lowered their reproduction rate. The forced absence of either the husband or wife in order to provide personal labor tribute also tended to have the same result. Abuse and labor also led to suicide and produced such despair that in some regions Indian women were accused of murdering their own children. Paradoxically the demographic catastrophe that followed the conquest eventually produced an improved socioeconomic status for some rural survivors, including women. Because of an abundance of land produced by the great epidemics of the sixteenth century, some Indian women in central Mexico found it easier to accumulate property. Their wills attest to this newfound prosperity.

Indian women also migrated along with men to cattle ranches, tobacco works, and mines. While their primary task was to provide services for their menfolk (drawing water, gathering wood, cooking), in some regions they were used in heavy agricultural tasks such as clearing land, preparing irrigation ditches, and raising crops. Women also worked as human carriers, hauling maize and water on lengthy journeys. In some mining districts they were also used in hard-pit labor and in hauling precious metal.

Nevertheless, those Indian women who continued to live in rural communities eventually benefited from Spanish law, chiefly laws that allowed women to inherit property from male kin. Increasingly in regions such as Yucatan women came to own houses, domestic animals, looms, and yarn. By the seventeenth century, a few extraordinary Mayan women, while remaining in their communities, were able to demonstrate economic independence and financial acumen, buying and selling goods and functioning as local bankers. By the eighteenth century in regions such as the Toluca Valley of Mexico, widows probably made up the largest group of independent landowners in the Indian communities.

Indian women also learned how to assert their claims to property and to just treatment in the Spanish legal system. By the eighteenth century Indian women living in Toluca (Mexico), for example, successfully invoked Spanish law to defend their landholdings against men questioning their right to inherit and purchase property. Indian women also learned to protect themselves against physical and sexual abuse committed against them by their kinsfolk by turning to Spanish courts to defend their right to just treatment. In general the courts championed the needy regardless of their gender.

In some regions elite Indian women who had remained in their communities were also able to maintain some traditional political roles. In the Mixteca region of Mexico (present-day Oaxaca) for at least the first one hundred years after conquest, women continued to inherit chieftainships (*cacicazgos*) from male kinfolk and to wield economic and political power. One such women, Ana de Sosa, the cacica of Tututepec, not only had vast landholdings and movable property but enjoyed tribute and personal service exacted from local Indians. Moreover, Ana successfully defended her entitlements in Spanish courts. Although the possibility of female political power waxed and waned in different regions, it never completely disappeared. In the eighteenth century, Josefa María Francisca of Tepoztlán (central Mexico) was an important leader of one of the town's political factions.

The question of acculturation and its relationship to gender in rural Latin America is just beginning to be understood. Probably women living in indigenous communities had less contact with Spaniards than did their menfolk, who worked seasonally on Spanish estates. As a result, rural women were slower than men to adopt Spanish ways, put on European-style clothing, or learn the Spanish language. Women's agricultural chores were probably more tied to pre-Columbian crops such as corn, maguey, potatoes, and quinoa, whereas men soon perfected the cultivation of European grains (wheat, oats) by working for the local landowners, or *hacendados*. Nonetheless, women and men both learned to raise European animals, although women were usually charged with tending to poultry and the so-called *ganado menor*, that is, sheep and goats.

Perhaps the most dramatic changes produced by the European conquest occurred in the sphere of religion. Indian women and men were forced to abandon their "heathen" ways and adopt Roman Catholicism. Women had had a relatively minor role in the religious ritual of pre-conquest societies, but this role was probably further reduced after the conquest. Nonetheless, the Catholic Church provided Indian women with new forms of religious expression and a degree of spiritual continuity. Preconquest female religious cults had linked women of differing social strata together; now *cofradías* (religious sisterhoods) gave these women a Catholic arena in which to organize their social and religious life. (See Document 4.) Like pre-Columbian forms of female worship, female cofradías were often devoted to a female saint. These native sodalities also provided a ceremonial life, as well as practical help in the form of burials, financial aid, and dowries for impoverished offspring.

The church, under the guise of freedom of choice in marriage, also tried to end the control of the Indian nobility over the marriage choices of commoners. At the same time the church worked to implement its kinship prohibitions on marriage, rules that were probably unintelligible to the Indian population. At first the church tended to accept Indian customs except when they were deemed to be repugnant to natural law and Christian morality. Slowly European ideas of marriage, legitimacy, and inheritance were introduced into Indian society, but they were probably not fully functioning until well into the seventeenth century.

The gradual change from multigenerational family to nuclear family households also affected the role of women. Instead of living in an extended family unit surrounded by parents, siblings, aunts, uncles, and cousins, Indian women increasingly found themselves living with only their husband and children. Some historians have suggested that this transition isolated women, cutting them off from a family life that provided companionship and a limited degree of authority within the larger group. Breaking up of multigenerational households also undermined cooperative labor arrangements based on the extended family. On the other hand, women in nuclear family units probably benefited from increased privacy and clearer direct authority over their children.

By the middle of the sixteenth century, the clergy's more tolerant view of Indian ability to be Hispanized gave way to Counter-Reformation moral stiffness. In Mexico the newly created Holy Office of the Inquisition hunted down men and women accused of deviation from the church moral and sexual code. Indian women were frequently accused of sorcery and of using their power of enchantment to work love magic. Although Indians would later be exempt from the arm of the Holy Office, women, especially older, peasant women, continued to be accused of working sexual magic in league with the devil.

The Spanish church and state also waged a campaign to end polygamy, outlawing the practice of one man taking several wives, but in some districts, such as Alto Peru, polygamy continued well into the seventeenth century. How this change affected the lives of Indian women also is far from clear. While one possible result was the end of the sociability of the household, another result might have been the end of rivalries between wives.

In rural Peru colonial authorities also attempted to end sexual and marital practices they considered immoral. Although they themselves were hardly chaste, both church and state increasingly condemned the widespread Andean practice of trial marriage, cohabitation that could last for years. In the 1570s Viceroy Toledo denounced the practice as "noxious and pernicious."[5] Later authorities would used sermons, the confessional, and even prison to dissuade Indian couples from living together. To judge from ongoing complaints, Spaniards were never able to convince Indian men and women of the virtues of premarital virginity, and trial marriage was never successfully rooted out.

Perhaps no Indian women were as tightly controlled as those who found themselves living on missions directly supervised by religious orders. Their entire lives, including their sex life, marriage, and morality, came under direct religious control. Mission priests viewed adultery, polygamy, and concubinage as immoral and worked to root out these vices while promoting Catholic marriage and morality. Fearing sexual promiscuity, the friars campaigned to stamp out informal unions and promote early marriage. Women were to marry at age fifteen; the result was that these Indian women devoted a greater portion of their lives to bearing and rearing children than did any other group of women in colonial society. Once married couples were forced to live in nuclear households. The friars' goals also served the Spanish state, which counted the married couple as the basic tribute-paying unit.

In frontier regions Spanish missionary priests, unable to understand why Indian women had no shame in being "unclothed from the waist up and the knees down," decried female nudity and encouraged women to adopt "proper" dress. Indeed the repeated use of the word "shame" when referring to nudity and the universal euphemism "shameful parts" reflect Spanish discomfort and fascination with people whose dress code differed greatly from theirs. Missionary teaching introduced European ideas of the weakness of women at the same time as it enforced traditional Indian concepts of female subordination. In the confessional priests also railed against what they saw as female tendencies toward infanticide, abortion, and neglect of their wifely duties.

[5] Francisco de Toledo, Ordenanza VIII, Ordenanzas para los Indios de todos los departamentos y pueblos de este reino, cited in Ward Stavig, *Amor y violencia sexual: Valores indígenas en la sociedad colonial* (Lima and Tampa: IEP Ediciones and University of South Florida, 1996), 64.

Mission priests went even further in protecting women from sexual temptation. In many missions there was a *casa de recogidas*, where women whose husbands were absent, or had fled, or whose general whereabouts were unknown, lived. In addition, widows, especially young widows without parents or other living relatives to protect them, were also housed in the casa. The casa de recogidas also served as a prison for female criminals – that is, for women who had in some way disobeyed the priests. Although they were not formally imprisoned, those deemed to have misbehaved were kept handcuffed and could leave the house only when accompanied by the *superiora*. On the other hand, recalcitrant women received better treatment than men; they were whipped only on their backs, only in private (within the confines of the casa), and only by other women.

Although responsible for female conduct, mission priests were enjoined to avoid all contact with Indian women. In the Jesuit missions of Paraguay priests were instructed to speak directly to women only with a witness present. The priest was never to be alone with or to touch any woman, and when handing the rosary to a woman, he used an Indian male as go-between. This did not stop priests from closely supervising the work of women. For example, priests managed to check the quality and quantity of the cotton thread spun by women, punishing those believed guilty of trickery.

The degree to which mission priests actually kept their distance from their female charges is hard to determine, although probably the Jesuits came closest to the ideal. On the other hand, firsthand observers such as Huamán Poma de Ayala depicted Catholic priests in general as sexual hypocrites. The text of his drawing *The Father Confesses* warned that "the fathers confess the Indian women in houses of the church and the baptismal font and the sacristy[;] in the dark and suspicious hidden places [they force] the single women to commit fornication and sin with them."[6]

Although much of the Indian population of America was brought into missions, along the frontiers of the empire, in regions such as Central America, northern Mexico, the South American Chaco, and the interior of Brazil, Indians continued to war against the Europeans. Repeated decrees forbade the enslavement of women and young children taken in "just" war, but this legislation did little to change reality

[6] Felipe Guamán Poma de Ayala, *El primer nueva corónica y buen gobierno* (Madrid: Siglo Veintiuno, 1980), 2:546.

In 1569, for example, two female Chichimec captives, aged twelve and twenty-five, were auctioned off to the highest bidder in San Luis Potosí. Women were also sold to the Europeans by hostile tribes, while a few were ransomed by their own people or given to Europeans in "marriage" by their father or chief. At least one mid-seventeenth-century Chilean report on the Indian slave trade suggests that adult women were twice as valuable as adult men.

Indian women were bought and sold, often ending up working as menial domestic laborers in the homes of the local elite. Their acceptance of assimilation varied widely. Some Indian women successfully escaped rejoining their tribes. Most spent their lives in formal or informal slavery, working as domestic servants or prostitutes for their master or mistress. Many found themselves in illicit sexual unions with their masters, but in some frontier regions where there was a scarcity of Spanish women, Indian women were also desirable wives. Soldiers stationed in remote military outposts in northern Mexico, for example, frequently took Indian brides, as did many of the Portuguese settlers of São Paulo. Occasionally an Indian woman emerged as a leader of her community or as an active mediator between the Europeans and rebellious Indians. Damiana da Cunha, for example, a Christianized Portuguese-speaking Caiapó woman from the Goías region in Brazil, not only adapted to European society but carved out a position of authority and respect for herself.

Along the European-Indian frontiers, raiding for women captives continued until the end of the eighteenth century. Conversely Indians also raided frontier settlements for "European" women, who they often took as wives or concubines. In certain regions, such as the Buenos Aires frontier, the result was the existence of a large group of Spanish women, aware of their linguistic and cultural differences, but assimilated into Indian society as spouses and mothers.

The conquest of indigenous societies by Europeans produced far-reaching changes in the lives of Indian women. Some of these changes were universal – a new culture, the Roman Catholic religion, new power relationships. Other changes varied widely by region, time, and the social class of the women themselves. The experience of an Inca princess married to a Spanish conquistador was totally unlike that of a Guaraní woman living in a Jesuit mission or a Chichimec woman enslaved and sold to the highest bidder.

Many Indian women were abused, especially in the early years of the conquest or in regions relatively isolated from government oversight.

But other women adapted with some degree of success to the new world that conquest had produced and learned to survive. By manipulating European laws and European customs, these women managed, within limited parameters, to prosper. On balance the European conquest produced both hardships and opportunities for the indigenous women of America.

CHAPTER 4

THE ARRIVAL OF IBERIAN WOMEN

You write to me that . . . you have a married daughter and four others to marry off as well as a son. It seems to me that these are many children to have to find positions for with the nobles of Spain. I know something about this, for I had to serve them, and seeing how little future there was in this made me come here. . . . we decided to come to Mexico City where God has been very gracious to us. The only thing we haven't been lucky in has been children, because the one that came here with us died, and I have had no others. Thus, because you have so many children . . . I would be most pleased if you were disposed to come here with my niece. We will take care of all family members who come here. And if you have any money left over that you don't need for passage, give it to your married daughter. . . . If you can manage it, come as soon as possible, for I am old, and as I can no longer go back to Spain, I would love to see my niece and her children before I die. . . . Please tell my niece not to invent any excuses; I am also a woman, and no stronger than any other, but God graciously brought me here and helped me, and thus will He do for her.[1]

Although the discovery and conquest of America was predominantly a male enterprise, Spanish women did have a limited role in the early settlements. In general during the period of Spanish conquest military expeditions sent to explore and conquer a region would be made up primarily of men, for Iberian women were considered superfluous during

[1] From a letter of Leonor de Aguilera to Francisco del Castillo, husband of her niece, Mexico City, 1591, cited in Enrique Otte, *Cartas privadas de emigrantes a Indias, 1540–1616* (Mexico: Fondo de Cultura Económica, 1993), 121–122.

battle. (Some exceptions to this rule were the woman who arrived in Mexico with Cortés's fleet and the five women included among the founders of the city of Puebla in 1531.) Once the initial conquest was complete a handful of Spanish women appeared. In the years following conquest, proportionately more Spanish women made their way to the New World. In comparison the Portuguese were slower to colonize and to send women to America.

The arrival of Spanish women in America was considered paramount by the crown for it believed that only Spanish women could transform the new settlements in the Indies into permanent colonies. Both crown and church thought that in addition to shoring up the institution of marriage, the arrival of European women would introduce Iberian cultural values into newly conquered regions. Women were seen as "civilizers"; it was they who would teach proper behavior and social forms to their menfolk, and act as the conservators of social gentility. Indeed, women were a metaphor for rootedness, and were portrayed as carrying the seeds and plants of the Old World to the New. Stressing the civilizing and stabilizing attributes of women, and foreseeing that they would populate the new lands with European Christian offspring, women's participation was encouraged in the second wave of colonizers. The crown's two-pronged policy encouraged married women to join their husbands in the Indies while enlisting unmarried women to come to the colonies as prospective wives for unmarried conquistadors. This campaign, it was hoped, would relieve Spain of having to support married women abandoned in Spain while ending the immoral behavior of the conquerors.

As early as 1498 thirty Spanish women accompanied Columbus on his third voyage to the Caribbean. The initial rate of immigration for European women was low; no more than 6 percent of immigrants were women in first decade, and women were only 10 percent of all colonists who came to America in the first thirty years after conquest. It is believed, for example, that between 1509 and 1519 only 308 Spanish women arrived in America. The majority of these early female migrants were from Seville and surrounding regions in southern Spain; most were women traveling in family groups, although there was always a large contingent of female servants. At first most were destined for Santo Domingo, the most "civilized" place in the Spanish colonial world, but as the conquest moved to terra firma, so did Spanish women. Wives, daughters, and nieces began arriving in New Spain as early as 1521, joining the men of their families who had taken part in the

conquest or were early settlers. Between 1509 and 1538 perhaps one thousand women left Spain for America. By 1540 European women were present in most Spanish American cities ranging from Mexico to Asunción.

Some Spanish women who came early in the colonization process found themselves involved in bloody turbulence. A handful of Spanish women took part in the civil wars that rent early Spanish Peru, participating in the various factions and at times losing their lives or their husbands to opposing groups of fellow Spaniards. The story of Leonor de Bobdilla, daughter of the Conde de la Gómera, is emblematic of noble Spanish women in the early days of the colonization. Married first to Nuño Tovar, she was widowed almost immediately when her husband left Santo Domingo to fight and die in the conquest of Florida. After arriving in Peru, she remarried Lorenzo Mexía, who died shortly thereafter at the hands of a Pizarro follower. During her lifetime she also witnessed the death of her firstborn and the executions of a son and a brother.

Over time increasing numbers of Spanish women and children arrived in the colonies. By 1530 Spanish women figured regularly in the lists of immigrants leaving for the New World; by 1550 they were a substantial presence. Female immigration to America rose to 16.5 percent by 1560 as increasing numbers of Spaniards, believing that their fellow settlers presented good opportunities for an advantageous marriage in America, began to import their unmarried sisters, cousins, and nieces. (See Document 1.) The arrival of Spanish women reached a high point of 28 to 40 percent of all immigrants by the end of the century, declining slightly by the seventeenth century. In the eighteenth century, when Spanish immigration picked up again, women constituted a mere 15 percent of the immigrant group. Immigration of Portuguese women to Brazil was always even lower. Probably between 1500 and 1700 no more than 100,000 Portuguese women made their way across the Atlantic, an average of about 500 per year. For approximately the same period it has been estimated that 2,900 Spanish women arrived in America each year.

To control the turbulent sexual morality of its men and create a stable society, the Spanish government soon instituted a reward system that encouraged husbands to send for their wives. In this way they also hoped to control men such as the sixteenth-century Central American royal judge, Pedro Ramírez de Quiñones, who carried on affairs with three married women while his wife stayed behind in Spain. Hernán

Cortés, the conqueror of Mexico who himself had delayed bringing his wife from Cuba, ordered all holders of encomienda grants to bring their wives to Mexico, an order repeated by the royal judges (*oidores*) ruling the colony after 1530. In sixteenth-century Chile, encomienda grants often stipulated that being married and "maintaining an honorable household and wife" were prerequisites for the award, while in Peru royal legislation made marriage and legitimate heirs the sine qua non of passing on an encomienda to the next generation. The crown also tried to restrict the emigration of married men who left for the New World without their wives. But try as the Spanish crown would to insure the stability of New World society by encouraging men to migrate with their wives once the initial period of conquest warfare was over, the crown's actual power was quite limited. Royal orders issued in the new colonies periodically encouraged all single men to marry with an equal lack of success.

At times married men who had sailed to the Indies alone believed their spouses to have died during their absence and entered into second marriages. Poor communications, confusion, or a desire to forget about a Spanish wife could and did lead to scandalous cases of bigamy. One such case was that of Francisco Noguerol de Ulloa, a young man from Galicia who made his way to Peru in 1534, leaving a bride behind. Fifteen years later, after receiving word from his sisters in Spain that his wife had died, he married Catalina de Vergara, widow of a royal judge. Only in 1554 did Noguerol find out that his first wife was very much alive. He was charged with bigamy.

Spanish women arriving in the sixteenth-century colonies in turn provided passage for other female kin. (See Leonor de Aguilera's letter at the beginning of this chapter.) Just as Spanish men coming to America represented a wide social spectrum, so did the Spanish women who followed. Not all Spaniards arriving in America were noblemen. The majority of these Spaniards, both men and women, were of middle- and working-class backgrounds, artisans and servants, as well as poor people of humble circumstances. Indeed female immigrants from regions such as Extramadura, where women were economically active, had often worked as bakers, vendors, candlemakers, innkeepers, midwives, or servants before coming to America. Women, as well as men, came to America as servants in the entourage of a noble, a priest, or government official.

Those single women whose families could provide them with a large dowry were exceedingly attractive marriage candidates once they arrived in the New World, although their social origins also played a part in determining whether men of rank and power took them as brides. For example, the six daughters of Leonel de Cervantes, an ally of Cortés and conqueror of Mexico City, all married encomenderos. The marriages of these Spanish women helped to reinforce the social glue of the early colonial society by creating family clans and kinship networks that exercised local political and economic power. In this way, for example, Bernaldino Vázquez de Tapia, a member of the Mexico City town council, or *cabildo*, was linked to several other cabildo members who were married to his nieces.

The wives of conquistadors and first settlers were usually markedly younger than their husbands. The typical pattern was the marriage of a young women still in her teens to a man often twenty or thirty years her senior. This age discrepancy increased the probability that a wife would outlive her husband. Once widowed those Spanish women who had inherited important encomiendas from their late husbands became attractive remarriage candidates. In addition, acquiring the protection of a second husband was important when a woman had to fight to maintain her inheritance. Two of the previously mentioned Cervantes sisters quickly remarried after their husbands died; one of them married for still a third time when her second husband died. It was not unusual for wealthy widows to turn to younger men as their protectors and second husbands.

In an attempt to normalize the sexual conduct of Spaniards in more remote areas, the state organized shipments of unmarried damsels with the goal of providing wives for the local conquistadors. Often the newly arriving Spanish women were greeted with a round of festivities. Then the local governor or other authorities got down to business – the business of arranging marriages for the recently arrived young women. These women were often encouraged to marry older battle-scared men. According to Garcilaso de la Vega in Peru, one young lady advised her crestfallen friends to marry these "rotten old men" because after their death they "will be able to choose a young man of our liking to take the place of the old one, as one changes an old, broken pot for a new one in good condition".[2]

Conditions were even more difficult for those women who partici-

[2] Inca Garcilaso de la Vega, *Historia general del Perú* (Lima: Librería Internacional del Perú, 1959), 1:115, cited in Luis Martin, *Daughters of the Conquistadores: Women of the Viceroyalty of Peru* (Dallas: Southern Methodist University Press, 1983), 14–15.

pated in the conquest and early settlement of more isolated regions. The chroniclers speak of white women enduring hunger and lack of basic necessities, as well as Spanish women being ravished by Indian chiefs or driven by hunger to leave camp to join the Indians. Chroniclers tend to underline the bravery, chastity, and fidelity of these women, although at times qualities such as love, power, leadership, and strength are also demonstrated. Even allowing for some dramatic exaggeration in chronicle and personal accounts, there is no doubt that Spanish women behaved heroically when circumstances warranted it. (See Document 2.)

At least one women was present in the Cabot expedition to the Río de la Plata, and probably six Spanish women lived in the ill-fated colony of Sancti Spiritus. We know of eight women who took part in the doomed expedition of Pedro de Mendoza, including the wife of a Canarian laborer, some women referred to as "doña," the Spanish title of respect for women from elite families, and some servants. One of the noblewomen, doña Isabel de Guevara, survived the disastrous attempt to found a settlement in Buenos Aires and joined the retreat upriver to Asunción. Years later she described the journey in a letter to Princess Regent Juana, stressing the heroic contribution of women throughout the ordeal. According to Isabel, because women were able to survive with less nourishment, when the men became too weak to carry on in the settlement,

> all the tasks fell on the poor women, washing the clothes as well as nursing the men, preparing them the little food there was, keeping them clean, standing guard, patrolling the fires, loading the crossbows when the Indians came . . . to do battle, even firing the cannon, and arousing the soldiers who were capable of fighting, shouting the alarm through the camp, acting as sergeants and putting the soldiers in order.

When the few famine survivors decided to seek refuge upriver, women continued to play an important part in the retreat. As the two ships moved upriver, the women

> worked the sail, steered the ship, sounded the depth, bailed out the water, took the oar when a soldier was unable to row, and exhorted the soldiers not to be discouraged.

Their Herculean efforts did not end when they reached Asunción, for now the surviving women had to turn to their tasks anew, making clearings with their own hands, clearing and hoeing and sowing and harvesting the crop with no one's aid until such time as the soldiers recovered from their weakness and began to rule the land, acquiring the service of Indian men and women.[3]

For women living along the frontier, life was especially arduous. Although life gradually improved, some regions of the newly conquered lands continued to experience a scarcity of food, clothing, and basic necessities for years after the conquest. As late as 1579 commentators spoke of a shortage of wine, oil, cloth, soap, and other goods in Yucatan. In regions such as Florida, Chile, and the Río de la Plata, where a state of war existed between Spaniards and Indians, life was also particularly dangerous for the few European women present. In 1582 at least one Spanish woman was reportedly captured during an Indian attack near the newly resettled town of Buenos Aires. Because it was difficult to attract women to these remote regions, unmarried Spanish women continued to be shipped to these areas. Often those willing to undertake the journey were women of exceedingly modest circumstances or ill repute.

In some regions widows and daughters of conquistadors found themselves so poor that they lacked the necessary dowry to attract suitable marriage candidates. According to one report from Yucatan, "the Spaniards have many young daughters waiting to marry who are suffering because they have neither prospective candidates nor the wherewithal to survive and as the region is so poor. . . . no military men with whom they might marry arrive." In Tucumán there were reported to be "more than sixty poor young women, daughters of conquistadors" who could not hope to marry men of an acceptable social station.

The situation was somewhat different in Brazil where white women were in even shorter supply in the sixteenth century. From time to time a few orphan women of good family were sent to the colony. Although they were quickly married, their numbers were so scant that it did little to correct the massive sexual imbalance among Europeans. In 1549 the Jesuit Manuel Nóbrega suggested that Portuguese prostitutes be imported to solve the chronic absence of white women in the colony.

Given this demographic reality, and the belief that only marriage to Portuguese women would create the necessary stability to assure the

---

[3] June E. Hahner, *Women in Latin American History: Their Lives and Views* (Los Angeles: UCLA Latin American Center, 1976), 18–20.

survival of its colony, the Portuguese crown not surprisingly pursued a pronatalist policy. Well into the seventeenth century the crown opposed the creation of a convent in Brazil, reasoning that because "women [were] more essential to the propagation of the species than were men,"[4] an institution that would remove potential fertile white females from the population could not be justified.

Even after the initial conquest and European colonization had ended, marriage continued to be a sign of stability. Colonial governments never stopped pursuing policies that encouraged European inhabitants to marry. The Portuguese crown, seeking to impose order in the raucous mining district of Minas Gerais in the eighteenth century, not only urged all important people to marry but considered restricting public service to married men. By the end of the same century the Spanish crown also saw marriage as a means of increasing colonial population and developing local economies.

By the final decades of the sixteenth century, because of the combined effects of immigration and birth, Spanish women were no longer in short supply in many regions of Spanish America. Increasingly Spanish men from a wide range of social backgrounds, from nobles to artisans, routinely married Spanish women who had either migrated from Spain or, more likely, had been born in the colonies. About this time Spaniard settlers also began founding the first convents in part as a refuge for daughters who could find no suitable marriage partners.

Thus, due to immigration and procreation the female population of European descent in Spanish America went from scarcity to parity and in some regions to oversupply. The rapidity with which a society of male conquistadores was transformed into one of male and female settlers varied from place to place, but the transformation was usually accomplished within two or three generations. While numerical gender parity was slower to be established in Brazil, there too the number of women of European descent came to equal that of men. Now Iberians could get on with the business of establishing a stable society with a clear racial hierarchy.

[4] *Documentos históricos da Bibliotheca Nacional do Rio de Janeiro*, 97 (1952), 19, cited in Susan A. Soeiro, "The Feminine Orders in Colonial Bahia, Brazil: Economic, Social, and Demographic Implications, 1677–1899," in Asunción Lavrin, ed., *Latin American Women: Historical Perspectives* (Westport, Conn.: Greenwood Press, 1978), 176.

CHAPTER 5

WOMEN, MARRIAGE, AND

FAMILY

"Mother, what is marriage about?"
"My child, it is spinning, bearing children, and crying."[1]

The centrality of the family – the nuclear family and the extended kin group – to social organization was a Mediterranean cultural value that the Spanish and Portuguese transplanted to America. This importance of family meant that marriage, the institution that created new families, was viewed by church and state as crucial to an orderly social organization in the colonies. Furthermore, marriage protected females and delineated the boundary between those children who were legitimate (and therefore had legal claim against the family's property) and those who were not. Although throughout colonial Latin America, legitimate marriage coexisted with other more informal relationships, marriage and the legitimacy it bestowed were marks of status, the indication that one was a person of rank rather than a mere plebeian, a Spaniard rather than a mixed-blood.

As a result, in colonial Latin America marriage was closely tied to race, social status, and economic conditions. Indeed, legal marriage was only overwhelmingly practiced by two socioracial groups, groups that paradoxically occupied widely separated positions on the social scale. One group with a strong tendency to marry was the white elite (here we can include those who aspired to its ranks). The other group com-

---

[1] José Francos Rodríguez, *La mujer y la política española* (Madrid: Editorial Pueyo, 1920), 179, cited in Johanna S. R. Mendelson, "The Feminine Press: The View of Women in the Colonial Journals of Spanish America, 1790–1810," in Asunción Lavrin, ed., *Latin American Women: Historical Perspectives* (Westport, Conn.: Greenwood Press, 1978), 199.

prised Indians living in rural communities. As we shall see, through marriage these groups were responding to very different types of social pressures.

Among the elite, marriage was the most desirable civil state for women, for it sheltered them and kept them from dishonorable pursuits. Nobles and elite merchants in Mexico City, wholesale merchants in Buenos Aires, elites in Santiago de Chile, as well as landowners, encomenderos, and bureaucrats in Peru, all formed part of a local Hispanic elite who overwhelmingly indulged in matrimony. Indeed, it was within legitimate marriage that most elite women spent their lives.

A woman's age at marriage fluctuated over time and across regions, although in general women married at an earlier age than men. Although canon law, the religious law of the Roman Catholic Church, allowed women to marry from age 12 (and men from age 14), marriage at such young ages was extremely rare. For example, in the eighteenth century most women in Mexico City married for the first time between the ages of 17 and 27, with the average age of marriage being 20.5 years. During approximately the same period the median age of first marriage for women in León (Mexico) varied from 16 to 18 years of age, with Indian women tending to marry younger than the population as a whole. In late-eighteenth-century Ouro Preto the average age for women at time of marriage was 22. Spanish women usually married men who were at least 7 to 8 years older, and therefore relatively mature and prosperous, or at least settled in a profession or calling.

Before courtship women were ideally to be virgins and were often referred to as "doncellas" or "niñas" regardless of their age. We know little about actual courtship customs, how couples met or how long courtship lasted. Flirting and social contact seems to have taken place in churches and especially at religious festivals held at night, for we have constant complaints by clergymen that the public made religious occasions into social ones. In those cases where marriage was not wholly arranged by the bride's parents, courtship probably consisted of brief conversations, secret notes and messages, and the exchange of gifts between the couple.

In general marriage patterns in colonial Latin America displayed a great degree of social endogamy. Women, be they the daughters of landowners, merchants, artisans, military officers, or government officials, tended to marry men from the same social group as their fathers.

The most common marriage pattern was between members of the same race, occupational group, social stratum, and parish. In a society organized by social and racial castes and corporate entities, these marriage patterns made sense.

Marriage was a family affair, and family interests, not romantic love, were given primary consideration. Although in theory both bride and groom were to enter into marriage exercising their own free will, both the age of the bride and family pressures encouraged many young women to marry the man chosen for them. Mariana Monroy, the wife of a *peninsular* living in late-seventeenth-century New Spain, claimed that her marriage had been her mother's idea, and that she, being only fourteen at the time, was too inexperienced to challenge her mother's wishes. Another woman in seventeenth-century Lima testified that her brother forced her to marry, threatening her with a dagger.

Regardless of the age of the bride and groom, once a suitable match had been found, a detailed marriage process began. The first step was the official engagement – known as "promise of future marriage" – a mutual binding promise given by the couple before two witnesses, which was viewed as being as valid as the marriage itself. The legal value given to betrothal protected women by obligating men to fulfill the terms of a contract. If a man failed to marry his intended after promising marriage, he could be sued for breach of promise and forced to marry. (See Document 7.) The only acceptable reason for a man to break off an engagement was the discovery that his intended was not a virgin. When an engaged woman changed her mind, the marriage did not take place.

Once the couple was formally betrothed, more public physical contact was permitted. In the eyes of the church, kissing, hugging, and touching (as long as it was not overtly sensual) between people engaged to marry was not considered to be a sin. There is much indirect evidence that, in spite of church opposition, once the marriage promise had been made, some couples began sexual relations. The practice of beginning sexual relations during engagement created a certain ambiguous space for women, endangering the future of any women who failed to marry her intended. Because of the importance of virginity, elite women who lost their virginity closed the option of marriage to anyone other than their lover. On the other hand, women from less exalted social backgrounds could occasionally force the man who deflowered them to pay for the loss of their virginity, using this money as a dowry for marriage to another.

Even more problematic than the loss of virginity was the accompanying risk of pregnancy, for while the former might be covered up, the latter was more difficult to hide. The situation of a young woman "afflicted by the growth of her womb" not only "made public her miserable state" but also produced "a notable loss of her honor, especially if "she had been publicly believed to be a virgin." Nonetheless, it was not unheard of to marry only when the woman became pregnant, thus protecting her honor while having proof positive of her fertility. Cases where a child was born within two or three months of marriage can be found in all colonial marriage registers. Even longer delays could result in an elite woman bearing a child out of wedlock, but marriage to the child's father usually followed, and the child was subsequently legitimized.

A woman might also invoke the power of the marriage promise if the man failed to marry her after the couple had been living together for long periods of time, or after several children had been born out of wedlock. Often the woman or her family did not challenge the man until he attempted to dissolve the informal union. Then, armed with the testimony of witnesses to a promise of marriage, the aggrieved woman appealed to local civil or ecclesiastical authorities. If she could prove that a promise of marriage had indeed been given, the authorities would order the man to marry. One historian has suggested that the power of women to make men comply with matrimonial promises diminished as judges came to insist on written rather that oral proof.[2]

A hesitant groom was not the only obstacle to marriage. Disapproving parents could also present problems. One solution was to appeal to the church, which from the mid-sixteenth through the seventeenth century defended the Council of Trent's doctrine of "free will" as the sine qua non of marriage, thus protecting a couple's right to marry. In the majority of parental opposition cases brought to the attention of the Mexico City ecclesiastical authorities, the church sided with the couples, at times going so far as to perform secret marriages or removing individuals from the custody of their parents to further matrimonial plans. But the church gradually abandoned its policy, siding more and more frequently with the parents in marital opposition cases. Couples now turned to a more daring solution: kidnapping, followed

[2] Patricia Seed, "Marriage Promises and the Value of a Woman's Testimony in Colonial Mexico," *Signs*, 13:2 (1988), 254.

by seduction, a strategy that tended to present the parents of the deflowered young women with a fait accompli. Under these terms, marriage, even to a mildly unacceptable spouse, was preferable to a dishonored daughter.

From time to time, elite women became pregnant under circumstances that made it impossible to marry. In some cases the intended groom was a government official or military officer who lacked royal permission to marry; in others the woman's lover was already married or had died or departed before a marriage could be performed. Because the existence of an illegitimate child created vulnerability for a woman and her honor, many of these women experienced "private pregnancy," often calling on close family members to help them, or traveling to another town to bear the child. Such women neither openly acknowledged nor raised the child, and the mother's name was omitted from the child's baptismal certificate. Other women chose to make their pregnancies more public, emphasizing that they had been formally engaged to marry, and thus had not lost their honor. Although their punishment was always a private family affair, both groups of elite women paid a harsh social price for their conduct: perpetual and total seclusion and a life of spinsterhood. Women from less exalted social groups, on the other hand, were sometimes able to marry even after bearing children out of wedlock.

Two other groups of women who tended to marry, although no doubt for very different reasons, were those living in traditional Indian communities or on missions. Here the proximity and control of Catholic clergy or the traditional values of these societies worked to encourage young women to have children within legitimate unions, although in the Andean region Indians continued their preconquest pattern of trial marriage.

For most other women, including castas, mulattas, mestizas, slaves, and very poor Spaniards, marriage, although the societal norm, was not a universal practice. Among these groups it was more common to find women entering into relationships, sometimes short-term, sometimes lengthy, without the benefit of matrimony. Marriage rates for the non-Spanish, nonelite population fluctuated as local conditions changed. In times of extreme economic hardship, for example, marriage rates for these groups tended to drop. In addition free women of African descent probably married more frequently than slave women.

Throughout colonial Latin America, racial intermarriage was

limited. White women tended to marry outside of their racial group less than anyone else. Women, on the whole, displayed a greater tendency to marry within their racial group than did men. Of all black women marrying in Mexico City between 1646 and 1746, for example, 79 percent chose black mates, but only 47 percent of black men selected black spouses. Race and class also affected the average age difference between husband and wife. In elite white couples the husband was often from six to twelve years older than his wife while in poor white, mestizo, mulatto, and black couples the husband tended to be only two to four years older than his wife.

Once married, women were charged with caring for their husbands, managing their households, bearing and educating their children, and joining their husbands in protecting the fortunes of their families. Although not envisioned as the leaders of the families, wives were not entirely passive or dependent; they could and did take the initiative, acting decisively and making choices. Wives of men who were absent for long periods of time oversaw household and property, functioning as junior partners in the family enterprise. In this role they might manage considerable amounts of money, oversee people, and de facto act on their own. These women also took responsibility for rearing their children, finding suitable marriage partners for their offspring, and amassing their daughters' dowries. The trust their husbands put in them was demonstrated when men granted their wives blanket power of attorney or named them as executrixes of their estate and guardians of their minor childrens' inheritances.

According to the Catholic Church, sexual relations were to take place only within marriage, and only for purposes of procreation. Sex solely for pleasure was condemned as was sodomy (including anal and oral sex) and masturbation, because their goal was not conception. Nevertheless, sex within marriage was viewed as a mutual obligation of both husband and wife, the so-called conjugal debt. Refusing to have sex with your spouse was a sin, and both husband and wife had the right to initiate sex. But women were to be subtle in requesting sexual relations with their husbands because this right conflicted with the social prescription that women be modest. There were also times when marital sexual relations were prohibited, including holy days and during the woman's menstrual period.

Even within marriage, a couple was not to engage in practices considered to be "against nature." This included "unchaste contact," especially contact that resulted in nonvaginal ejaculation, excessive petting ("putting one's hands in dishonest places"), and sex talk. Vaginal sex was the norm, but some sexual positions were considered to be "dirty and ugly" because they were considered to be "animal-like."

In theory all female sexuality was to occur within marriage, but in practice there were varying codes about female sexuality depending on the social group of the woman. Elite women were subject to strong private control exercised by their families. The elite also subscribed to a double sexual standard; women were to be pure, whereas men were to be sexually adventurous. Among the elite a woman's having sexual relations before engagement was a serious blot on her honor. Nonelite women, on the other hand, were subjected to weaker public control of their sexuality. The same double standard affected attitudes toward adultery. In general, men's adulterous escapades were accepted both by society and by their wives, who no doubt feared abandonment should they present any opposition. Female adultery was not only far less socially acceptable than male; it was far more risky. If a married woman was caught in the act with another man, her husband had the right to kill her. His vengeance was considered to be justifiable homicide.

The Catholic Church's insistence that sex be closely linked to pro-creation forbade all practices aimed at preventing pregnancy. Indeed, there is no direct evidence for any practice of birth control, although colonial folk medicine had a panoply of herbal remedies supposedly guaranteed to prevent conception or induce early abortion. Rue (*ruta graveolens*) was one such plant reputed to be a contraceptive and abortifacient. We can only imagine that some of these remedies proved efficacious.

The state of gynecological knowledge was rudimentary at best. Although most women were attended at birth by midwives, the pro-fession of midwifery was excoriated for its superstition rather than its science. Every woman faced a high probability that she might die in one or another childbirth, for difficult births, infection, and ignor-ance resulted in high maternal mortality. As a result the average age of death for the majority of women was probably about thirty years old. Nonetheless, most married women could expect to give birth to five or six children, although not all of them would survive early infancy. Among the elite, families were often larger, with more frequent preg-nancies (the result of better nutrition and wet-nursing practices) and greater survival rates. By the eighteenth century an elite woman might expect to bear nine or ten children, and families of thirteen or four-teen, while unusual, were not unheard of.

Not all married couples lived in harmony, and marital conflict was not unknown in colonial society. Women believed that marriage was an indissoluble pact and turned to family members and civil and reli-gious authorities when they judged their husbands to have neglected their moral responsibilities. Women also expected their husbands to provide a minimal level of sustenance, including bed and board. When abandoned, women, citing universally shared ideas of a husband's obli-gation to provide for his wife, sued their husband for *alimentos* in the local courts.

Marriage gave a husband the power to exercise his patriarchal authority, including disciplining and punishing his wife as long as he was not arbitrary or excessive. In the moral economy of marriage a wife had the right to expect just and loving treatment in return for her obe-dience, while her husband had the right to use "moderate" physical punishment to secure obedience from an obdurate or wayward wife. In other words, husbands were considered to be within their legal and moral rights when they physically punished their wives, for this was the accepted method of correcting "wayward" women and making sure they conformed to the norms of proper female behavior.

Their husbands' physical power was reflected in the level of physi-cal abuse that colonial women endured. Women were beaten, stabbed, starved, and even tortured by their mates. An informal social agree-ment dictated what treatment was too severe, and family members or neighbors would intervene when the husband had transgressed these bounds. But husbands were not the only ones who exercised the right to discipline their wives. Mothers- and sisters-in-laws were also accused of physically and psychologically mistreating wives, especially those wives who were young and living under the same roof as their in-laws.

But some husbands clearly went beyond acceptable canons, subject-ing their wives to long-term mistreatment and humiliation and thus embittering their lives (*la mala vida*). An abused woman occa-sionally ran away, seeking shelter with family members or retiring to convents, or petitioned church authorities in an attempt to change her husband's conduct. In these briefs a wife stressed that she had been treated unjustly by her husband and punished too severely or too arbi-trarily, calling attention to how her husband's conduct had ruined her life.

In general women were carefully controlled during legal clashes with their husbands. Because men usually had a near monopoly of physical, economic, and legal power, they could easily force any unruly wife into legal seclusion, depositing her in a convent or private home, and thus controlling her physical movement and social interaction. To counter their husband's power, women could and did turn to male kin – fathers, brothers, brothers-in-law – to defend them.

Church authorities were usually reluctant to end a marriage and would counsel couples to attempt reconciliation. In the most egregious cases, however, church law provided protection for women by allowing them to institute legal separation proceedings. Among acceptable reasons for separation were extreme physical or spiritual danger, including gross mistreatment, threat of murder, and wanton adultery, as well as forcing a wife into crime, paganism, or heresy. Separation was not the modern equivalent of divorce. The church granted only separation of *cuerpo y bienes* (body and goods): the couple was no longer required to live together, and a woman's dowry and half of the property acquired during the marriage was turned over to her. But neither party could remarry while his or her spouse was still alive.

Nonetheless, ending a marriage through separation was rare in colonial Latin America; when it occurred, it was almost always the woman who requested it. During the divorce proceedings the woman was placed in a convent or private home (*depósito*) and closely monitored; no such restrictions were imposed on men. Suing one's husband was risky business, for if the woman was found to have made groundless charges, she could lose all her property, including her dowry. Women suing for separation also ran the risk of their husbands countercharging female adultery. Once a woman obtained a legal separation, she was usually considered to be a social pariah and isolated from polite society. Men separated legally from their wives suffered no such social sanction. In addition to social ostracism, for many women separation brought relative economic impoverishment.

In spite of the weakness of their situation, the French observer François Depons was amazed by the "blind protection afforded by the Spanish laws to females in opposition to their husbands."[3] When an aggrieved woman turned to the civil and ecclesiastical authorities,

[3] François Joseph de Pons, *Travels in Part of South America, during the Years 1801, 1802, 1803 and 1804 Containing a Description of the Captain-Generalship of Carraccas* (London: Richard Phillips, 1806), 37–38.

these judges were ready "to believe everything that an imagination can suggest against her husband." Furthermore "no proof is required of [her] assertions; she is believed on her word. The husband, in such cases . . . is either cited to appear . . . or he is instantly, and without further inquiry, thrown into prison, where he continues until his liberation is requested by his wife."

The Catholic Church never gave any woman the right to marry again while her husband was still alive, but there are examples of women who conveniently forgot about their original vows, appearing for a second time before the wedding altar. Although far fewer than men, female bigamists, like male ones, tended to be among the geographically mobile poor. María Felipa, a mestiza living in San Andrés Chalchicomula (Mexico), deserted her first husband (a man she had married at age twelve) and, accompanied by her encouraging mother, moved to Mexico City. There she found work as a spinner (*hilandera*) and eventually began a relationship with José Ignacio Gamboa. After nine months of living together, Gamboa proposed matrimony. María Felipa, her mother at her side, appeared before the priest, swearing that she was "free and not tied by marriage" and was wed to Gamboa. Only two years later when an ex-neighbor from San Andrés arrived in Mexico City was the bigamy discovered.

As a result of the state of medical knowledge about childbirth, disease, and illness, widowhood was a common phenomenon in colonial Latin America. But very different social patterns obtained depending on whether the man or his wife was the survivor of the marriage. Because they were desperate for another wife to manage the household and mother their orphaned children, widowers frequently remarried. Among the elite, men often took brides ten to fifteen years their junior. Non-elite widowers also remarried, perhaps needing the domestic labor of a wife even more urgently than those with servants; they too usually chose single women considerably younger than they.

Because of the age disparity between husbands and wives, women were more frequently widowed than men. In addition, some dangerous or unhealthy professions tended to create a surplus of widows. In the formative years after the conquest, when Spanish women were at a premium, widows remarried with great frequency. Such was the case in Peru in the 1540s, years immediately following the civil wars, which had left many Spanish women husbandless. By the seventeenth century in most of Latin America, only those women who had wealth, social position, or unusual sexual attraction could hope to remarry after widowhood, although there were always regional exceptions to this pattern. Montevideo, in the years after its founding as a military outpost, continued to suffer from a shortage of women, making widows as attractive as single women in the marriage market.

Widowhood was almost an expected stage of the female life course. Many older elite women might expect to spend the last twenty years of their lives as widows. A few found themselves in a good economic position, in control of their dowry and property acquired during marriage (*gananciales*), well attended by family and servants, guardians of their minor children, and able to draw on male family members and *compadres* for advice and support while they ruled their families. In these cases the patriarchal family, so mythologized in Latin America, was transformed into a matriarchal family.

But widowhood did not usually translate into economic independence and familial power. Widows could find themselves involved in complicated litigation associated with their late husbands' estates, vexed by trying to provide social and economic positions for their children and plagued by debts. They could also discover they were at the mercy of rapacious in-laws, willful children, and bad financial advice. Paradoxically in many of the cases involving widows there is a strong suggestion that the wealthiest and poorest possessed the greatest independence in the managing of their property.

Although marriage to an earthly or heavenly spouse was a social ideal, a large group of women could not achieve this goal. The alternative to the choice between marriage and nunnery was spinsterhood. In part the problem was demographic, for by the seventeenth century women were overwhelmingly concentrated in the cities, where they tended to outnumber men; in general for every one hundred women there were anywhere from eighty-two to eighty-eight men. In regions where men were engaged in endemic warfare or where women were left behind as men moved out to the frontier, spinsterhood was also quite common. Some of these women subsequently migrated to the nearby towns and cities, further increasing the numbers of women in urban settings.

In general women remained spinsters more frequently than men. Even in those communities of relatively low "definitive spinsterhood" 8 to 10 percent of all women never married, while among men the rates ranged from 6 to 7 percent. A distinction must be drawn, however, among spinsters who remained single and celibate, those who remained single, and those who were involved either in long-term or serial common-law marriages.

Celibate spinsters were found primarily among the real and would-be elite. Among these groups, spinsterhood also resulted from elite impoverishment – for example, a girl might be orphaned without sufficient dowry to attract a socially suitable candidate. In addition, encouraging spinsterhood for a daughter or two was a way to lessen the effect of the laws of partible inheritance and the continuous splintering of family wealth. Spinsters not only forewent a dowry; they frequently left their portion of the family wealth to nephews and nieces. Because their class code of honor called for female premarital virginity, these unwed women sought protection in the homes of their kin, although at times they headed households and lived with female companions and orphan girls. Depending on their economic circumstances they spent their lives running their own establishment or as gentile companions or glorified servants (referred to as *agregadas* or *dependientes*).

The majority of nonelite spinsters subscribed to a more casual attitude toward marriage. As a result relatively low rates of marriage were found throughout colonial Latin America. Mid-eighteenth-century Tucumán had a crude marriage rate of only 3.5 marriages per 1,000 population. For Buenos Aires, the marriage index for the period 1726–1820 was approximately 7.79. There is some suggestion that in Spanish America marriage rates began to climb by the end of the eighteenth century, no doubt the result of a clerical campaign to stamp out the "evil life-style" of so many colonials. Marriage was so far from universal in colonial Latin America, however, that there continued to be regions in which marriage was the exception, not the rule. For example, more than 83 percent of the population over the legal age of marriage in eighteenth-century Vila Rica was single.

While there was a lack of marriage in colonial Latin America, there was no lack of sex. Relatively few nonelite people married, but this did not mean than many adults remained chaste. In spite of the efforts of the Catholic Church to encourage marriage, concubinage was widespread throughout the colony and was the prevalent pattern among the poor. For the majority of colonial peoples there was no advantage in taking the sacrament, for they had no lineage, legitimacy, or inheritance to protect. Formal church-blessed marriages were expensive, and often difficult to arrange in rural areas sporadically served by the clergy. In addition, wealthy men, married or single, often entered into sexual relations with women of less socially valued groups. Concubinage was the generally accepted social norm, especially between people of different social or racial groups. In 1725, for example, the Portuguese Overseas Council, bemoaning the loose morals in the boom region of Minas Gerais, reported "The majority of the [white] residents of those lands do not marry because of the free and easy ways in which they live, it not being easy to coerce them to separate from their black and mulatto concubines."[4]

In both urban and rural Latin America single women were commonly involved in "marriage-like" relationships, which could last from a few months to several years. Poor people settled for consensual unions, but unions nonetheless. The norm in colonial Latin America was widespread concubinage (*amancebamiento*), with couples sharing bed and board as though a marriage existed. When, in the late eighteenth century, the bishop of Venezuela attempted to instill a new moral climate in his diocese, he investigated more then fifteen hundred individuals accused of sexual misconduct; 80 percent of these cases involved premarital sex, fornication, concubinage, and adultery.

Among those women who could be found living in concubinage were a goodly number of widows, as well as working women – poor Spaniards, castas, and Indians living outside their communities – from the lower middle and lower classes of society. These women were frequently from the same or a lower social strata than their respective lovers. Among them were women involved with men who could not marry – priests, or government bureaucrats forbidden to marry in the colonies – or men already married.

Women involved in concubinage (also called *mala* or *ilícita amistad*) tended to have even less power than women who married. Often the woman in the relationship was of an "inferior" condition or race, perhaps a slave or a poor Indian woman. Although these women had entered freely into the relationship, hoping to improve their lot and perhaps receive some modest benefit, testimony in criminal cases points repeatedly to the difficulty they faced when they tried to end the relationship, as well as the physical abuse they suffered at the hands of their lovers. Nonetheless, there are also examples of women who found love, prosperity, and some degree of social advancement in long-lasting concubinage relationships.

[4] Donald Ramos, "Single and Married Women in Vila Rica, Brazil, 1754–1838," *Journal of Family History*, 16:3 (Fall 1991), 261.

Spanish women with any social pretensions tended not to become concubines, for such a relationship meant a loss of status, respectability, and honor. (For an exception to this rule, see Document 10.) But poor Spanish women did enter into concubinage and at times had a series of long-lasting lovers. On the other hand Spanish men could and did have concubines without any loss of position. For women, concubinage was a sign of moral turpitude; for men, it was another display of their macho nature.

The public role of women, especially women who worked, left them open to constant suspicion that they had entered into a mala amistad, for this was a society in which "virtuous" women were careful to never be alone in public. Proof of mala amistad often consisted of testimony that a women had entered a man's home at unusual times (or vice versa), that a man and woman visited each other regularly, that they ate or drank together at the same table, that a woman cooked for a man, that she took care of his clothing, or that he gave her money or other gifts. Of course there was more direct proof, such as witnesses who saw a couple sleeping in the same bed.

Periodically, the church undertook campaigns to stamp out concubinage. The records are full of cases where couples were repeatedly called up before the court but continued to live together. Punishment was generally light and gender-specific; men paid a small fine whereas women were imprisoned for a short while. Usually there was a large degree of indifference toward the sexual conduct of poor women and slaves. Even when the authorities periodically decried immorality, regardless of their rhetoric, they ended up tolerating what was essentially an endemic pattern. Indeed concubinage continued to be so widespread as to be banal.

While the church publicly preached against unmarried couples living together, common people believed that it was an acceptable practice, not a mortal sin. Many saw a couple's concubinage as a temporary, transitory relationship that would eventually give way to either marriage or the end of the relationship. Others believed in the Spanish folk adage that it was "better to have a good mistress than a bad wife." Moreover, in spite of the threat of punishment and the officially sanctioned moral behavior, many lower-class women clearly preferred mala amistad to marriage, seeing their relationship as one that afforded them a greater degree of independence. Isabel, the Indian concubine of Sebastián Moreno, testified in 1606 that "she was getting along very well with this man and furthermore wanted to be with him, but she didn't want to marry because when he became her husband he might make her life very difficult."[5]

Consensual unions were in large part responsible for the high illegitimacy rates found throughout colonial Latin America. In Lima during the sixteenth and seventeenth centuries, illegitimate births ranged from 20 to 40 percent of all births. Mid-seventeenth-century Charcas in the mining district of Mexico had an illegitimacy rate of 28.7 percent of births, while San Luis Potosí, another Mexican mining town, had a rate of 51 percent. Comparable samples taken from mid-eighteenth-century parish registers in Buenos Aires show illegitimacy rates between 23 and 37 percent. Both concubinage and illegitimacy were tied to race. Between 1778 and 1784, for example, illegitimacy rates for the city of Córdoba ranged from 45 percent for white births to 54 percent for casta (mixed-blood) births. Portuguese America showed much the same pattern: between one-fourth and one-half of all free births were illegitimate in mid-eighteenth-century Ouro Preto. In São Paulo total illegitimacy averaged about 39 percent of all births.

Illegitimacy, while far greater than in Spain or Portugal, also varied from urban to rural areas. In Río de Janeiro, 45 percent of all urban births were illegitimate, whereas in the rural regions the numbers ran between 12 and 19 percent. These numbers reflect both a surplus of women as well as weaker social controls in the cities. Comparisons of data on illegitimacy in colonial Latin America suggest that marriage, or the lack of it, had a social, racial, and geographical component. While factors such as the rural or urban nature of a region, the state and type of economy, the sex balance, and race all influenced single motherhood, there was always a close correlation between bearing illegitimate offspring and social status.

Concubinage produced a social stain not only on women living in mala amistad but also on their female illegitimate children. Women born from unsanctified unions tended to marry less frequently than did their brothers and were themselves more likely to bear illegitimate children. For example, only 3.6 percent of women marrying in eighteenth-century Zamora, Mexico, were illegitimate, whereas for men the percentage rose to 5.5. Nonetheless, among the colonial masses, previous sexual experience did not affect a woman's chances, limited

---

[5] Archivo Arzobispal de Lima, Amancebados, Legajo 1, 1589–1611, Proceso contra Isabel india y Sebastián Moreno, 1606, quoted in María Emma Mannarelli, Pecados públicos: La ilegitimidad en Lima, siglo XVII (Lima: Ediciones Flora Tristán, 1993), 123.

though they might be, to marry. It was not uncommon for a woman to have illegitimate children, often by men other than her husband-to-be at the time of marriage. Among slave women in eighteenth-century Brazil, the wife usually had at least one child at the time of marriage. The masses of colonial Latin Americans clearly had a much less high regard for female chastity than did the elites.

Regardless of their official or unofficial marital status, in specific regions of Latin America women were often found as heads of household. Indeed women, usually single or widowed, headed a substantial number of households throughout the colonial world. Although the need to preserve their honor often prevented elite women from forming matrifocal households, female-headed households were especially visible in urban districts. In mid-sixteenth-century Mexico women headed one-fourth of all families while in late-seventeenth-century Lima, 27 percent of all households were female-headed. In São Paulo, 29 percent of all households were presided over by women in 1765; this number rose to 45 percent by 1802. According to the 1804 census for Ouro Preto, 45 percent of all households were headed by women and 83 percent of these female heads had never been married. Indeed, a large number of urban households consisted of single women with their fatherless illegitimate children, children born of an "unknown father." In general women who headed households tended to be poorer and darker than the population of women in general.

While the female population of cities continued to grow and represented an increasing percentage of heads of household, in rural districts, even those close to cities, single women were less likely to be in the majority and less likely to form their own households. Instead, most female-headed households were made up of widows. In rural districts near São Paulo city, for example, in 1765 and 1802, although 27 percent of all households were headed by women, 17 to 20 percent of total households were headed by widows and only 3 to 6 percent by never-married adult females. Both male and female tasks were essential to the survival of subsistence-level farms, which often incorporated production of foodstuffs with domestic manufacture. When a woman found herself without a man in rural Latin America (the result of death, immigration, or abandonment), she usually invited sisters and cousins to join her and share the rural chores, or sought refuge in the home of kinsfolk or neighbors.

Regions on the economic periphery of Latin America or once wealthy areas in economic decline had a disproportionately large

number of matrifocal households. Indeed as the local economy deteri-
orated, the percentage of female-headed households tended to increase.
Even in the wealthier cities as one went down the social scale, there
was a growing probability that the head of the family would be a
woman, probably single or widowed. Among the lower classes of colonial society, single mothers, often heads of household, were ubiquitous.
Because of race and social status, for these women neither marriage nor
the convent was an option. In general, single motherhood was primarily an urban phenomenon, for only in a town or city setting could single
women find employment to maintain themselves and their children.
The overarching social presumption was that these women were all
sexually available.

Survival was hard for these women and they often were forced by
their limited economic circumstances to live with other women in
similar circumstances in the poorest and least desirable housing on the
outskirts of urban settlements. Frequently these women banded
together to share work, rent, and child care duties. To the degree that
they were forced to work to support themselves and their children,
these women were economically independent. They were also among
the poorest segment of colonial society, often living on the margins of
colonial cities or along unhealthy embankments, in *casitas*, lean-tos and
shacks. We can only imagine the impact of poverty and lack of male
role models in the identity formation of their children.

Single mothers tended to have fewer children in their homes than
married mothers. Perhaps they bore fewer children because their male
partners were not always present, perhaps fewer children survived, or
perhaps young children were living outside the home. Single women,
because of poor maternal diet and working conditions, probably suffered a higher rate of stillbirth, and their children experienced higher
infant mortality. Lastly, the fact that poor women apprenticed their
children outside their home must be taken into account. Preliminary
analysis of colonial censuses also shows that, on average, single women
were older mothers than married women, suggesting that single women
practiced some form of birth control or abortion.

Not all single women chose to raise their children. Indeed, a growing problem throughout colonial Latin America, a problem linked
to female poverty, ideas of race and honor, and perhaps to manumission, was the growing numbers of children, almost always illegitimate, abandoned shortly after birth. In São Paulo, for example,
approximately 41 percent of illegitimate children were abandoned. In

Córdoba, 42 percent of all children brought to the baptismal font were abandoned, while between 15 and 30 percent of all infants born in Quito suffered the same fate. In the case of Mexico, 5,000 infants were abandoned between 1767 and 1821, with more than half of them listed as "Spanish" and abandoned because of the dishonorable circumstances of their birth. Interestingly there seemed to be no systematic tendency to abandon girl babies more than boys. In fact, in Mexico City of a group of 619 children abandoned between 1767 and 1774, 58 percent were male.

One response to the problem of abandoned children was the creation of *casas de niños expósitos* throughout Latin America. Modeled after Iberian institutions, foundling hospitals were found in the major cities of all colonial Latin America. These hospitals served two populations: women who were forced to give up their children because of problems of survival and women who used the institution to defend their honor. Foundling hospitals thus provided a refuge for illegitimate chidren of the very poor as well as unwanted children whose very existence would besmirch the reputation of the mother and by extension her whole family.

In spite of the Hispanic view that foundling children were a responsibility not to be shirked, mortality rates in these institutions were catastrophic. Only about 10 percent of those sent to the *casa de niños huérfanos* survived. The eighteenth century witnessed a growing interest in foundling hospitals and enlightened attempts to improve their administration, but conditions in these hospitals remained dismal. Still another response to the growing numbers of mothers who abandoned their infant children was a call for more social control. In 1761, for example, the Ouro Preto town council attempted to control the problem of abandoned children by naming inspectors to watch over single mulatto and black pregnant women.

There is no doubt of the importance of social class in any woman's experience of marriage and motherhood. Elite women, while subject to rigid patriarchal control, were sometimes able to use their social status for their advantage, introducing a degree of flexibility into the gender norms of colonial society. Middle-group women, like most of their elite counterparts, were probably under strong social pressure to marry and lead "virtuous" lives. Poorer women clearly enjoyed more sexual freedom and independence, but the price of that freedom was often exploitation and poverty.

CHAPTER 6

ELITE WOMEN

> The marriage arrangements of the wealthy are usually such shame-
> ful [economic] pacts that they should take place in the Consulado
> [Merchant's Guild] because of their economic content, than in the
> church because of their religious content. Instead of the desires
> and compatibility of the bride and groom, the first thing that is
> looked at is money.[1]

Although elite women were by definition a small, select group, they
played important social and cultural roles and were intimately involved
in the transmission of status and property and elite strategies of survival
and recruitment. Honor, on both the personal and family levels, was of
central concern to the elite and those who hoped to join its ranks. In
the eyes of the elite, honor was linked to social standing and to virtue.
To be honorable, the Hispanic social code called for women to be pure
and sexually beyond reproach, publicly discrete, and timid in their
behavior. A woman who failed to fulfill these norms was shameless.
Her conduct not only defiled her own honor but also that of her
husband, or that of her family. This code both linked the protection of
a woman's honor to that of her kin and their present and future claim
to an exalted social position and required that women be watched over
by men.

Because the ideal elite woman was to be virginal before marriage and
chaste afterward, her sexuality, activities, and education were closely
supervised. Elite girls were brought up out of the public's sight, and left

[1] José Joaquín Fernández de Lizardi, *El Periquillo Sarniento*, book V, chap. 6, cited
in Juan Javier Pescador, *De bautizados a fieles difuntos* (Mexico: El Colegio de
México, 1992), 224.

their homes only to go to mass. They were raised to respect and defer to their parents, especially their father. Their parents stressed the Hispanic honor code, which tied female sexual behavior and woman's virginity to her family's honor. A young woman was also taught to have her family's economic and dynastic interests at heart. These standards of behavior affected every elite woman in colonial Latin America for she was a women, part of a family, and a member of the local elite.

As a result of honor and family interests, the elite comprised a very married segment of society. In the case of the nobility of Mexico, of the 292 men and women who held noble titles during the colonial period, 225 (or 77.1 percent) married at least once. Only 10 percent of the wholesale merchants in late-eighteenth-century Buenos Aires failed to marry. In Santiago de Chile, only 17 percent of elite men and 27 percent of elite women were not married by age forty-five, a pattern not unlike that found among elite European families. Furthermore, fragmentary data suggest that daughters of the elite tended to marry at a younger age than other Spanish women. As a result, the age difference between bride and groom was largest in the wealthiest and most socially prominent segments of colonial society, where young women were routinely married to mature, established men. Daughters of the wealthy Buenos Aires merchants, for example, usually wed before they had reached their nineteenth birthday, marrying men more than twelve years their seniors.

Marrying a daughter at age seventeen or eighteen provided several important advantages to the elite. Because of their youth, these girls were far more malleable than women in their twenties. It was therefore easier, in spite of theoretical free will in the choice of marriage partners, to influence their decision. Because they were still legally minors and therefore under their parents' control, their ability to defy their parents' wishes was severely curtailed. (Once a woman had reached twenty-five, the age of legal consent, she was free to marry with or without her parents' approval.) Lastly, their youth helped insure that they were virgins and probably fecund at the time of marriage. Virginity, as we shall see, was a quality much desired in honorable young women.

For the elite of colonial Latin America marriage was part of a strategy employed in cementing family alliances and furthering family and kin interests. Marriage was used to create crucial social, political, and economic ties with individuals and groups seen as important for a family's survival or to recruit members into an occupational elite.

Because marriage was of interest to the future of family and its economic interests, marriage of an elite woman was far too important to
her family to be left to chance or to her choice, and unions were customarily arranged. Thus, the landed elite routinely sought out other
wealthy landowners when choosing the children's marriage partners,
whereas merchants, especially in times of expansion of commerce,
married their daughters to promising Spanish immigrants who had
apprenticed in local commerce and were ready to join the ranks of
wholesalers. One historian describing the marriage pattern of elite
mining and mercantile families in eighteenth-century Guanajuato
(Mexico) has spoken of the "almost Sabine seizure of its females" by
peninsular Spaniards.[2]

Marriage was a way for the family to assure that a daughter would
be taken care of while perpetuating the family interests. In this elite
marriage market, women were both pawns and active agents of the
interests of their family, kin group, and social class. Young women were
educated to be modest, obedient, chaste, and faithful to the needs of
their families and their future husbands. They were trained to be used
by their families as agents of recruitment. Marriage (and more infrequent remarriage) of women was carefully controlled.

Elite young women throughout colonial Latin America were both
protected and manipulated for family goals, a situation that tended
to preclude amorous matches. In spite of church doctrine that
underlined free will in contracting a marriage, the daughters of the
elite married men who met the requirements and social expectations of their families. Mariquita Sánchez, the daughter of an important Buenos Aires merchant, described marriage among the elite as
follows:

> The father arranged everything [related to his daughter's mar-
> riage] to his liking. He told his wife, and the bride about [having
> chosen a marriage candidate for his daughter] three or four days
> before the wedding . . . The poor daughter would not have dared
> to raise the least objection. She had to obey. The fathers thought
> that they knew what was best for their daughters, and it was a
> waste of time to try to make them change their minds. A pretty
> girl would marry a man who was neither handsome nor elegant,
> nor fine, and who, besides, could have been her father. But, he

[2] David A. Brading, *Miners and Merchants in Bourbon Mexico, 1763–1810* (Cambridge: Cambridge University Press, 1971), 306.

was a man of sound judgment and good business sense. That was all that was important.[3]

It was feared that young men and women, especially women, blinded by romance and sexual passion, would disregard their families' interests, and make disastrous choices. Marriage was linked not to love, but to legitimate offspring and inheritance of property. Indeed, marriage based on love was potentially threatening to the social and racial hierarchy because it could result in socially undesirable unions between people of different races, social backgrounds, morality, and economic positions. Marriage tied to romantic love had no place in the value system of the elites. A good marriage partner was one chosen by one's parents or guardians, a candidate whose social and economic credentials had been examined and whose incorporation into the family would help further the family's interests. Parental power might have been informal, having no standing in church law, but it was power nonetheless.

Daughters had to be controlled, and their marriages arranged. Parental control over the choice of a woman's marriage partner was enhanced by the protection and isolation afforded elite girls. Before marriage, elite young women tended to be secluded or at least tightly chaperoned wherever they went. Seclusion both protected a woman's chastity and deprived her of opportunities for romantic encounters. It also limited courtship. Nonetheless some elite women managed to become sexually involved despite these controls. (See Documents 7 and 10.)

Because marriage was a crucial part of the strategy a family used to preserve its wealth and power, elite parents sometimes chose to marry their daughters to kinfolk, thus protecting assets against the effects of partible inheritance by stanching their flowing outside of the family circle. Although church law stipulated that the bride and groom were not to be related to each other within four degrees of consanguinity, the same church was more than willing to grant special exemptions to its own rules. As a result, kin marriage, including first-cousin unions as well as marriage between uncle and niece, was not unknown. One historian has described a "thicket of constant cousin marriage" in colonial Bahia, where cousin marriage was the rule rather than the exception.[4]

---

[3] María [Mariquita] Sánchez de Thompson, *Recuerdos de Buenos Aires Virreynal* (Buenos Aires: ENE Editorial, 1953), 59–60.

[4] Stuart B. Schwartz, *Sovereignty and Society in Colonial Brazil: The High Court of Bahia and Its Judges, 1609–1751* (Berkeley: University of California Press, 1973), 339.

In mid-eighteenth-century Caracas one-fourth of all elite couples married their first cousins. Another common strategy was to marry several sisters in one family to several brothers in another.

Another tactic used to protect the family's fortune was to discourage some adult children from marrying. Preventing all one's children from marrying acted as a counterweight to high fertility and its negative effect on inheritance. For females this meant that one or two daughters might be persuaded to enter a convent. Parents had to decide if a daughter had a better future as a bride or a nun. The number and promise of her suitors, the state of the economy, and her health and personality all entered into the final equation.

Parental control was not always exercised by a male parent. At least one study of elite marriage patterns has shown that in an economy in decline men often waited until the death of their fathers, and the receipt of their paternal inheritance, before marrying.[5] In many cases, their mothers, usually younger than their fathers, were still alive and could exercise much influence in the choice of marriage partner. Because of the average colonial life-span, parental control was as frequently exercised by widowed mothers as by fathers, both searching to protect the prospective bride and her kin.

The colonial elite and those of the middle groups who could afford it normally provided the bride-to-be with a dowry. Although dowries were always assigned a monetary value, they often contained goods and property that reflected the social and economic status of the bride and her parents. Brides of modest circumstances usually brought some clothing, a few domestic animals, and practical kitchen utensils to the marriage. A more affluent bride might be given a small house and a slave, while the wealthiest received several pieces of real property, large amounts of cash, several slaves, elaborate furniture and silverware, personal jewelry, and luxurious clothing. In rural areas herds of cattle or sheep might be included in a young woman's dowry. Interests in mining, commerce, and manufacturing or the right to a hereditary office was also part of some exceptional dowries. Although dowries always belonged legally to the bride, husbands could benefit from the property and cash contained in the most lavish of these grants.

The total value of the dowry depended on the social position and prosperity of the bride's family, the status of the bride (legitimate

---

[5] Robert J. Ferry, *The Colonial Elite of Early Caracas: Formation and Crisis, 1567–1767* (Berkeley: University of California Press, 1989), 223–235.

or illegitimate, orphan), the need to attract a groom, and general economic conditions. One historian has argued that in seventeenth-century São Paulo members of the local elite were so eager to marry their daughters that they granted inflated dowries to ensnare Portuguese new-comers.[6] Overall a dowry was a basic ingredient in cooking up an accept-able marriage. When the bride was from a respectable family that had suffered economic setbacks, a small dowry would be provided by an interested relative or family friend. Modest dowries were also provided by local religious or civic funds usually charged with protecting poor but decent girls of European extraction. In some cases where a women's dowry took the form of an investment in a business in which she had expertise, a dowry could give the bride power within the marriage.

Neither the custom of granting dowries nor the amount of dowry settled on a woman was uniform throughout Latin America. Although a general practice in the seventeenth century, dowries began to decline in mid-eighteenth-century Mexico. Although the majority of brides still came to the altar with a dowry, those from less affluent families were increasingly not endowed at the time of marriage. The same pattern seems to be present in eighteenth-century São Paulo. On the other hand, dowries grew larger and more ostentatious in eighteenth-century Río de la Plata. Whether these differing patterns reflect local economic conditions, growing availability of commodities, or the increasing defiance of young women in choosing marriage partners remains unclear.

The luxury goods in dowries and the detailed descriptions of these items give us a glimpse into elite female consumption patterns. Dowries often included clothing, jewelry, and articles of personal adornment. Flora de Azcuenaga, daughter of one Buenos Aires merchant and wife of another, was given a dowry consisting of petticoats of Brittany linen, skirts of cambric and Flemish lace, silk brocade robes, silk dressing gowns, a dress of silver and gold silk tissue, jackets, cloaks, fine hand-kerchiefs, and linen blouses as well as ornate fans, elaborate diamond jewelry, topaz hair ornaments, and strings of pearls. The dowry also included jacaranda furniture, a clavichord, luxurious bed linen, mirrors, and twenty-five pounds of silverware to furnish her new home.

It is clear from the analysis of dowries and wills as well as from reports by foreign travelers that colonial women enjoyed displaying their

[6] Muriel Nazzari, *Disappearance of the Dowry: Women, Families, and Social Change in São Paulo, Brazil, 1600–1900* (Stanford: Stanford University Press, 1991), 30–31.

wealth in fine clothing and jewelry. (See Document 3.) Reports by late-sixteenth-century European visitors spoke of women dressing in great luxury. Observers of fashion in eighteenth-century Montevideo, a new and relatively poor town, spoke of women dressed in rich garments of silk and fine wool, which, although not as expensive as those worn in Peru, were embroidered with gold, silver, or silk. Peruvian women were said to be so fond of precious stones that they covered themselves with "extraordinary ornaments of pearls and jewels . . . pendants, bracelets necklaces and rings."[7] A miniature of the upper-class Buenos Aires matron, Maria Eugenia Escalada de De Maria, painted in 1808 shows her with a gold comb and two strings of pearls held in place by a pearl and diamond pin in her hair; diamond earrings in her ears, a string of pearls from which a diamond flower hung and a medallion hanging on a large gold chain around her neck.[8] Elite colonial women bedecked themselves with earrings, necklaces, bracelets, rings, pins, and chains. They also prized decorated fans and small silver snuff boxes.

Personal jewelry served several ends, combining adornment with a marker of social distinction and religious piety. In addition to the articles of luxe used by a small group of women, women of all social classes and racial groups wore religious jewelry including crosses, medals, and reliquaries. Chief among these was the rosary, whose beads could be strung on gold, silver, or far more modest materials such as base metals, silk cord, or cotton thread. The very wealthiest displayed rosaries whose beads were made of solid or filigreed gold, adorned with pearls and precious stones. A poor woman's rosary might cost her three or four reales while a wealthy woman might count her prayers on beads valued up to three hundred pesos. Women also wore magical amulets such as alligator teeth set in silver (believed to ward off poisoning), figas (to ward off the evil eye), and jet beads.

By the eighteenth century, another article of conspicuous consumption often displayed by elite women was personal servants, sometimes free, often slave. According to one French visitor to early-nineteenth-century Caracas,

> A white woman of moderate fortune goes to Mass on church days
> with two female Negroes or mulattos in her suite, though she does

---

[7] Amadeo Frézier, *Relación del viaje por el mar del sur* (1717) (Caracas: Biblioteca Ayacucho, 1982), 223.

[8] This painting can be found in the Museo Histórico Nacional, Buenos Aires.

not possess in other property an equivalent capital. Those who are notoriously rich are followed by four or five servant women, and there remain as many more for each white of the same house who goes to another church. There are families in Caracas with twelve and fifteen female servants.[9]

Elite women did not live in total isolation. The wives of high-ranking government officials took a surprisingly active role in public cere-monies. They accompanied their husbands to investitures, masses, bap-tisms, and funerals, as well as bullfights and official ceremonies. During the seventeenth century the countess of Lemos, wife of the sitting viceroy of Peru, governed during her husband's six-month absence in Arequipa and Puno. In an advanced state of pregnancy, she attended a high mass at the cathedral, "accompanied by the oidores, alcaldes of the court, comptrollers, and the secular cabildo," six days before the birth of her third child.[10]

Despite legal limitations, the wives of important political figures were occasionally accused of exerting influence behind the scenes. As early as 1529 the wives of powerful government officials in Mexico City were charged in private letters of being mad, greedy, dissolute, and in command. Almost three hundred years later, Francisca Villanova y Marco, wife of the viceroy Amat y Borbón of New Granada, was attacked by a hostile crowd because she had greedily established a monopoly over local commerce, controlling the price of many of the basic necessities of life in Bogotá. Women such as these were clearly interested in business and involved in local politics. (See Docu-ment 5.)

Surviving personal correspondence also shows elite women to be deeply involved in a social life that extended to family, friends, and compadres. Visiting, playing cards, attending tertulias, masquerades, concerts, religious plays, civic and religious processions, and ceremonies – all these activities were part of their lives. According to Francois Depons, women in Caracas "always receive company seated on a sofa ... these visits are always paid between five and eight o'clock in the evening. Husbands very seldom accompany their wives on such occa-

[9] François Joseph de Pons, *Travels in parts of South America during the years 1801, 1802, 1803 and 1804 Containing a Description of Captain-Generalship of Carrac-cas* (London: Richard Phillips, 1806), 102.

[10] Robert Ryal Miller, trans. and ed., *Chronicle of Colonial Lima: The Diary of Josephe and Francisco Mugaburu, 1640–1697* (Norman: University of Oklahoma Press, 1975), 133.

sions; they go without any retinue, merely followed by two or three servants."[11] On weekends women went to their country homes where they
entertained friends, gambled, and drank; men and women joined
together in the festivities.

Charged with caring for their households and the well-being of
various servants and retainers, including those who lived on their rural
estates, elite women visited the homes of these servants as well as
nearby Indian towns, pausing to eat a snack, gossip, catch up on local
happenings, and purchase food or medicinal herbs. Elite women were
rarely alone; they seldom moved about without a slave, Indian, or
mestiza hovering nearby. Within their households elite women acted
as cultural instructors, teaching their slaves and servants Spanish
customs, traditions, and behavior. But they also learned from these
women. It was reported that by the late eighteenth century Quechua,
the Indian language of Bolivia, was seeping into the speech of
"respectable" women in Cochabamba, a result of their daily dealings
with market women and servants.

Because elite women married young, many of them spent a relatively
long part of their childbearing years within marriage. The result was a
large number of pregnancies, births, and, depending on social class, surviving children. In Spanish and Portuguese America, elite families had
both high birthrates and high survival rates, the result of good diet,
housing, and health combined with younger age at marriage and the
widespread use of nursemaids. Venezuelan-born Francisca Moreno de
Mendoza, daughter of a brigadier and wife of a captain, married at age
fifteen and bore sixteen children, approximately one child every thirteen months, for the next twenty-one years. She was not unique. The
average elite woman bore eight to ten children and saw five or six of
them survive to adulthood. Among middle groups women married later
and had fewer children.

Although elite women had little say in the choice of their husbands,
there is evidence in the rare letters that have survived to suggest that
over time strong affection, tenderness, trust, and even love developed
in some of these marriages. In the late sixteenth century Sebastián de
Pliego wrote beseeching his wife to come to New Spain from Granada.
His words reflect concern and love: "I can't live without you. . . . I will
say no more than that I wish to see you with my eyes before I die. All

---

[11] De Pons, *Travels in Parts of South America*, 39–40.

that there is would not pay for the tears I have shed for you day after day."[12] The eighteenth-century letters of María Antonia Trebustos to her husband Pedro Romero de Terreros, future count of Regla, were also studded with expressions of love. She repeatedly addressed him "my esteemed and dearest little daddy," "dearest object of affection," "my only love and my heart's only solace," "little father of my life and of my heart," and the "precious jewel of my life."[13] María Antonia spoke of herself as "the dearest one who loves you" and "your little girl" and declared her love over and over: "Any way of life would suit me if only I could be with my dearest." "I am suffering from not seeing you," "I kiss your beautiful little hands, as always, idealizing you and wanting to see you."

Elite men could hold the most stereotypical vision of women but could nonetheless view marriage as the solution to a host of economic and social problems. Such was the case of don Antonio de Porlier, an eighteenth-century Audiencia official and a misogynic critic, who believed that "the nature and normal disposition of women is so full of impertinences, extravagances, frailties, lack of consideration, excesses, sillinesses, gossipings, presumptions, shallowness, indiscretions, and other weaknesses, that one must have complete Christian resignation in order to put up with them."[14] In spite of these heartfelt views, Porlier married a Salta-born woman who brought both a large dowry and important social connections. Paradoxically, although not part of the original equation, years of marriage, the birth (and often the death) of children, and shared travails produced love, companionship, and mutual respect. When Porlier's wife died suddenly, he wrote to friends that "through this blow I have lost my consolation, my companion,

---

[12] Letter of Sebastián de Pliego, in Puebla, to his wife Mari Díaz in Medina-Bombarón, Granada, 1581, in James Lockhart and Enrique Otte, trans. and eds., *Letters and Peoples of the Spanish Indies: Sixteenth Century* (Cambridge: Cambridge University Press, 1976), 127.

[13] Archivo histórico de la Compañía Real del Monte, Pachuca, Correspondencia del primer conde Miravalles, letters of April and May 1757, quoted in Edith Couturier, "The Letters of the Countess of Miravalle and the Question of Colonial Women's Biography" (unpublished paper, 1994), 20, 21, 27.

[14] Antonio Porlier, *Advertencias cristiano-políticas que dio Don N. a un amigo suyo cuando salió de Madrid provisto para una plaza de ministro togado en una de las Audiencias de la América*, 109, quoted in Daisy Rípodas Ardanaz, *Un ilustrado cristiano en la magistratura indiana: Antonio Porlier, Marqués de Bajamar: Viaje de Cádiz a Potosí (1758–1759)* (Buenos Aires: Prhisco-Conicet, 1992), 61.

my escape from the care of house, children, and family, and the good example that she provided daily of her many virtues and talents."[15]

By the eighteenth century remarriage for women, regardless of their social status, was rare. Exceptions, of course, existed. For a widow to remarry, she usually had to be young enough to bear children and wealthy enough to attract a second husband. While remarriage for women was relatively uncommon, approximately 10 percent of all women marrying were widows. A widow's wealth often proved an irresistible attraction, especially for newcomers seeking to establish themselves in America. Simón Piñate, for example, an immigrant from Huelva, Andalucia, to Venezuela in the early eighteenth century, used his marriage to the widow María Caldera and her inheritance of a cacao hacienda to develop a sizable fortune. The greater the value of property controlled by a widow, the greater the pressure on her to remarry, but there is a suggestion that at least some of these young, wealthy widows had an active role in deciding on their second mate. Wealthy widows brought their dowries, their family connections, half of their first husbands' estate, and their increased experience to these second marriages. Widows also tended to marry single men rather than widowers, perhaps another indication of their ability to choose their second husbands more freely.

Among the more extraordinary widows was Ignacia Javiera de Echeverz y Valdés, the second Marquesa of San Miguel de Aguayo, and widow of Francisco de Sada y Garro, the third conde de San Javier. Before she died in 1733, the marquesa married twice more, first to Pedro Gaspar Enríquez de Lacarra, conde de Ublitas and marques de Castelnau, and then, after being widowed for a second time, to José Ramón de Azlor, captain general of Coahuila-Texas. Ignacia Javiera was also among those elite females whose second marriages were to younger men.

Older women, often widowed, served as matrons of their families, protecting the interests of their children, and taking an active role in their personal and professional decisions. Although no specific legislation granted special authority to mothers, in the absence of fathers women of all social classes attempted to defend their families' interests.

---

[15] *Vida de don Antonio Aniceto Porlier, actual Marqués de Bajamar, escrita por él mismo para instrucción de sus hijos, Madrid, May 25, 1807*, cited in Daisy Rípodas Ardanaz, "Una salteña, 'fiscala' del Consejo de Indias: Doña María Josefa de Asteguieta (1745–1779)," *Boletín del Instituto San Felipe y Santiago de Estudios Históricos de Salta*, 41 (1992), 52.

Indeed, it can be hypothesized that poorer widows, more dependent on their adult children for economic survival, were even more motivated to develop strategies to insure the continued material and affective support of their children.

One of the few arenas in which elite women could take an active public role was that of church-sponsored charity, usually directed at other more needy women. Under the direct or indirect guidance of the church, secular women joined together to support orphanages, schools for needy girls, women's shelters, and women's hospitals. Under the leadership of the Hermandad de la Caridad, seventy-three elite women in Buenos Aires, for example, each undertook to donate a bed and linen to the Hospital de Mujeres; fifty of them also donated funds to cover one day of the inmates' board. Embedded in the myriad of social institutions promoted by women and men was the idea that women, because of their frailty, needed special social protection and control. The same idea of protection and aiding needy women was also reflected in the funding of special charitable dowries for "honest but needy girls" who wished to marry or join a convent.

Elite women and those who aspired to join their ranks were both the victims of and players in a strict paternalistic system. They were subject to tight control of their virginity before marriage. Their choice of marriage partners was limited and often manipulated to further the social position and fortunes of their families. Dedicated to a life of childbearing, they were expected to be a model of Catholic virtue. They were also required to acquiesce to a double standard of sexual conduct, which allowed their husbands freedom while strictly enforcing marital fidelity for them.

But elite women did not live in isolation. Rather they enjoyed a life of sociability and comparative luxury. They were better fed, housed, clothed, and attended than any other group of women. Surrounded by servants and slaves, they were rarely called on to perform any type of arduous physical labor. While much of their social life was spent gossiping, visiting friends, and participating in church-sponsored charities, they also enjoyed the opportunity to exert their influence, albeit guarded, among their family and friends.

CHAPTER 7

THE BRIDES OF CHRIST AND
OTHER RELIGIOUS WOMEN

In the name of all powerful God and with his Divine Grace Amen. Be it known that I, Sor Juana Isabel San Martín de la Santísima Trinidad, born in this city, age 23, and legitimate daughter of don Manuel de San Martín and doña Isabel Hidalgo, inhabitants [of Buenos Aires]; being sane of body and with just reason and mental powers because of the infinite grace of God Our Lord, and finding myself a novitiate in the Monastery of Saint Catherine of Sena about to profess [as a nun], which I have anxiously desired for many years because I know that the difficulties and dangers of the world are an obstacle to serving God and achieving a state of perfection; having consulted frequently with God-fearing people of instruction who have approved my decision; I therefore have decided to draw up my last will and testament and renounce the temporal things of this world.[1]

Colonial Latin America was a deeply religious society, a world in which all were called upon to subscribe to one dogma and one set of religious beliefs, that of the Holy Roman Catholic Church. The church was spiritually, ritually, and physically present (or perhaps omnipresent) throughout the colonies. Religion entered in many spheres of daily life, helping to organize both the beliefs and the social actions and interactions of all inhabitants of the region. Religion helped to define and enforce gender roles. Thus, it should come as no surprise that religion deeply affected Hispanic women, providing them with life choices, the

---

[1] From the renunciation and will of Sor Juana Isabel San Martín de la Santisima Trinidad, Buenos Aires, 1813, in Archivo General de la Nación (Argentina), Escribanias, registro 4, folios 327–329v.

arenas in which to organize their spiritual and social lives, and the opportunities to display personal piety.

Entering the convent of Santa Catalina de Siena that day in 1813, Juana Isabel San Martín was making a lifetime decision that thousands of women in colonial Latin American had made before her. Like all elite women, she had been encouraged "to take a state" – marry a man or marry God. Most chose the former, but an important group of women, like Juana, elected to enter female monasteries. In doing so she was becoming a member of the only clearly identifiable female group in colonial society. Why were convents important to colonial women? What type of life awaited Juana Isabel and thousands of other women who had preceded her inside its walls? Why did women choose the cloistered life of the convent? What other types of religious participation existed for women who sought a spiritual life while stopping short of taking the veil?

Colonial Latin American convents served multiple roles. Convents offered all women a surrogate family and an alternative life style, while also relieving society of the burden of sustaining surplus elite women. They served religious needs by fostering religious piety and providing a religious outlet for women. Convents also provided a respectable repository for elite women who did not or could not marry, for those who were considered socially anomalous, and for wealthy widows. Having a daughter or granddaughter in a convent formed part of a family strategy, identifying the family as part of the elite that shared deeply religious values while reflecting on the wealth and honor of the family. In short, convents were an integral part of colonial society, tied to "white" society, responding to the needs of this group, and reflecting the social and racial world view of the colonial elite.

Convents were quintessentially urban institutions. Indeed it was considered unthinkable that a group of women could live alone in the country. Only the cities could provide convents with the protection, services, religious advisers, and patrons they needed to survive and prosper. Convents would eventually be found in all the principal and secondary cities of colonial Latin America except those which lacked a sufficient population base or were considered to be in unsafe areas.

Nuns began to arrive in the Spanish American cities within twenty to thirty years of their founding. The first convent in Mexico City, Nuestra Señora de la Concepción, for example, was established within nineteen years of the conquest (1540), and the first one in Lima, within twenty-six years. In Puebla the first female monastery was founded thirty-seven years after the city's founding. Only twenty-five years later demand for more spaces had so outstripped supply that a second convent for "women who wish to take the religious state and leave the world" was set up.

Only in poorer, more dangerous, and more isolated frontier towns were convents slower to develop. The first convent in Santiago, Chile, a Franciscan nunnery of Poor Clares, for example, was established almost 70 years after the creation of the city, while Buenos Aires waited 165 years for its first convent to be founded. The number of convents eventually created in any one city varied according to the prosperity of the region and its population, with wealthier cities tending to have more establishments.

As the earliest convents were being set up in Spanish America, the Catholic Church was changing the power structure of feminine monasteries. The great Counter-Reformation church council, the Council of Trent, enacted a series of reforms aimed at bringing female convents under the control of male religious orders. From the mid-sixteenth century on, convents were subordinate to the general chapters of their corresponding male order. In addition, the council established strict principles concerning the novitiate, profession, communal life, and strict enclosure of female religious.

In spite of, or perhaps because of, stricter rules sequestering nuns, convents continued to grow in number and size during the seventeenth century. Paradoxically, the growth of convents in the seventeenth century might have resulted from a contracting economy, which made it preferable to send daughters to the convent rather than to have them marry beneath a family's aspirations. Thus, convents responded to the need of the elite to shrink its numbers. In Mexico alone thirty-eight convents were founded before the eighteenth century. While nunneries continued to be established in the eighteenth century, in general they stabilized their population between 1650 and 1750 and began a gradual decline in numbers thereafter.

In Brazil, unlike Spanish America, convents were founded later. Four convents were eventually set up in Salvador, Bahia, but the city waited more than 120 years before the creation of the first female monastery in 1677. Before this date Brazilian women seeking to join a convent journeyed to Portugal to take religious vows. The Portuguese state hesitated to found female monasteries because it believed they would exacerbate a shortage of white women in the colonies, but colonial elites eventually pressured the state to fill what they saw as a religious and social need.

By the eighteenth century a multiplicity of feminine orders could be found in the cities of colonial Latin America: Concepcionists, Poor Clares, Capuchines, Augustinians, Dominicans, Urbanists, Clarissas, Cistercians, Brigidas, Hieronymites, and the Company of Mary. These convents fell into one of two general classifications: barefoot orders, also called descalced or Capuchin orders; and "shod" or calced convents, whose members were allowed to wear shoes. The former, far fewer in number, were committed to a more austere life of poverty and prayer.

The founding and support of convents served as a means by which wealthy, prominent women expressed their religiosity while enhancing their social status and preparing for their future. There are many examples of wealthy widows who provided the impetus and funds to found a particular convent and then themselves took religious vows. Doña Ursula Luisa de Monserrat, sole heiress of a major fortune in eighteenth-century Bahia, founded the convent of Nossa Senhora das Mercês and became its first abbess. Convents could also be founded by socially prominent males, married couples, or groups of devout women. Some convents were founded as such, while others grow out of other charitable institutions. The Santa Clara convent in Cuzco, for example, was originally set up in 1551 as a home for mestiza orphans. During the next decade it became a Franciscan convent, and by 1564 housed thirty-two nuns, twenty of whom were Spaniards and twelve mestizas.

It is impossible to calculate the total number of nuns who entered the convents of colonial Latin America. In just one region of Spanish America, New Spain, there were over twenty-four hundred religious women in convents at the beginning of the nineteenth century, with probably over nine hundred nuns in Mexico City alone. At approximately the same time there were two hundred nuns in Bahia, the capital of Portuguese America. Probably throughout all of Spanish and Portuguese America six thousand women lived within the walls of the convent at the time of independence. Nonetheless, nuns represented a small fraction of the entire population. In Mexico City they were approximately .7 percent of the city's population whereas in Bahia they totaled less than .2 percent.

The number of nuns within each convent varied greatly, with the stricter descalced convents tending to be small establishments, usually housing between fifteen and thirty-five nuns. Calced convents averaged between fifty and one hundred nuns, although some had as many as two hundred or three hundred women who had taken the veil. In general descalced orders, with their more ascetic life-style, attracted about half the number of novices as calced orders. The maximum number of nuns allowed into any convent was set by the rules of the convent itself and sometimes also limited by the crown. The Destêrro convent of Bahia, for example, was held to no more than one hundred nuns. In Portuguese America these quotas did not stop wealthy parents who desired to have their daughters enter a convent. They simply continued to send them back to Portugal to take their vows and enter a convent there.

To enter a convent as a novice, a girl was examined about her religious vocation and her free will in choosing to profess. Each potential novice also had to show proof of age, baptism, and purity of blood. Postulants were to be white, devout, properly brought up, legitimate, and racially pure. Some of these requirements could occasionally be overlooked, but others were rigorously enforced. Racial purity usually was essential. Legitimacy, however, was desirable but not necessary; indeed, a convent was the perfect place to shelter a high-born but illegitimate young woman. The prospective nun also had to demonstrate that her family had sufficient economic resources to provide for her within the convent walls.

The length of the novitiate varied by convent and the age of the girl, but this trial period always lasted at least one year. During this time prospective nuns learned the rules of the community as they adjusted to monastic life. At the end of the period, each postulant was examined in religion, prayers, and general conventual rules. In the final profession a nun took the four vows of obedience, chastity, enclosure, and poverty and was symbolically married to Christ.

The age at profession for most nuns is difficult to determine, although some partial information does exist. Theoretically some convents were open to girls from the age of twelve on, but among nuns entering the Catalina convent of Buenos Aires during the eighteenth century whose birth date is known, the average age was slightly over twenty-six years old. The youngest woman taking vows was sixteen, while the oldest was forty-five. Even if we except the few widows in the group, the average age of profession was well above the average marriage age for elite women, which suggests that the convent, for at least some women, was a solution turned to when the prospect of marriage was already dim.

The number of women seeking entry into a convent reflected local conditions, including the sex ratio within the elite and general level of local prosperity. In regions with an abundance of women – often regions in decline that had experienced an out-migration of men, leaving eligible males in short supply – the convent could be a very attractive solution for elite women. Economic decay, large families, and shrinking fortunes made the convent a good alternative to marriage, and families unable to provide a fitting dowry for their daughters encouraged them to look to a religious life. During the 1740s and 1750s, a period of economic decline in the sugar-producing regions of northeastern Brazil, the number of novitiates seeking entry into Bahian convents rose sharply. One Bahian nobleman cited his entailed estate as the reason he was unable to marry his daughters to men of the requisite social stature and was therefore sending them to the convent. In a letter requesting the establishment of a convent, the cabildo of Buenos Aires explained the economics of sending daughters to the convent, pointing out to the king that "most of the honored citizens [of this city] support this project, taking into consideration that in order to marry off a daughter with a modicum of decency one needs much more fortune than for two daughters to become nuns."[2]

Certain convents such as the Destêrro in Bahía overwhelmingly attracted the regional elite, welcoming the daughters of landed and mercantile magnates. Other convents drew women from middle social sectors such as daughters of hacienda administrators and government bureaucrats. When daughters of people of more modest social background – shopkeepers, artisans, and tradesmen – entered the convent, these women were always racially "pure" and of legitimate birth.

The majority of convents, those of calced orders, required that nuns have both a cash dowry and a yearly income, thereby further limiting the number of women who could enter as nuns of the black veil. A nun's dowry varied within and between convents. In the early seventeenth century, nuns entering the Santa Catalina convent of Cuzco usually brought dowries ranging from 2,000 to 3,300 pesos, but one woman, the daughter of a wealthy count, was provided with a 17,000-peso dowry. Over time dowries tended to increase in size. In Mexico City, nuns typically brought between 1,000 and 2,000 pesos in the sixteenth and most of the seventeenth century; by the end of the seventeenth century the dowry had risen to 3,000 pesos, and by the eighteenth century, the minimum dowry required at convents such as

---

[2] Cayetano Bruno, *Historia de la Iglesia en la Argentina* (Buenos Aires: Ediciones Don Bosco, 1971), V, 42.

Jesus María was 4,000 pesos. While these dowries represented substantial sums, they were usually less than the dowry needed to marry a daughter to a socially acceptable husband.

The size and importance of the dowry depended on what type of nun one became, for there were two different types of nuns in each convent, a reflection of the hierarchy of colonial society. The elite within any convent were the nuns of the black veil. Beneath them in prestige and power, although often as numerous, were the nuns of the white veil, women of more modest social origins. These women entered the convent with smaller dowries and enjoyed less leisure time and comfort than regular professed nuns. In addition to their religious roles, they also performed domestic duties within convents.

Some convents demanded that dowries be paid immediately; others permitted payment in installments. Still other convents allowed the nun's family to take a lien or mortgage on its property, promising to provide interest payments until the dowry could be paid off. By the eighteenth century, poor, honest Spanish women who lacked financial backing were given special licenses to beg for alms in order to amass the requisite white-veil dowry. One historian has calculated that approximately half of the women allowed to raise money in this fashion were successful in their quest to take religious vows. Although lacking in personal fortune, these women tended to be those whose families had strong kinship or friendship ties to the wealthy elite or churchmen.

In addition to dowries, entering a novitiate and taking final vows, occasions for celebration and lavish feasts, were expensive. Profession was a marriage, and it was feted as such. In some convents food, music, pageantry, and general rejoicing formed part of the celebration. One nun, mother María Luisa de San Bartholomé, calculated that her entering the Conception convent of Puebla had cost her father "more than five thousand pesos in gold coin." In addition to her three-thousand-peso dowry, there had been "gratuities, board and lodging, living expenses, and other expenditures" associated with her entry and profession, as well as the price of a "decent cell."[3]

Discalced orders followed strict vows of poverty and accepted novices without dowries. To enter the Capuchine convent of Buenos

---

[3] Archivo del Convento de la Concepción, Puebla, Testamento de la madre María Luisa de San Bartholomé, 1686, cited in Rosalva Loreto López, "La fundación del convento de la Concepción: Identidad y families en la sociedad poblana (1593–1643)," in Pilar Gonzalbo Aizpuru, ed., *Familias novohispanas: Siglos XVI al XIX* (Mexico: El Colegio de México, 1991), 170.

Aires, for example, a woman need only have "a simple ironed-legged cot with a wooden board and bedstand, modest personal linen, religious habits, and useful utensils." Some convents that did not require dowries asked for a yearly income to support the nun. Additionally the personal incomes of the nuns (*reservas*), often generated by income-earning property, covered expenses beyond those provided for by the convent. These funds allowed the wealthiest nuns to buy sumptuous habits, adornments, and special foods such as chocolate.

In some convents nuns were permitted to inherit property from their family. In almost every case the total value of this property was usually less than what the nun would have inherited had she chosen marriage instead of the convent. Convents that allowed nuns to hold private property also allowed them to manage it, administering, renting, and selling land and houses and lending cash. These nuns continued their religious lives while taking on additional responsibilities and business activities, much as did some women outside the convent.

One sterling example of a nun with extraordinary business acumen was Catarina de Monte Sinay, a member of the Dêsterro convent in Bahia. In her last will and testament drawn up in 1758, Catalina listed working capital equal to half of her wealthy convent's total annual income.[4] This money was invested in loans made to individuals in Bahia, Ilheus, Rio, and Minas Gerais; in rental property, including five substantial residential buildings; and in a pastry business, which she ran using the labor of twelve slaves (six men and six women) from within the convent.

While some nuns engaged in business, others undertook a life of self-denigration, atoning for their sins and those of their fellow citizens by suffering in imitation of Christ. One of Catarina de Monte Sinay's sister nuns, Victória da Encarnação, was such a woman, known for her good deeds, miraculous powers, and austere life-style. Victória practiced mortification of the flesh, eating only bread and water, wearing a hair shirt during the day, flagellating herself at night, and performing the stations of the cross while carrying a cross herself every week. Clearly, within the confinement of a convent, a woman had a choice of different life-styles.

Life within the convent also varied greatly depending on time, place,

---

[4] Arquivo do Convento de Santa Clara do Destêrro, Bahia, Caixas 1 and 2, cited in Susan Soeiro, "Catarina de Monte Sinay," in David G. Sweet and Gary B. Nash, eds., *Struggle and Survival in Colonial America* (Berkeley: University of California Press, 1981), 266–271.

and religious order. In theory women undertook a religious life to dedicate themselves to the service of God. Their primary roles were to praise God and perfect their own spiritual life. Nuns also accepted a life governed by a communal rule and punctuated by a ritual of canonical hours that alternated periods of silence, prayer, meditation, and fasting.

Life was particularly hard in discalced convents where food was more austere (only fish and vegetables), fasting more regular, and comforts nonexistent. In their search for religious perfection, discalced nuns linked self-restraint, humiliation, suffering, and self-mortification of the flesh. Seeking to appease God, they practiced flagellation, exalted mystical experiences and visions, and followed a life of contemplative prayer. The liturgical day for a discalced nun might begin with midnight prayers in the convent church choir. After praying for an hour, the nuns returned to their cells to sleep but were awakened at 5:00 A.M. to attend mass and receive communion. Fifteen minutes were allotted for a brief breakfast; by 6:30 the nuns were again at prayer followed by an hour of spiritual exercises. From 8:30 to 11:00 the nuns returned to their cells, and, after cleaning, devoted themselves to manual tasks in a communal room, scouring the convent's floors, or washing linen. While they worked, they prayed or listened to a religious talk. Before their 11:15 lunch, the nuns once again returned to their church for a period of private reflection and examination of their conscience for personal defects.

While they ate, the nuns listened to religious readings such as biographies of exemplary nuns; during Advent and Lent, they practiced public acts of penitence. After returning again to the church for the Miserere, they had the hour from 12:00 to 1:00 P.M. for communal "recreation," which usually consisted of conversation on spiritual matters or edifying religious stories. The next hour was dedicated to private prayer or rest; by 2:00 the nuns were back in the church for Vespers. From 3:00 to 5:00 were hours again spent at manual tasks, followed by prayer and spiritual exercises to help guide their thoughts until 6:45. Dinner followed, and then another hour of prayer. By 8:00 P.M. the nuns returned to the cells to sleep until midnight prayers. Once a week the nuns met to examine their faults and failures publicly and were given special penitential exercises for the coming days.

While also following a routine of prayer and meditation, nuns in calced orders usually enjoyed a far more comfortable life. Despite the vow of poverty, women in calced convents were allowed to keep their private possessions – slaves, silver, decorations, cash. Some convents, such as the Poor Clares of Salvador, were famous for their costly extravagant life-style, replete with finery, jewels, and personal servants. These women fashioned a life of comparative extravagance within the convent walls, decorating their cells with imported furniture, dressing in habits decked with ribbons and embroidery, dying their hair, wearing makeup, and consuming luxury goods. Nuns not only purchased private rooms or suites within the convent, they paid to renovate their quarters. Although these women had renounced the secular world and retired to a cloister, they were allowed private quarters, servants and slaves, and fine clothing.

Nuns lived within enclosed walls to protect them from worldly contamination, and most convents followed strict rules governing who could enter their walls. But while regulations kept all but those providing the most essential services outside the convent, a rather colorful array of people would gather at the convent's entryway (portería) to visit, peddle, and generally provide entertainment. Nuns were allowed to distribute food to the needy, gossip with visitors in reception rooms (locutorios), and exchange goods through the convent's door. The convent of Santa Catalina in Córdoba marketed pots produced by slaves within the convent walls. In addition, special festivities were held to celebrate noviates taking the veil, and sumptuous feasts marked the saints' days of each convent.

Although convents in the sixteenth century were rather austere retreats, during the seventeenth century there were increased charges of riotous living within the convent walls. Baroque poets mentioned lascivious nuns having illicit relations with monks and priests, and charges of solicitation and molestation were brought before the Holy Inquisition. In Spanish America at least one nun and friar were denounced for having illicit carnal relations that resulted in the birth of a child, and one Bahian nun had an affair with her chaplain, who entered her room through a trap door in the convent church. In general these piquant adventures were very rare. Periodical scandals did not prevent the elite from continuing to send their daughters to the convent. One historian has suggested that the social and economic advantages of sending a daughter to the convent far outweighed any possible moral contamination.

Indeed for many nuns life in the convent was a bit too comfortable. There were several failed attempts during the seventeenth century to reform the convents, but only in the mid-eighteenth century did crown and church attempt a major reform of Spanish American female monasteries. Reacting to what they viewed as a too worldly life-style, church authorities attempted to restore the austere common life within the convent. Nuns were pictured as overindulging in luxury, having large numbers of servants and slaves, and enjoying such frequent contact with the outside world that the spirituality of the convent was undermined. Exhorted to return to a simpler life, several nuns success-fully resisted, claiming that they had not joined an order to live in a self-sacrificing community. In spite of the pressure of church and state, no major changes were enacted, although the relationship between convents and their bishops was severely strained.

The geographical immobility of nuns was much greater than that of lay women. The only exception were those few senior nuns who were chosen to help found an offshoot convent. Although at first nuns arrived in Latin America from Spain and Portugal, later convents were founded by nuns arriving from established monasteries in closer-by colonial cities. For example, in 1745 a convent of Cataline nuns was begun in Buenos Aires by five nuns sent from the same order's convent in Córdoba. Three of the founding nuns were themselves natives of Buenos Aires. In 1749, another convent, that of the Capuchine order, was established in Buenos Aires by nuns coming from Santiago de Chile.

After taking her final vows, a nun did not expect to leave the convent. She had made a commitment for life, a commitment that on the average lasted almost forty years. But entering a convent did not mean that a nun was isolated from her family and friends; indeed, many nuns found a rich and familiar social life within the convent. Often several close relatives from the same family entered the same convent. In this way, sisters, cousins, aunts, and nieces reproduced within the cloister many of the patterns of sociability they had known outside. Some elite families sent two, three, or four women from every genera-tion to the convent. The Soledade convent in Bahia, for example, housed five sisters from the same family. Over three generations, the Pires de Carvalho family of Bahia sent nineteen of twenty-six women in the family to the convent. In Buenos Aires, six sisters from the de la Palma family entered the Catalina convent within an eight-year period. Because nuns tended to be drawn from the same social class, they often knew each other before joining the religious community. If men from these same families were in the clergy, nuns could also keep up contact with their brothers, uncles, and cousins while never leaving the cloister.

In addition to the private property owned by nuns, convents, like monasteries, earned income from real property and mortgages (*censos*), which they accumulated through gifts from generous benefactors and investments. Convents amassed ample portfolios of urban property as well as a few pieces of rural real estate. Nuns, elected by their peers, took a role in managing these properties or at least overseeing their administration. (See Document 8.) Convents also served as bankers, landlords, and slave masters, making loans, managing urban and rural property, and administering slaves. Again it was nuns who supervised these complex tasks, demonstrating financial and managerial talents. Not surprisingly, having a daughter, aunt, or sister in the convent often facilitated a family's access to credit.

A handful of nuns also had the opportunity to exercise leadership and responsibility, because convents were self-governing units administered by an abbess, who was helped by other cloistered women. They not only governed their own community but determined who qualified for entry into their world. But nuns also sought and received spiritual and temporal guidance from financial advisors (*síndicos*), religious confessors, provincials, bishops, and archbishops. Many nuns undertook to record their spiritual autobiographies only when encouraged to do so by their confessors. All convents were under the governance of the local bishop or archbishop, and any nun seeking exemption from the communal rule had to petition this churchman.

Nonetheless, groups of nuns did occasionally rebel against their abbess or reject change sponsored by the church hierarchy. In the mid-seventeenth century Mexican nuns in the Franciscan convent refused to obey an order limiting the number of servants they could each have in the convent. More than one hundred years later, nuns in several Mexican convents protested against the church's attempt to institute stricter communal living arrangements within the convent walls. These uprisings were all conservative reactions against attempts to modify the nuns' way of life.

Equally conservative was the eighteenth-century rebellion by the Capuchine nuns of Buenos Aires over admission of a nun of doubtful racial antecedents. Although committed to a life of penury and privation, the nuns were not about to allow a suspected mulatta to join their august order. They succeeded in defying both the abbess and the bishop, effectively closing down the entry of novices for twenty years. As this example shows, convents were not divorced from lay society or from its values. The politics of larger society could also be reflected within the convent. Politics within the convent was often linked to political machinations of the society at large, and family feuds could continue within the convent walls. For example, at the same time as the crown was prosecuting Martin Cortés, the second marques del Valle, and his followers for high treason, Elena de la Cruz, a Conceptionist nun and member of a family allied to Cortés, was called up before the Mexican Inquisition in 1568 for heresy. Furthermore, just as nuns demonstrated camaraderie, they also displayed envy, greed, and partisanship.

In spite of the constraints on their life, nuns could find room for self-expression and self-fulfillment within the convent walls. It is quite possible that life in the nunnery was less confining for elite women than the other socially acceptable option, marriage. In spite of being cloistered, nuns were not inactive. Here women read, wrote, and worked with numbers. Nuns had a level of literacy far above that of any other group of women, and hundreds of nuns left writings that attest to their education and spirituality. Nuns chronicled their convents, wrote the histories of exemplary nuns, authored their own spiritual biographies, recorded mystical experiences, and wrote poetry and plays. They also wrote and directed religious plays for their own edification and entertainment.

There was also music within the convent walls. Nuns wrote, directed, and performed sacred music, and played a variety of instruments, including the clavichord, harp, flageolet, and flute. Nuns sang in convent choirs, entertaining an elite public, including at times high-ranking government officials and the viceroy. At Christmas some convents held religious pageants or musical recitals to which the city's notables would be invited. Sometimes poor girls with exceptional musical ability were accepted into a convent as nuns of the white veil.

Nuns also practiced an array of feminine arts including sewing, embroidery, baking, and selling special confections. The candies and pastries produced by the nuns were often known locally by suggestive if not salacious names such as "raise-the-old-man", "little kisses," "maiden's tongue," "men's sighs" "love's caresses," or "nun's belly." In some convents nuns were encouraged to make handmade silk roses and religious tableaux to decorate their cells.

Joining a convent allowed women to find both a spiritual and social life. Colonial Latin America was a deeply religious society, and Hispanic Catholicism always viewed piety as an especially female attribute.

Many young women had a true vocation, seeking to emulate the Virgin Mary, Catholicism's most cherished religious icon and the special intercessor with Christ, guide and protector. Some women joined to escape the sinfulness and danger of world. Others wanted to also enjoy economic power, social prestige, and a coherent community. Still others saw the convent as an acceptable way to escape a life under the direct authority of either their father or their future husband, while also avoiding both the more routine and more dangerous aspects of domestic life. Still others took vows under parental pressure, or to fulfill their family's larger social strategy. Entering the convent was a most personal decision, undertaken for a variety of reasons and usually preceded by a period of self-examination.

A few women were moved by both spiritual and intellectual motives. Such was the case of Sor Juana Inés de la Cruz (1648–1695), probably the most extraordinary woman in colonial Latin American history. Born out of wedlock in a small town near Mexico City, as a child Juana Ramírez was identified as a genius and brought to the viceregal court. At about age eighteen she decided to join a convent, explaining that she had no interest in marriage and instead wished to pursue a life of the mind. After a brief unsuccessful experience in a discalced monastery, she entered the convent of San Gerónimo. In the years that followed Sor Juana wrote secular and religious poetry, plays, philosophical treatises, and theological critiques, spoke to visitors who came to the convent's grille on subjects ranging from mathematics to science to music, and defended the right of women to use their intellect. Although silenced by her bishop in 1690, Sor Juana remained in the convent until her death during a plague epidemic, five years later.

Convents housed more than nuns. They were also temporary residences for girls and women in need of protection, shelter, and support regardless of their marital state. Large and complex communities, they provided shelter to a considerable segment of the urban female population. La Concepción convent in Lima had a total of 1,041 inhabitants at the beginning of the eighteenth century, although only 318 of these women were nuns, novices, or lay sisters. In early-eighteenth-century Lima, approximately 10 percent of the population (3,865 women) lived in one of seven convents. Probably the number of women in convents reached its peak between the mid-seventeenth and mid-eighteenth centuries, declining slightly from then on.

Like the cities in which they were located, the convent was a world that mirrored the social, economic, and racial hierarchy of the larger society. At the top of the convent's social pyramid were the religious: nuns of black veil and nuns of white veil. Next came the secular inhabitants: *recogidas* (*recolhidas*) and *educandas*. The former included illegitimate daughters of prominent citizens; unchaste daughters; adulterous wives; abandoned or divorced women; orphaned girls; single women seeking solace or protection; women temporarily alone or unprotected by a male guardian, such as the wives of absent merchants; widows; and lay women, often kinsfolk of the nuns, who wished to join them. Educandas were young girls sent to the convent to receive a basic education.

The presence of these students underlines the fact that convents were also female educational institutions. Some convents such as La Concepción in Mexico City were originally envisioned as training centers for Indian women. Many other calced orders also did some degree of teaching. Generally the education provided for the convent's clientele, the daughters of the local elite, consisted of basic reading, prayers, and sewing skills. In the mid-eighteenth century the Order of Mary began to function in Latin America. Founded specifically to improve the educational standards of nuns and women in general, this order made education the center of its activities. But regardless of the order, all convents contributed to improving the level of female education and perhaps also created a feminine identity.

Even those convents which did not have a formal educational establishment usually raised orphan girls and others. These girls were always of Spanish origin and, though usually poor themselves, often had some benefactor willing to cover their basic expenses. Among their ranks could be found illegitimate daughters of prominent men, sisters of nuns, and poor but decent young women caught in trying circumstances. Those without benefactors could be sponsored by a nun; in these cases the girl was expected to attend to the nun much like a servant.

All of these women tended to be white, reflecting the society's deeply held belief that only white women needed to be protected. The racial bias of convents was so strong that even those houses originally founded to serve noble Indian women and mestiza daughters of prominent Spanish conquistadors, such as the Santa Clara convent of Cuzco, became sanctuaries primarily for European women. Only at the bottom of a convent's social pyramid were there nonwhite women: servants and slaves, including Indian *donadas*, servants who took private vows of chastity and pursued a religious life. Female slaves, used to clean and cook, to sell sweets to the public, to run errands, and to carry messages to and from the convent, were also common in the wealthiest convents. In the middle of the eighteenth century, the 94 nuns of Dêsterro nunnery had a total of 219 personal servants.

One of the more exceptional colonial convents was the Monastery of Corpus Christi in Mexico City, founded in 1724 for Indian women. Although noble Indian women had been allowed to enter certain convents in Peru, in New Spain only one non-Spanish woman had become a professed nun prior to the eighteenth century. This woman, Luisa de Tapia, had joined the Royal Convent of Santa Clara, a convent founded by her mestizo father. According to his restriction only one Indian woman, his daughter, was to be admitted to an essentially Spanish institution.

The creation of a truly Indian convent, reserved for the daughters of *caciques* and *principales*, the nobility of Indian society, was proposed by the viceroy of Mexico, the marqués de Valero. Although some Jesuits and members of the Mexico City Audiencia opposed the idea, arguing that Indian women could not be trusted to fulfill the obligations of a nun because they were sexually promiscuous, unstable, melancholic, and slow to learn, the viceroy prevailed. Corpus Christi was founded in 1724; two other Mexican Indian convents, Nuestra Señora de Cosamaloapán in Morelia (1737) and Nuestra Señora de los Angeles in Oaxaca (1782) followed.

Postulates to the Corpus Christi convent were required to be full-blooded Indian, legitimate, daughters of nobles, never linked to idolatry, at least fifteen years old, able to read Latin, trained in domestic arts (sewing, embroidery), never betrothed or married, and virtuous young women. Corpus Christi was a mendicant convent – that is, an institution dependent on alms rather than nuns' dowries – and, like other similar convents, it was small. The convent did not house secular women or students and had perhaps twenty members at any time. Reflecting its relative poverty and the social position deemed fitting for Indian women, its nuns were not permitted private incomes, servants, or private cells.

From 1724 to 1821 the convent admitted 147 novitiates, of whom 105 eventually professed. These women were overwhelmingly from Mexico City. Although requirements emphasized Indian racial purity, the actual proof of Indianness needed to enter was both cultural and racial. The novitiates were in the main daughters of Indian titleholders and members of the civil bureaucracy, but many were also from modest economic circumstances. Forty-seven percent of the postulants were orphans and some had been employed as servants before joining the convent. The nuns of Corpus Christi fiercely protected the Indianness of their establishment and successfully countered an attempt by Spanish nuns to integrate (and eventually to take over) the convent by going to court.

Convents were not the only religious institutions providing temporary or permanent refuge for women. Other institutions – *beaterios*, *recogimientos*, and orphanages – allowed women to live in a female environment where they pursued a structured religious life. Beaterios, congregations of unordained laywomen pursuing private religious devotions, most resembled convents, but unlike convents they required no dowry and no irrevocable religious vows were made. Because beaterios were never subject to the formal mandate of the provincial of a religious order, these institutions and the women within them, often of more modest social origins, were often suspected of lacking order and being somewhat uncontrollable.

Beatas affiliated with the Franciscans were actually the first religious women to be present after the conquest of the New World. Six women were sent to Mexico in 1530 by the queen of Spain to serve as teachers for the daughters of noble Indians, but they soon turned out to be too independent and too influenced by Illuminism. Accused by Bishop Zumárraga of teaching their Indian charges to be idle and uninterested in serving their husbands, the beatas soon returned to Spain. The bishop then turned to Clarissan nuns, who promised to be more virtuous, tractable, and supportive of authority.

Nonetheless, beatas continued to be present in the cities of Latin America. By the seventeenth century, Cuzco was reported to have nine beaterios while Lima had six. The requisites for becoming a beata were flexible and varied from place to place. Some beatas took vows of chastity and poverty while also promising to lead a life of prayer; others did not. Some beatas followed the rules of a religious order, but this was not true of all. Indeed some beatas lived in groups while others lived alone. Beatas were uncloistered and often subsisted by begging alms, selling their handicrafts, and even performing domestic chores. In Cuzco members of Indian beaterios often cleaned the churches of the monasteries with which they were informally tied.

Generally beatas were unmarried women or older widows. They were usually white women of modest social origins (frequently daughters of artisans and small farmers), although mestiza, Indian, and mulatta women also joined their ranks. All were searching for religious expression but for personal, social, or economic reasons had stopped short of making a complete and formal religious commitment. Beatas cared for orphans and abandoned children and provided schools for poor girls, but because they were neither cloistered nor under the close supervision of a religious order and were of modest social origin, they were often accused of being "wayward" women and suspected of immoral behavior. Furthermore, because beatas were not directly subject to male authority, the Inquisition in both Spain and America viewed them, especially those whose spiritual devotion led them to religious ecstasies and mystical visions, as a threat to religious orthodoxy.

Perhaps the most famous Latin America beata was Rosa de Santa María, a late-sixteenth-century *limeña* canonized by 1670. Rosa was not only the model beata, she also inspired several contemporaries to pursue her style of spirituality. All were mystics who fasted regularly and experienced repeated "vertiginous trances and shining ecstasies." At least five of Rosa's followers were examined by the Lima Inquisition on charges of heresy, because, in addition to curing the ill, these beatas claimed to save souls from purgatory, foretell the future, enter into raptures, and fly over the city. While some of these beatas were married, all had avoided sexual contact with their husbands, preferring instead to enjoy erotic visions of Christ and "mystical pregnancies," which they believed resulted in the birth of saints.

Religious ecstasy was always viewed with suspicion by the church, and several beatas in New Spain were also called before the Inquisition during the sixteenth and seventeenth centuries on charges of "following the sect of the *alumbrados*."[5] Like their counterparts in Lima these women were accused of entering into direct communication with Jesus Christ, the Virgin Mary, and a host of other male and female saints; undergoing raptures and mystical trances; following deviant religious practices; falsely claiming to have stigmata; and being fed by manna from heaven. Many of these Mexican beatas were poor Spanish women, often sickly and tormented by sins of the flesh, who had sought solace in religious excess.

Although both mysticism and the Inquisition became less important in the eighteenth century, most beatas never ceased to be viewed as marginal religious women; those who also claimed to be visionaries and miracle workers came perilously close to heresy. Ana de Aramburu, a

---

[5] The *alumbrados* were a heretical sect that had first appeared in sixteenth-century Spain. They believed that one could obtain a perfect state of grace through prayer and were often suspected of being secret Protestants.

beata called before the Mexican Inquisition in 1801, was said to enter in trances, sweating blood replicating the wounds of Christ and floating in the air. In this state she spoke directly to God, prophesizing the future and performing miracles. For at least three years Ana was protected by priests who housed her in Puebla, Toluca, and Mexico City, where she earned a loyal following among women, who like her, were of humble background. But she eventually crossed the line into heresy by claiming to have traded her heart for Jesus'; suggesting that the Virgin Mary was not pure; and counseling other women to follow their heart, and not their confessors, to find God. Accused by the Inquisition of being in consort with the devil, of sexual perversions with other beatas ("the three of them were all mixed together, at times fulfilling the part of the man, at times of the woman, and even helping each other with their hands"), and of "riling up the public." Ana was imprisoned and then remanded to a hospital because of an advanced case of venereal disease.

Nonetheless, some beatas, inspired by a special religious zeal, took leading roles in founding local religious institutions. Sor María de la Paz's dynamic religious leadership led to the creation of a House of Spiritual Exercises, founded in Buenos Aires in 1780. Sensing a religious void that resulted from the ouster of the Jesuits in 1767, Sor María, a well-born woman from Santiago del Estero, created a casa to shelter men and women in search of spiritual solace. She personally took charge of building the casa, raising funds, and petitioning individuals, churchmen, and the city fathers for support. With her guidance those attending spiritual exercises followed a strict sixteen-hour schedule of prayer and contemplation. Under Sor María's direction, the institution also gradually replaced the women's public jail (where men and women had been housed in quarters described as a "frightful place . . . totally lacking in hygiene"). As the storehouse for women accused of criminal behavior, Sor María personally took on the task of reforming wayward women. Shortly before her death in 1799, Sor María named her successor, another *beata*, the childless twice-widowed Margarita Melgarejo, who had become a penitent, living austerely and subjecting herself to bodily privations after the death of her second husband.

Another place of protection for women were the recogimientos (in Portuguese, *recolhimentos*), secular houses of refuge for impoverished women. The first recogimiento was probably founded in Mexico City in the mid-sixteenth century, when the viceroy, seeking to provide protection for "the many mestiza girls who roam around lost, with no one to look after them," set up a lay home. The goal of these shelters was to provide a secure retreat for women in difficult personal circumstances and thus help them avoid falling into "dishonest" ways in order to survive.

Poor but honest widows as well as white and mixed-blood young women waiting to "take a state" sought protection in the recogimiento. In addition, fathers, husbands, and brothers deposited wayward daughters, wives, and sisters seeking divorce in these houses for weeks, months, or years. Women whose personal behavior was viewed as "pernicious and insolent," female adulteresses, bigamists, prostitutes, and other criminals were remanded by the court to the recogimiento to be punished, repent, and reform. Some recogimientos changed character over the years, beginning as homes for repentant prostitutes and ending as protectors of economically needy women. Others continued to welcome a mixed clientele, providing protection to women regardless of the circumstances. The demand for these institutions is reflected in the fact that a city of twenty-one thousand inhabitants such as Bahia had three recolhimentos by the eighteenth century.

Most of the principal cities of colonial Latin America also had at least one orphanage. In the sixteenth century orphanages were founded to serve the young daughters of the elite, but over time they came to accommodate a more diverse population. As the goal of the orphanage was to marry off its wards, female orphans were provided with a rudimentary education (basic literacy and needle skills) and, if possible, modest dowries. By the eighteenth century some of these casas de niñas huérfanas began to accept day students in addition to orphaned inmates and soon emerged as educational institutions for elite young women.

In the major cities of colonial Latin America still other institutions were created to protect special groups of women. Lima, for example, had a retreat for divorced women, both a *hospital de niños huérfanos* (hospital for orphaned children) and a *colegio de niñas expósitas* (school for abandoned girls), and three hospitals for women (one for white women, another for the poor, and a third for convalescents). One historian has calculated that by the end of the seventeenth century approximately 20 percent of the women of the city of Lima lived in church-sponsored sex-segregated institutions.

There were still other ways in which women could participate in religious life. Elite women attended mass daily and often became members of third orders. Women of all social groups and civil states joined lay organizations, especially religious cofradías dedicated to sponsoring the care and cult of a patron saint, as well as underwriting the cost of religious services and popular celebrations. Some cofradías boasted an elite membership, but most, like their Iberian counterparts, were linked to specific artisan guilds or occupational groups. Cofradías not only provided a spiritual dimension to the lives of their members; they also helped to articulate their members' social lives, while providing care for the widows and orphans of deceased members. So ubiquitous were cofradías that by the end of the eighteenth century 425 of them were registered in the archbishopric of Mexico alone.

Different cofradías were open to women of various social and age groups. In Mexico City, the Congregación de San Pedro welcomed elite Spanish women, usually the wives or widows of men of high social rank. A list of new members shows that women made up approximately one-third of its associates. Cofradías were also frequently organized along racial lines. There were cofradías dedicated to serving the spiritual needs of Spaniards, others for Indians, and still others for blacks in almost every city of colonial Latin America. While some cofradías welcomed both male and female members, others were sex-specific. The cofradía of Our Lady of Monserate of the town of Andahuaylillas in southern Peruvian Andes, for example, was open only to unmarried Indian women. Likewise, all officeholders in the Cofradía de Jesús Nazareño in the southern Mexican village of Yajalón were Indian women. Throughout America, Spanish, Indian, or black women, especially widows, took an active role in these cofradías, including joining their governing councils.

Women were also active benefactors of these organizations, providing funds to undertake the cofradía's charitable work. Although not in the majority, several women members appear in the account roles of the prestigious Archicofradía del Santísimo Sacramento of Mexico City, donating thousands of pesos. Many of their contributions specified charitable actions to help women. One of the most generous patrons was Elvira de Mayorga, who provided funds in 1618 and 1633 to dower orphan girls. Isabel de la Barreda, another generous patron, earmarked some of her 1659 gift for burying poor Spanish widows and saying masses for their souls.

The care and protection of unprotected widows, orphans, and poor but honest girls was a special concern of many cofradías. By the end of the eighteenth century, an average of 90 girls were dowered annually by the cofradías of Mexico City; each received 300 pesos. Between 1768 and 1808 the Archicofradía of Nuestra Señora del Rosario in Mexico City awarded dowries to 417 young women (an average of 26 dowries per year). Approximately 41 percent of these women used their dowries to marry, 31 percent remained single, and 28 percent took religious vows.

In the rural regions of colonial Latin America there were still other religious roles for Indian women. In towns and missions, women were trained by priests to teach the catechism and prepare people to receive sacraments. In addition it was usually the most devout women who were given the duty and honor of looking after the local church.

In all its myriad forms, the Catholic Church provided women with a religious and social community and a rich religious life. Depending on one's point of view, church-sponsored convents, orphanages, and schools either protected women in need of shelter or created repositories for those believed to be potentially disruptive to the social hierarchy or misfits in the established elite patriarchal social order. These institutions allowed for the removal of elite women who diverged from the sanctioned models, while they also presented these women with a way to escape from the restrictions of a patriarchal society.

CHAPTER 8

WOMEN AND WORK

The poor females perform all the drudgery, waiting upon [the men]
with the greatest humility.[1]

Colonial women were not only wives, concubines, spinsters, mothers,
and nuns; they were also participants in the local colonial economy.
Unfortunately the place of women in the economy – as investors, con-
sumers, and above all as a work force – has tended to be ignored by historians. We are just beginning to understand the role played by women.
This chapter will look at female participation in various sectors of the
colonial economy paying special attention to the importance of social
class, ethnicity, and physical location in women's economic pursuits.

Because of their number in colonial Latin America, an active economic role for women is not surprising. By the eighteenth century
and possibly before, women were in the majority in virtually all
the cities of colonial Latin America. For example, by 1778 in
Córdoba, Argentina, 54.8 percent of the population was female; in
late eighteenth-century São Paulo (1798), women accounted for 53.3
percent of the total; Quito also became increasingly female and by
1797 had only 53 men per 100 women.

The ratio of women to men differed by place and social or racial category, but from the seventeenth century on, women were in the major-

---

[1] Alexander Caldcleugh's description of women in the Argentine pampas,
although made shortly after independence, was also true of the colonial period.
*Travels in South America during the Years 1819–20–21: Containing an Account of
the Present State of Brazil, Buenos Ayres, and Chile* (London: John Murray, 1825),
1:251, cited in Richard W. Slatta, *Gauchos and the Vanishing Frontier* (Lincoln:
University of Nebraska Press, 1992), 57.

ity in virtually every urban nonwhite group. In São Paulo, for example, women predominated in the free population (83.52 men for every 100 women), whereas in the slave population the sex ratio was almost equal (99.04 men for every 100 women). Among the casta population of Córdoba, there were only 71.3 men for every 100 women.

Throughout colonial Latin America, the nature of female economic participation was closely tied to race and class. Colonial ideas of propriety forbade elite women from working in public, but occasionally wealthy women were active in commerce, mining, or business. Usually they were widows who had been left sizable assets by their husbands, or daughters who had inherited from their fathers. Although many elite women were content to allow their brothers, uncles, or sons to manage their inheritances, some decidedly took a more active role. These noteworthy women bought and sold houses, haciendas, and slaves; employed managers and foremen; and closely administered their property and goods.

Wealthy women – usually widowed or single – also invested in companies that manufactured artisanal goods or sold goods to the public. Three women, for example, invested a total of 25,000 pesos in a silversmith shop in Mexico City. Women also owned liquor stores (*vinaterías* and *pulquerías*), although they usually used men – either kinsmen or hired agents – to run the business. Six pulquerías in 1784 Mexico City were owned by two daughters of the conde de Regla, and in a 1795 survey of pulperías in Mexico City, 7 percent of the shopowners were women. Women also inherited, owned, or invested in stores, factories, and other property. Doña María Paulín y Aguirre, daughter of Francisco Javier Paulín, Mexico City's most important *obrajero* (textile factory owner) during the last half of the eighteenth century, and widow of the merchant, Francisco Saldaña, owned both her late husband's store in the Portal de los Mercaderes (worth 55,771 pesos), a factory in Posadas (valued at 29,443 pesos), and another one in Mixcoac (valued at 23,534 pesos) at the time of her death in 1789. In Querétaro, one woman was listed among the sixteen obrajeros owning factories producing coarse cloth in a 1793 report, while in Veracruz, Doña Manuela Lazcano, widow of a local merchant, invested in a grocery story in Mexico City. At least some of these women were as successful as María Magdalena de Mérida, the Caracas-based widow of a military man, who increased her husband's sizable estate by 2,000 pesos in the form of silver coin, a house, a lot, and a shop within five years of his death.

In theory, women of the better classes did not work, but Spanish single women, widows, and women with absent husbands were often forced into some type of economic activity to maintain themselves. (See Document 9.) Because of the importance of enclosure in assuring a woman's reputation, upper-class women when faced with the need to earn money attempted to work in their homes using male surrogates whenever possible. Some used brothers, sons, and kinsmen to manage rental properties. Those less affluent preferred to earn a livelihood by renting rooms in their houses or sending their slaves out to work for day wages. For example, Doña María Josefa Flores, a widow living in late-eighteenth-century Buenos Aires, had three single Spanish men boarding with her and her children. Because these economic activities avoided direct entry into the public space, they were acceptable for those who aspired to be among the finer class.

Middle-group women also tried to stay at home, shielded from public gaze. The more literate among them sometimes taught young girls or took in sewing. Those widows who had worked alongside their husbands in retail trade sometimes became shopkeepers themselves, running their late husbands' businesses from a small corner store in their homes. Widows of booksellers routinely continued their husbands' business. In certain regions permission to own *pulperías* (general stores) or to sell tobacco products was reserved for Hispanic widows who conducted their businesses from shops located in or near their homes. In colonial cities women owners of tobacco stands (*estancos*) were ubiquitous. For example, one-third of all sellers of tobacco products in Mexico City were women. Women were, in general, the owners of the more modest establishments, but some of them were able to garner enough profits to make modest investments in real estate and other property. Until the creation of government-owned tobacco factories in the late eighteenth century, women were also active in cigarette production, owning and working in small family workshops and also rolling cigarettes on a putting-out basis.

The same was true of the wives of artisans, especially the wives of master craftsmen. After their husbands' deaths, some of these women who had no doubt participated, unofficially, in the craft became artisans themselves, working in the shops they had inherited from their husbands. Although most guilds never formally allowed female members, they often turned a blind eye to widows continuing in their husbands' footsteps. The widow of the first printer in Mexico carried on his business after his death, and the widows of several master

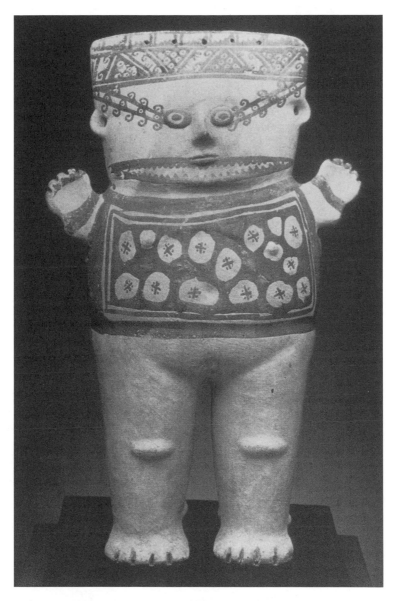

1   Effigy of a female figure from the Chancay culture of the central Andes, A.D. 1000–1470. Courtesy of Michael Carlos Museum, Emory University, Atlanta, Georgia.

2   During the period of Inca rule, middle-aged women wove common cloth in the service of nobles. After the conquest female weavers would continue to produce cloth for their Spanish encomenderos on the same type of backstrap loom. Felipe Huamán Poma de Ayala, *El primer nueva corónica y buen govierno* (1612–1616).

3   A portrait of Isabel the Catholic, fifteenth-century queen of Castile, and sponsor of Columbus's voyages of discovery. Painting by Bartolomé Bermejo, Courtesy of Royal Palace, Madrid.

4   A colonial folk painting depicting Santa Rosa de Lima, a Peruvian beata of the late sixteenth or early seventeenth century. Although Rosa is dressed as a nun, as a beata she never took formal vows. Gloria Kay Giffords, *Mexican Folk Retablos* (University of Arizona Press, 1974).

5   Women filled various roles in the colonial economy. This mulatta market
vendor is shown selling fruit in an eighteenth-century casta painting. "De
tente-en-el-aire y mulata nace albarazado," Seville series, private collection.

6   A rural Indian woman. Although her husband seems to be a peasant farmer,
she is shown wearing ornate earrings and a necklace. "De sambaigo e india
produce albarazado," Courtesy of Museum of Natural History, Vienna.

7 A black woman street vendor selling prepared food in a mid-eighteenth-century casta painting. She is well dressed, wearing jewelry and sandals, and is shown with her Spanish artisan husband and frock-coated child. Luis Berrueco, "De español y negra sale mulato," circa 1750, private collection.

8   In this casta painting, a mixed-blood woman spins yarn, while her mate works at a cobbler's bench. The spinner is barefooted, but porcelain dishes are displayed in the cabinet. Their child is busy potting a plant. Unknown Mexican artist, "De coyota e indio, chamiso," circa 1780, private collection.

9   A woman packs cigarettes being rolled by her husband in their tobacco shop. As befitting a small shopkeeper she is well dressed, wearing a pearl necklace and earrings; a beauty mark is painted over her eye. Unknown Mexican artist, "De español y albina, torna-atrás," circa 1760–1770, private collection.

10 Two elegantly dressed Brazilian ladies and a child dressed in the same fashion in late eighteenth-century Brazil. Carlos Julião, "Noticia sumária do gentilismo da Ásia con dez riscos iluminados . . . ," prancha XIII, circa 1785, Courtesy of Biblioteca Nacional, Rio de Janeiro.

11   An elite woman of La Plata (Bolivia) being served mate by her mestiza servant. The mistress's finery includes several necklaces, a plumed hat and a fine linen handkerchief. The servant, while more modest in her attire, none-theless is wearing jewelry, a lace blouse, and fine shoes. Unknown Bolivian artist, dress of a lady of the city of La Plata, circa 1790, Courtesy of Museo Soumaya, Mexico City.

12   A rural Indian woman from the town of Charasani (Bolivia) with her husband and child. Although modestly dressed, she wears a distinctive hat and holds a purse or small basket. Unknown Bolivian artist, dress of an Indian of the village of Charasani, circa 1790, Courtesy of Museo Soumaya, Mexico City.

weavers continued to do the same throughout the colonial period. Widows owning and running bakeries with slave labor became common throughout colonial Spanish America; three of the forty-eight bakers in late-eighteenth-century Mexico City were women.

As we can see, women's economic activities were more publicly visible as one went down the social scale. Among artisans, women's presence in the cloth trades and in specialized food production had grown large enough by the late eighteenth century that guilds began to admit women. During the 1790s five widows controlling twenty-one looms were included among members of the guild of cotton weavers of Mexico City. A few women also were listed as journeymen in this guild and that of sackcloth weavers. Female silk spinners were so numerous in Mexico City that in 1788 they were allowed to organize their own guild. At the time they listed 23 masters, 200 journeymen, and 21 apprentices. The guild of female brandy (*aguardiente*) producers and sellers of Cartagena in New Granada also actively pressed for its rights.

Women were also active in domestic, nonguild weaving. Some urban women owned looms at which they worked in their own homes, selling their products to local merchants or to the public. In the countryside whole families might be involved in weaving. In certain zones women spun and carded wool, while men did the actual weaving. In other regions both men and women were producers while in some places all facets of weaving were in the hands of women. In Mexico alone, between 1777 and 1780, women composed 21 percent of the domestic producers of fabric and wove 12 percent of the total output.

Another major venue for female employment was the marketplaces of cities and towns throughout colonial Latin America. Female food vendors and market women were found in every city in colonial Latin America, and women owned small retail businesses such as food shops, greengroceries, and general stores. In the major urban markets, women sold fruits and vegetables, bread, flowers, and meat as well as cloth, woven goods, yarn, and cotton, each woman working from her customary stall. In the Quito market, Indian and mestiza women also sold ham, salt, cheese, and tobacco, items supposedly limited to licensed *pulperos* (grocers).

Depending on time and place, the market women of colonial Latin America were either Indians, mestizas, mulattas, or blacks. Indian women formed the majority of small traders at the weekly town fairs held in Mexico and Peru, whereas both Indians and mestizas sold in the Quito market. There was some ethnic variation. One observer of the Lima market remarked that Indian women customarily placed their goods on blankets and mats on the ground, whereas black and mulatta women displayed their goods on wooden tables. Black and mulatta women, both slave and free, also peddled foods they had prepared at home – doughnuts and other sweets, cheeses, beverages – as well as fruits, vegetables, and fish on the streets of the coastal cities of Spanish and Portuguese America.

Did the daily experiences of market women develop female solidarity? Although lasting friendships were probably formed, the historical record is also full of territorial conflicts among market women. Those women with centrally located stalls aggressively defended their places, seeking to keep any and all interlopers from moving in. Those relegated to the fringes of the market sought to reposition themselves whenever they could. Some of these conflicts also had clear racial overtones. Between 1599 and 1636, for example, the market women of Mexico City, principally Indians, fought to keep black and mulatta women from selling food. The *indias* argued that African American women sold only ill-gotten goods. Spanish authorities eventually sided with the indias, prohibiting any black women from selling in the market.

Certain urban occupations were closely identified with women of specific racial groups. Indian and mestiza women specialized in the sale of wine or locally produced alcoholic beverages. Peasant women in regions such as Oaxaca produced *pulque*, transporting the fermented agave cactus drink to nearby towns, where they sold it in market stalls. In cities and towns, some market women were full-time pulque vendors, whereas others dispensed the drink from their own homes. Women also worked in the rather boisterous pulquerías of the cities of Mexico. This trade tended to be a profitable though sometimes violent one. In addition to being at the mercy of irate or highly inebriated customers, female alcohol sellers were periodically subjected to government policies that sought to control drinking by regulating its sale. Although the beverage of choice changed from one region of Latin America to another (*chicha* in the Andes; *aguardiente* in Brazil), women's participation did not vary.

In spite of their visibility in the market, a larger group of colonial women probably labored full- or part-time in the "domestic economy," producing the services and goods that provided for the welfare of household units. The domestic economy employed wives, daughters, various dependents (agregadas and dependientes), and poor female relatives as

well as servants and slaves. The home was the most important arena
for female labor.

The duties of women within the household were directly related to
the social position of the male head of household and the relationship
of the individual women to the head. Among elite families, wives and
daughters held supervisory roles, directing dependents, poor female
relatives, servants, and slaves. Elite women oversaw household
expenditures and themselves produced some handiwork, but the bulk
of labor was provided by the women they supervised. In households
of lesser social standing and wealth, the line between the domestic services provided by wives and daughters and other women within the
household was far from distinct. Working within the home, most
women were only indirectly remunerated for their services. All but
salaried servants worked for only food and housing.

Domestic chores ran the gamut from cleaning to cooking to child
care, and in the nonmechanized world of colonial Latin America all of
these tasks were time- and labor-intensive. Many items of domestic
consumption – candles, soap, bread or tortillas, alcoholic beverages –
were produced within the home. Given the prevailing level of technology, even preparing a simple meal involved considerable time and
effort. Some more specialized skills such as spinning and weaving,
sewing, starching and ironing, and hairdressing were provided either by
women within the household or by independent female contractors.

Domestic service was also the major wage-earning employment
option for women, especially single women between the ages of ten and
twenty-nine. The race of those women who provided domestic service
varied by region and time. Among Spanish women coming to America
in the sixteenth century there was more than a sprinkling of women
who listed their occupation as "maid." These women were sometimes
indentured laborers, who, after working for a stipulated period of time,
usually married Spanish artisans and remained in the colonies.

Although some Spanish women sought employment as domestic
servants in America, by the beginning of the seventeenth century as a
general rule white women no longer worked in such low-prestige
employment. As agregadas or dependientes, they did continue to hold
overseeing or housekeeping jobs. But the more servile domestic chores
were increasingly performed by women of color: Indians, slave and
occasionally free black women, mestizas, and mulattas. In some regions
of colonial Latin America domestics were overwhelmingly black and
mulatta slaves. In other areas household servants were Indian and

mestiza, although even in such Indian zones of Spanish America as Guatemala City, African and African American household slaves were in demand as status symbols. Only in the homes of the highest-ranking individuals in Spanish society – viceroys, archbishops – would one find Spanish servants; often they had come to America as part of their master's entourage. (See Document 6.)

In addition to room, board, medical care, rudimentary religious instruction, and at least one set of clothing, nonslave domestic servants received some nominal salary, which varied greatly according to a woman's age and skills as well as her location. In Peru Indian women earned as little as six silver pesos per year as domestics, whereas in Mexico City female servants were paid two pesos per month. Nurse-maids and wet nurses tended to be the most highly paid of the female domestics, often earning more than twice the wages of ordinary servants. Juana, an Indian from Cuzco, for example, agreed to work as a nursemaid for two years in exchange for food, health care, ten gold pesos, and three pairs of buttons. Women of proven skill who were in demand within a household could exact better working conditions and more generous salaries, but all domestic servants were at the constant beck and call of their masters (or mistresses). Their lives were often ones of submission, humiliation, and verbal, physical, and sexual mistreatment.

Female domestic servants could be found not only in the home but also in convents. In Lima, for example, nuns in the city's most prestigious convents were served by black servants and slaves. Women were also employed in domestic-like services in hospitals and orphanages, where they commonly worked as nurses, cooks, and laundresses.

The use of wet nurses was widespread among the elite, although there were some rare cases in which an elite mother nursed her own child. Those usually selected for this job were young women who had recently given birth to healthy children. Wet nurses who claimed to be of Spanish extraction were especially highly prized, in part because of the belief that a baby would imbibe certain traits in the milk it drank, in part because of their very rarity. Nonetheless, it was slave women and indias who routinely served as nursemaids (*amas de leche* or *leite*), suckling the infants of the elite from birth until age two or three, and then becoming "dry" nurses who continued to care for their older charges. Foundling hospitals throughout Latin America also employed wet nurses. Usually hired by the local city council, these women typically earned a monthly or quarterly wage. As a group these wet nurses were repeatedly accused of incompetence or neglect of the children in their charge; although city councils often spoke of improving their education, no changes were ever enacted.

In the sixteenth and seventeenth centuries young Indian women were taken from their villages to work as domestics in nearby urban centers. By the eighteenth century, the opportunity for domestic employment was a major factor in attracting poor rural women to the city, although some Indian women in central Mexico sought refuge in the city after losing their property to male relatives and neighbors. In Mexico in 1804, Humboldt mentioned the great number of "country women come into the cities to serve in houses."[2] Throughout the colonial period, in-migration of female domestic labor, whether forced or voluntary, was a major factor in producing a sexual imbalance in the region's urban population.

Domestic service drew young single women to the city and provided employment for up to 75 percent of them. Adolescents' first jobs as domestic servants in private homes or convents often served as the female equivalent of male apprenticeship. For some these jobs were temporary, lasting only until marriage. Although women with children usually found domestic service too confining, marriage, either formal or informal, did not insure that poor women would not have to earn their own living. Seeking employment that would allow them to live with and support their families, these women often resorted to self-employment.

Poor women reentered the labor market as self-employed washerwomen, candlemakers, laundresses, cleaning women, seamstresses, weavers, embroiderers, nurses, and cooks. Commercializing traditional female work and transferring domestic services to a more public sphere, women sold their labor for wages. This work was often precarious and usually poorly paid. In addition, a surplus of women supplying these services tended to depress wages. Many women were listed in censuses as working "by their efforts" or "by their labor," suggesting that they combined a variety of part-time occupations in order to survive.

Because of the universal assumption that women working outside the home were without honor, few legally married women could be

[2] Alexander von Humboldt, *Political Essay on the Kingdom of New Spain* (New York: I. Riley, 1811), 1:191.

found in this type of employment. Probably only the poorest married women were forced by economic necessity to endanger their husband's honor. In the Mexico City tobacco factory, for example, 72 percent of women workers were single or widowed. Women whose jobs took them into the street were also presumed to be engaged in nefarious or immoral activities. In 1704 the bishop of Rio de Janeiro attempted to prohibit all women from being on the streets at night, implying that they were engaged in immoral behavior. This ban was overruled by the Overseas Council, which pointed out that many poor women needed to work at night in order to support themselves and that this was not necessarily a sin.

Whether provided by domestic servants or purchased from specialized workers, some skills such as washing and ironing clothing were always considered to be women's work. Other work was performed by women for only female clientele; only female seamstresses sewed for women, while male tailors sewed for men, although the actual work involved was virtually the same. A good seamstress needed to combine the skills of artist, geometrician, and engineer as well as showing imagination, stamina, and manual dexterity. Nonetheless seamstresses were paid far less for their work than tailors.

Another exclusively feminine occupation was that of midwifery, a practice that frequently passed from mother to daughter. In the Iberian Peninsula and Spanish America there were no standards for midwifery, although in Brazil slave women were prohibited from the practice because it was feared they could cause harm. Midwives, who were always women and frequently women of color, were viewed by the male medical establishment as poor, ignorant, illiterate, superstitious, and having no more authority than having given birth themselves. They were repeatedly accused of giving their patients strange brews and dangerous herbs, pressing and jiggling the fetus in the womb to put the infant in its place, and applying clysters and other "bizarre" remedies. Even those midwives who were most successful were labeled as practicing "an indecent occupation."[3] These women nonetheless delivered most of the children born in Latin America.

Probably the midwife's role in the birth process differed little from

---

[3] When the Mexican midwife María Ortiz attempted to join a prestigious cofradía, although she offered the organization cash and an altar worth one thousand pesos, she was rejected because of her occupation. Asunción Lavrin, "La congregación de San Pedro, Una cofradía urbana del México colonial: 1604–1730," *Historia mexicana*, 29 (1979–1980), 572–573.

that described by João Imbert, in his *Manual do fazendeiro (ou tratado doméstico sôbre as enfermidades dos negros)*.[4] The midwife was called to the side of the pregnant woman as soon as labor had begun. She would first arrange the mother's limbs into one of several positions, then offer her relics to kiss, place rosaries on her body, encourage her to pray to her patron saint, and exhort her, at the proper time, to push. After the birth of the child, the midwife often massaged the head of the child to improve its shape, and then cut the umbilical cord. Midwives also dispensed prenatal advice, provided psychological support for women in labor, eased the delivery by massaging a woman's stomach, and performed emergency baptisms for newborns not expected to survive.

Midwives were also often suspected of being *curanderas* or folk healers, an occupation held in even lower repute by male doctors. Midwives not only knew how to bring children into the world; they were also reputed to have special knowledge to prevent conception or induce abortion. It was also believed that midwives knew how to prevent the conception of female children.

By the end of the eighteenth century the elite of Mexico City were using *médico-parteros*, signaling the entrance of male doctors into the realm of pregnancy and the beginning of the masculinization of a traditional female profession. The use of male doctors probably did little to reduce maternal mortality. While midwives used potions, doctors believed in the "fluction" theory, seeing illness as caused by an abnormal flowing of blood or excrement and treating it with bloodletting. Some doctors recommended that women be bled in the third month of pregnancy and at any time that they threatened to miscarry. Others thought that expectant mothers should be bled from their arms and ankles before the seventh month of pregnancy. While a few advised baths or exercise to relieve the swollen legs of the later stages of pregnancy, all believed that when all else failed, a good bloodletting was a viable solution.

In colonial Latin America the vast majority of women who worked did so in order to survive. Although there were some exceptions, their work did not usually make them prosperous or independent nor was it a means of social ascension. Working women freely circulated through the city, buying and selling goods and services, stopping to meet friends,

---

[4] The Imbert manual was published in Rio de Janeiro in 1832, and is cited in Stuart B. Schwartz, *Sugar Plantations in the Formation of Brazilian Society: Bahia, 1550–1835* (Cambridge: Cambridge University Press, 1985), 404.

flirting with men, or even carousing in bars. But this freedom and the fact that they worked in public stigmatized working women both socially and morally, for by definition they were unprotected, lacking in honor, and assumed to have been corrupted by their dealings with men.

Some working women were indeed "corrupt," for prostitution was still another occupation that allowed poor women to earn money. Prostitution could be quite lucrative. In late-eighteenth-century Mexico City, for example, a prostitute earned between one and three pesos per sexual encounter. Furthermore, prostitution was seldom punished, for church law failed to distinguish between sex for sale and simple fornication and the state tended to treat prostitutes more leniently than their procurers. Prostitutes were especially in demand in ports, market towns, and cities, all urban settings with a large transient male population.

Some women were more or less permanently employed as prostitutes, whereas others periodically supplemented other wages or weathered periods of unemployment by selling sexual services. Black women working as cooks and laundresses on ships sailing between Chile and Peru at the end of the sixteenth century, for example, also worked as prostitutes. Two centuries later, when Ana Maria Villaverde, a twenty-two-year-old widow from Puebla, was laid off from the Mexico City tobacco factory, she turned to prostitution to support her family. The fact that she could earn more than three times as much as in her tobacco factory job no doubt added to the lure of this way of life. Occasionally a women entered prostitution with the full knowledge of her husband, who served as her pimp.

Prostitutes not only were viewed as being dishonorable; they also were especially at risk to contract syphilis and gonorrhea. Indeed, if extant hospital records are accurate, venereal disease was probably endemic among urban poor women. In early-nineteenth-century Córdoba, approximately one-quarter of all women seeking medical treatment in the local women's hospital were diagnosed as having second- or third-stage venereal disease.

In order to instill virtue while providing economic sustenance, Enlightenment policies encouraged poor women to become productive members of society by entering the work force through jobs considered appropriate to their sex. The late eighteenth century saw the creation of a new industrial workplace for women – the tobacco factories of the Royal Tobacco Monopoly in major cities throughout Spanish

America. These factories reorganized the production of tobacco products and increased the number of employment opportunities for single women, widows, and abandoned wives in government-sponsored manufacturing.

One of the principal attractions of tobacco factory employment was that it required few skills to roll cigarettes. Indeed, women had always been seen as superior cigarette workers because of the size and agility of their hands. They were also believed to be a more dependable and passive work force. In the Mexican tobacco factory of Guadalajara and Oaxaca only women were used as cigarette makers, while in Mexico City and Querétaro the percent of women rollers gradually increased. By 1809, 72 percentage of all cigarette workers in Mexico were women. In Mexico City alone the female work force totaled nine thousand. Once employed in the tobacco factory, women were not limited only to cigarette rolling. Although never allowed to participate in cigar manufacture, some women rose to lower-level administrative positions such as guards, forewomen, and heads of sections. Doña María Fuentes, for example, began factory work in 1771 when she was hired as a paper sorter. She soon advanced to wrapper, and then guard and forewoman; by 1784 Fuentes was promoted to head forewoman.

Factory work allowed women to take on leadership roles and to better their salaries, while also giving them new opportunities for socialization. Furthermore, in the case of the Mexico City Tobacco Factory, after 1793 a nursery for young children was available to all employees. But factory work also meant working under unhealthy conditions in dusty, cramped rooms with the air full of tobacco dust. A work force subject to poor diet, harsh living conditions, and tobacco dust found itself particularly susceptible to contagious diseases, especially tuberculosis.

The wages paid to female workers in most occupations varied widely by occupation, time, and place. At times women worked for little more than room and meager board. Such was the case of Chilean contract laborers who were forced to indenture themselves to avoid vagabond legislation. With the advent of government-sponsored industry in the eighteenth century, women found they could earn a larger, steadier income by working in a state factory. But the actual income varied widely, depending on the tasks, rapidity, and number of days worked. Cigarette rollers could hope to earn between 4 reales and 1 peso per day, while female supervisors earned between 140 and 600 pesos per year. In general male workers always earned more than females, although women often had larger work loads. In addition, as the work force became increasingly feminized, working conditions became increasingly exploitative and piecework rates for tasks declined.

The urban centers of colonial Latin America were not the only places where women worked. Women were also found in large numbers in mining towns. In late-eighteenth-century Potosí, for example, 51.7 percent of the inhabitants were female, including large numbers of Indian women who accompanied their husbands to the mines. Although specifically exempt from the forced labor draft (mita), these women came to Potosí to help their husbands by hauling and sorting minerals, brewing and selling chicha, and working as domestic servants. They also provided essential household services (cooking, cleaning) for the male laborers. In some areas such as late-eighteenth-century Vila Rica, female prospectors panned for gold. Women also owned small farms on the outskirts of town, where they typically produced surplus food for the urban market.

Although in a majority in colonial cities, women were often in the minority in the countryside. Age pyramids show that among rural people the discrepancies between the number of males and females was dramatic in groups age thirty to thirty-nine and above, an indication of the effect on mortality of women of childbearing age. Indeed, these data suggest that rural women survived the births of their first children, only to die as a result of bearing a fourth or fifth child. In more settled regions there were often fewer women because of the continual migration of women to the cities. In frontier regions, often perceived as dangerous, untamed places, women were also in the minority. But even frontier zones were far from having an absence of women; 44.5 percent of the rural inhabitants of the eighteenth-century Buenos Aires frontier, for example, were female. In some rural districts, especially those regions that supplied male migration to newer frontiers, women were in the majority. At the beginning of the nineteenth century (1803), the population of the captaincy of São Paulo, for example, was 92,521 men and 95,858 women.

On large rural establishments such as estancias and haciendas, people tended to live in patriarchal-type families (a nuclear family plus other individuals living under the tutelage of a paterfamilias). The more ubiquitous subsistence farms were usually inhabited by nuclear families. Small farms were overwhelmingly dependent on members of entire families – men, women, and children – for labor in order to survive. As a result "marriage" was the almost universal norm, although in some zones this was marriage without the benefit of clergy. Only when a man took a "wife" was there enough labor to set up an independent household.

Women filled a variety of roles in rural Latin America. Elite women who owned land sometimes took an active role in its administration. Approximately 10 percent of the *lavradores de cana* of colonial Bahia were female. On large haciendas and ranches, nonelite women were sometimes employed at specific tasks. As early as the sixteenth century, Indian women were employed in the Cortés hacienda as tortilla makers in charge of soaking kernels of corn, grinding them by hand, and finally making tortillas to feed the cowboys. Although paid a wage, these women worked from sunup to sundown. Female black slaves were used both on rural plantations and in obrajes. In the countryside as in the cities, women's work was an integral part of colonial socioeconomic structure.

As in urban settings, rural female commercial activities were over-whelmingly an extension of traditional female roles: child care, food production and preparation, producing and caring for clothing, care giving, and providing sexual services. Female chores tended to be arduous, time-consuming, and repetitive. For example, preparing tor-tillas, the corn-based staff of life of Mexico and Guatemala, involved shelling the corn, washing the kernels, soaking and then heating them, rewashing the softened maize, grinding and regrinding it on a stone *metate*, forming the round thin cakes, and then baking them on a griddle. One historian has calculated that producing this bread, if it were made at least once a day, took up to thirty-five to forty hours a week.[5]

On small rural farms most of the production was for domestic subsistence consumption, and here women played an essential role. Peasant women shared the chores of farms and ranches with men. Active in growing food crops, women worked in the planting and har-vesting of wheat and corn. They also were in charge of processing and storing food, and grinding wheat into flour, and corn into cornmeal. Women took an active role in caring for domestic animals, such as chickens and pigs, and other ganado menor. In some regions women also raised sheep and goats, which allowed for a small production of wool for domestic use. Women participated in the shearing of sheep

[5] Arnold J. Bauer, "Millers and Grinders: Technology and Household Economy in Meso-America," *Agricultural History*, 64:1 (Winter 1990), 3.

and then carded, spun, and wove the coarse wool into ponchos and other garments. Tallow (*sebo*), grease (*grasa*), and smoked dried meat products in small amounts were also produced by rural women working alongside their menfolk.

In addition to domestic chores, field work, and spinning, weaving, and sewing, women also produced local alcoholic beverages, made pottery, processed agricultural commodities (such as flax, honey, rice, and hides), made candles, and provided medical services. Indeed, because of the female domestic economy, relatively few goods or services consumed in the countryside were purchased. In rural regions, men, especially poor men, were dependent on the work of women for their material comfort. Women, on the other hand, were enmeshed in a continual round of harsh daily chores. A traveler who observed the hard work of rural women on the pampas also remarked that women were often ill-clad, dirty, unkempt, and prematurely aged by the harsh conditions of rural life.[6]

Indian women living on missions worked alongside men in constructing the mission complex, performing daily mission duties, tilling the fields, and tending the livestock. In rural communities, Indian women had an active role in growing and processing foodstuffs and in weaving. After the coming of European conquerors, the traditional female role of weaver was gradually commercialized. Although Indian women continued to produce cotton cloth used to pay the Spanish tribute, they were under constant pressure to produce ever wider pieces of cloth and to forgo the quality of intricate weaving for the quantity of simpler production. Although tribute payment in kind was gradually replaced by tribute payment in coin in central Mexico, in regions such as the Yucatan Peninsula, women wove cotton cloth as part of the tribute obligation well into the eighteenth century. In addition to tribute weaving, a variety of cotton cloth used for armor, bedding, religious garments, altar cloths, and clothing for the growing non-Indian population was also produced by Indian women weaving at home. Women either sold these goods to Spanish merchants or other middlemen or marketed them themselves in town fairs.

By the late sixteenth century, Indian women living in districts under the control of Spanish corregidores often found themselves enmeshed in a type of "putting out" system, not all that different from similar work systems used in Europe. Women received a supply of raw cotton from

[6] Alexander Caldcleugh, cited in Slatta, *Gauchos*, 57.

the Spanish administrator and were required to produce finished goods woven to the administrator's specifications. Although these women were paid a piece wage for their work, they received far less than the true value of their product. Because they were in essence working for the local political boss, these women had little power to negotiate either salary or terms of employment. It was been suggested that the growing resentment of Indian women forced to provide lopsided profits for Spanish bureaucrats led to a large female participation in the mid-seventeenth-century attacks against the corregidores of Oaxaca.

Weaving continued to be a cottage industry throughout the rural areas of Latin America. In some regions women were spinners and weavers; in other areas such as Bolivia women prepared, finished, and marketed the textiles, while men did the actual loom work. Their tasks included cleaning, plying, and spinning wool or cotton into yarn; stretching and dyeing the woven cloth; and transporting it to market and selling it – tasks that required more labor than the actual weaving. As a result, women working in cottage industries tended to outnumber men by three to one.

By the late sixteenth century, another proto-industrial setting, the obraje or textile factory, emerged in several regions of Spanish America. Located in both urban and rural areas, in the Indian communities of Bolivia, Peru, and Ecuador as well as in towns such as Tlaxcala, Queretaro, and Puebla in Mexico, obrajes moved workers from their homes to primitive factories. Both men and women worked in the obrajes; at times there was a sexual division of labor, but men and women could also be employed at the same tasks. Women were especially prized as wool sorters, carders, and spinners in the Jesuit obrajes of rural Quito, whereas the Fábrica de Pintados in Mexico City employed women to grind and mix dyes. In most obrajes both men and women wove, but because salaries tended to be based on the amount of textile produced, in general women were paid half of men's wages. Women, both slave and free, were also sent to labor in obrajes as punishment for misbehavior.

In the obraje, women workers were usually under the control of a female foreman, often the wife of the obraje manager. According to some reports, these women overseers were especially demanding. The wife of one obraje owner in Bolivia was described as keeping an Indian woman "almost a perpetual slave, spinning cotton and wool. She hardly finishes spinning one bag of wool, when she is handed another. She receives only one real, instead of the customary day's pay of two reales."[7] The same female overseer was said to force "all the women on the hacienda to weave . . . but they get no payment except a little salt or wheat."[8]

In spite of the contribution of women's labor, rural zones tended to have far fewer female heads of household than urban ones. In general women were better able to survive as heads of household in wealthier, more settled regions. But even in settled regions, female heads of household tended to be widows, not single women. Indeed only relatively wealthy widows with able-bodied sons prospered in rural regions. It is difficult to determine whether those women who remained on the land as the nominal heads of large haciendas or ranches actually managed their rural property. The fact that women generally lived with at least one adult kinsman suggests that the actual day-to-day administration of their property was left to others. Poor widows, those whose husbands had not owned land or who held a small plot, were forced to migrate to towns or cities in search of employment, or to take refuge with kinsfolk.

Although most women worked simply to survive, occasionally a woman of humble origins, through hard work, shrewd dealings, clever investments, marriage, or luck, emerged as a successful businesswoman. Mencia Pérez, an illiterate mestiza who combined good business sense with assets inherited from two husbands, was by the end of the six-teenth century the wealthiest person in the town of Huemantla and one of the most prosperous in the province of Tlaxcala. Another such case was Micaela Angela Carrillo, an impoverished mestiza widow living in the eighteenth-century Puebla region. In conjunction with her legitimate sons and illegitimate daughters, she rented maguey plants, tapping the sweet tasting sap to produce pulque. Carrillo retailed the drink in her home and also wholesaled the beverage to shops in Puebla. Gradually she invested her profits in small pieces of property, emerging as an important local landowner.

Women could be found working on the ranchos of the countryside, in the streets of the city, and in the homes of prominent local citizens. In cities and towns, middle- and lower-class women worked as teach-

[7] Archivo Histórico Municipal de Cochabamba, Expediente por el yndígena Esteban Pablo contra su patrón Manual Almarás en la hacienda Caporaya, 1795, folio 7v, as cited in Brooke Larson, *Colonialism and Agrarian Transformation in Bolivia: Cochabamba, 1550–1900* (Princeton: Princeton University Press, 1988), 200.

[8] Ibid., folio 10, as cited in Larson, *Colonial and Agrarian Transformation*, 200.

ers and midwives; ran inns, boardinghouses, and taverns; and owned small stores (*tiendas, pulperías*). Poor white women, mulattas, mestizas, blacks, and Indians also sold foodstuffs and prepared foods in the market, worked as laundresses and ironing women, and cultivated their small garden plots. As dependientes, slaves, agregadas, day laborers, as single, married, or widowed women, they occupied a socially tenuous position, for the economic circumstances that forced them to work also exposed them to social prejudice, visited upon them by men of the same social class. In colonial society, women who were forced to defy the female norm of the protected, cloistered woman left themselves vulnerable to ridicule and abuse.

A woman's participation in the colonial work force was closely tied to her social class. The poorer a woman was, the more likely that she would be found working publicly. Geographical location was another important variable, for in towns and cities women found greater and higher-paying employment opportunities. In addition, female participation varied greatly by the sector of the economy, with many more women working in domestic rather than commercial or industrial jobs. For the vast majority, women's work was based on the commercialization of traditional female roles: food preparation, marketing, laundering, candlemaking, weaving. Nonetheless, women of all classes formed part of the work force. Whether single, married, or widowed, whether involved as owners, managers, or workers, women were an important part of the world of work in colonial Latin America.

CHAPTER 9

WOMEN AND SLAVERY

I declare that when I married doña Margarita Mexia, she brought with her as her dowry 1,000 pesos and a black slave named Catalina de la Cruz, and that the said slave has produced seven other slaves [*piezas de esclavos y esclavas*] named Nicolasa Ramos, a twenty-year-old black woman; Alfonso José, a suckling child; José Ramos, an eighteen-year-old black man; Antonio Lugardo, a mulatto boy, 14 to 15 years old; Ignacio José de Ramos, a dark mulatto boy, 4 to 5 years old; and Margarita Ramos, a fair-skinned mulatto girl, between 2 and 3 years old. I declare them all to be slaves, subject to service.

Inventory taken at San Miguel de Almolonga, 1 July 1699: Among other property belonging to Don Nicolás Ramos de Bustos, we take inventory of the following slaves:
Catalina, 38-year-old black woman, married to Manuel de
    Rueda, free mulatto
Nicolasa, daughter of the abovementioned Catalina, 18 years old
José, 14-year-old black, son of Catalina
Antonio, a 12-year-old mulatto, son of Catalina
Margarita María, 8 years old, daughter of Catalina
Ignacio José, 5-year-old mulatto, son of Catalina
Margarita de Guadalupe, a mulatta girl, daughter of Catalina,
    between 2 and 3 years old
Alfonso José, 8 months old, son of the abovementioned
    Nicolasa [Catalina's grandson].[1]

---

[1] From the last will and testament of Don Nicolás Ramos de Bustos, Jalapa, Mexico, 9 June 1699, in Archivo Notarial de Jalapa, tomo 1694–1699, folios 596–606, cited in Fernando Winfield Capitaine, comp., *Esclavos en el Archivo Notarial de Xalapa, Veracruz* (Xalapa, Veracruz: Universidad Veracruzana, 1984), 102.

Just as the women of the conquered pre-Columbian Indian populations found their lives changed forever as a result of the coming of European conquerors, the position and role of African women were permanently altered by their enslavement and transportation to the New World. Far from their communities of origin and torn from their culture, slaves were forced to recreate a new social and religious world. They did this by accepting Hispanic forms while maintaining parts of their African heritage. Although they were viewed as legally inferior to the indigenous population, most slaves probably had closer day-to-day contact with their masters than did Indians. This was particularly true of enslaved women.

The first female slaves to arrive in America came directly from Spain in the retinue of the conquistadors. Margarita, slave of Diego de Almagro, for example, accompanied him on his 1535 expedition to conquer Chile. She returned with him to Peru and was manumitted in accordance with his will after he was executed for treason. Although we have no idea as to the relationship that existed between Margarita and Almagro, she eventually became a shopowner in Cuzco, and established a chaplaincy to say prayers for the soul of her ex-owner and his followers.

Most black slaves, however, did not come to America from the Iberian Peninsula. Instead they were shipped from Africa, as merchandise in a trade that eventually saw 3.5 million people forceably moved across the Atlantic. Beginning in the sixteenth century, slaves were shipped to Spanish America from several places along the west coast of Africa. Peoples from the Senegambia and Guinea-Bissau regions predominated in the early trade, replaced by slaves from Angola during the seventeenth century. The human trade to Brazil was always closely connected to Angola, although there was some regional variation. Women made up 30 to 40 percent of all Africans forceably transported to America.

Slavery was experienced differently for women born in Africa than for their American-born counterparts. Kidnapping, enslavement, and the mixing of individuals from several regions of Africa tended to cut people off completely from their families and their lineages. Furthermore African-born women could maintain their ethnic or tribal identity for another generation only if men from the same tribe were available in the New World. Slavery no doubt weakened the importance of family ties for the first generation of slaves, although in later generations slaves were able to construct new kinship ties.

Some African customs such as the use of bridewealth, the role of parents and kin group in choosing a marriage partner, and the prohibition of cousin marriage were completely abandoned. Other customs that depended less on the survival of a family or kin group endured. Slave mothers, for example, continued the West African custom of prolonged breast-feeding (weaning their children only after age two) in spite of their master's opposition. It is also possible that women continued the African custom of abstaining from sexual intercourse during this period of breast-feeding. Nonetheless, there was a general weakening of African culture among creole-born slaves who were usually the offspring of parents from different African tribes or the result of racial mixing.

In order to understand the experience of enslaved women, we must consider the setting in which the female slave found herself. There was a marked difference between the demography of urban and rural slavery, which influenced everything from work to patterns of sociability. Sex ratios were often very skewed among the slave population. Men usually outnumbered women in rural zones, especially those regions which continued to receive slaves from Africa. In virtually every city of colonial Latin America, however, there were more female slaves than male slaves.

In urban settings female slaves were overwhelmingly used as domestics. Their labor was considered so essential to the running of a household that one or two female slaves were frequently included in dowries given to wealthy new brides. Female slaves were trained as cooks, household servants, washerwomen, seamstresses, and laundresses and thus possessed skills that greatly enhanced their market value. Moreover, ownership of one or more domestic slaves was proof of wealth and social status. It was common for at least two or three female slaves to accompany their white mistresses in her daily appearance at mass. The most trusted slave women chaperoned the young women of the family when they left the house to visit women friends. Slave women were also used to run errands, to carry packages, and to deliver messages. In a very real sense, slave women were used as a point of contact between protected elite women and the public space.

Slaves, in addition to their labor, were a capital asset. Age and reproductive potential affected the value of a female slave, for by Iberian law the child of a female slave was also a slave. A healthy, fecund slave woman could increase her owner's wealth. Catalina de la Cruz, the Mexican slave who appeared in the will and inventory at the beginning of this chapter, provides a dramatic example of such increase. Her six children and one grandchild, slaves all, were worth far more than the original value of the young childless Catalina.

Black and mulatto slave women who had recently borne children, whether or not the child survived, provided still another attraction: they could be used as wet nurses for the newborn children of the elite. The attraction of a slave wet nurse was that her owner could more closely monitor her diet and actions. Sometimes, to keep a slave woman producing milk after her own child had died, she was given an orphan to nurse for a few weeks or months. Pasquala de Ansules, the black slave of the expectant doña Ignacia de Campos, recounted how "still in bed, having given birth to a child who died, her mistress went to the Children's Hospital and brought her back a girl to suckle."[2]

Female slaves were also employed outside the house as day laborers (jornaleras). Spanish widows frequently lived by collecting the daily wages that their slaves earned. Women slaves were rented out by their owners to suckle children, peddle trinkets, or work as seamstresses. Still others, especially in the urban centers of Spanish and Portuguese America, took to the streets with trays loaded with food and drink. In certain regions, slave women were strongly associated with the sale of one particular item, such as fish in Brazil. At times skilled and semi-skilled slaves maintained and rented themselves, supplying their owners with a fixed monthly income and absorbing their own expenses for housing and food. To the degree that this work gave women the opportunity to move about freely and to pocket some of their earnings, jornaleras had a privileged position in the slave world.

Black female servants, both slave and free, also worked as cooks, laundresses, and prostitutes. Indeed, prostitution was another occupation often associated with free and slave women of color. Using the widespread practice of day laborers, some masters encouraged slave women to sell themselves. Others engaged in the world's oldest profession by their own volition, because selling sexual services was a profitable business. Earnings from prostitution have even been suggested as the reason that so many urban female slaves were able to buy their own freedom. Municipal authorities attempted to curb female prostitution by ordering that all black women, both slave and free, be prevented

[2] Archivo General de la Nación (Lima), Inquisición, Fundaciones, Legajo 1, Expediente de Micaela Francisca de Atocha, 1670, cited in Mannarelli, *Pecados públicos: La ilegitimidad en Lima, sieglo xvii* (Lima: Ediciones Flora Tristán, 1993), 291–292.

from going into the street after nightfall. Such restrictions usually failed. Although municipal authorities railed against the exploitation of slave women for prostitution, they totally ignored the sexual exploitation and abuse that occurred within the master's house. From the beginning, European men sought sexual favors from black slave women, both at home and in the street.

By the social and moral definitions of the Iberian world, women of color because of their racial "stain" had no claim to honor. "Virtuous" sexual conduct was seen as being outside the ken of slaves, and the moral code that privileged virginity in women did not extend to any black or mulatta woman. Society did not attempt to limit the sexuality of slaves, but slave owners themselves controlled the sexuality of slave women by restricting their freedom and enjoying unimpeded access to their bodies.

Because they were legally the property of their masters, slave women had even less power to resist the sexual advances of their masters than did Indian women. Sexual abuse of female slaves was common, although these crimes were generally not reported to the local authorities. Even those who attempted to seek some legal redress were usually foiled by a system that gave precedence to a white man's testimony. One example will suffice. In 1814, Manuelita, a seventeen-year-old quadroon slave, was sent to work as a domestic in the home of a prominent Lima merchant and his well-born wife.[3] One day while the wife was at mass, the master, Don Baltasar, raped Manuelita. She in turn filed a complaint in the ecclesiastical court, requesting that she be freed because her owner had corrupted her virginity. Her plea was rejected when her master countered that she was not only lying but was using a common false accusation that other female slaves had also attempted. Manuelita was returned to her master, who continued to force sexual relations on her, eventually getting her pregnant. Again she tried to publicly denounce her owner's immorality but again her pleas for justice were rejected.

Despite Manuelita's lack of success, this case and others demonstrate how women of color used the legal system to press for their rights, limited as they were. Slave and free women, especially those who were acquainted with Iberian customs, spoke Spanish or Portuguese, and lived in cities, initiated legal proceedings against their owners and

---

[3] Christine Hünefeldt, *Paying the Price of Freedom: Family and Labor among Lima's Slaves, 1800–1854* (Berkeley: University of California Press, 1994), 21.

others for mistreatment. Although they were usually unsuccessful in their pursuit of justice, these cases show that female slaves were aware of their legal rights and willing to fight to protect themselves and their children. In addition, female owners sometimes joined with their female slaves to complain of rape or sexual abuse of the latter.

In a system that gave masters unlimited access to their slaves, it was not unknown for slave women to become the concubines of white or mulatto men. In some cases sexual liaisons could benefit slave women, for they could use their position to improve their day-to-day treatment and eventually to gain manumission. In other cases, especially when there was a jealous wife in the picture, just the opposite could occur. Inés Mulata, for example, was sold when she was three to four months pregnant, because her master's wife was convinced that he was having an affair with the girl. The wife pressured her husband to sell the girl with the stipulation that she could not return to Lima. In other instances the legitimate Spanish wife might insist that her husband sell or exile any illegitimate brown-skinned offspring. Relationships with white or whiter men also conveyed a degree of prestige on the slave woman while producing lighter-colored offspring from the union. In Cuba one proverb held "rather mistress of a white man than wife of a negro."

Nonetheless, slave women were subjected to a gruesome catalog of physical abuse – beatings, torture, even death – at the hands of male and female owners. It was not unheard of for a female slave to be sexually mistreated by her master and then physically abused by his jealous wife. They were also indifferently fed, clothed, housed, and looked after. On the whole, slaves belonging to religious orders tended to receive better care than those in private hands. The Jesuits, for example, provided their women slaves with midwives.

Although crown and church encouraged slaves to engage in Holy Matrimony, the very ability to marry depended on the location of the female slave (city or plantation), the sex ratio among slaves, a slave's personal preference, and, of course, the master's or mistress's desire. Slave owners were often opposed to marriage because marriage made it more difficult to sell a slave. In addition, couples living in informal consensual unions were not subject to the church's policy forbidding the separation of the couple.

In spite of the resistance of white society, some female slaves did marry. Those slaves who married usually belonged to persons of higher social status. Slaves owned by religious orders were also encouraged to wed. It is difficult to know how much freedom of choice slave women had in the decision of whom to marry. In general African-born women tended to couple with men of the same African ethnicity, while American-born slave women preferred men also born in the colonies. Slave-free marriages were not uncommon; in Mexico City, for example, 39 percent of mulatta female slaves married a free spouse. Women slaves were usually in their late teens or early twenties at the time of marriage, although their husbands tended to be substantially older.

In theory marriage bettered a slave's condition because a married person could not be prevented from having a married life. Marriage also created social networks that could help achieve manumission. Nonetheless, it has been suggested that concubinage with a free man was a more advantageous choice for a slave women; it provided her with greater security than did marriage to a slave and more directly improved her chances of being manumitted. While the church and state encouraged slaves to marry, slaves overwhelmingly remained single. For example, of 1,696 black females sold in Lima between 1560 and 1650 only 9.5 percent were married. By contrast 19 percent were unwed mothers or mothers-to-be. Slaves no doubt believed that in spite of theoretical protections, formal marriage provided no guarantee that their families would survive intact. Neither church nor state, for example, could stop their masters selling off their children.

More than resisting marriage, female slaves actively resisted those who would control their decisions and their private lives. Urban slaves both sought to prevent their owners from forcing them to marry against their will and sued masters, mistresses, and slave or free family members who attempted to prohibit them from marrying. Whenever possible slaves chose marriage partners from within their own ethnic group. Slave women also appeared before ecclesiastical courts to stop masters from separating them from their husbands. On the more isolated rural plantations, masters were better able to pressure their female slaves to marry mates chosen for them; some slave owners forbade marriage of their slaves to slaves on other plantations.

Although there was no lack of sexual contact between women of color and white men, legitimate marriage was very uncommon. The same civil and church authorities that encouraged slave marriage discouraged interracial union. Nonetheless, sexual contact between slave women and white men was widespread and persistent. One seventeenth-century observer believed that Spaniards in Peru preferred black women to white ones because they had been suckled by black nursemaids. In general these relationships were casual and fleeting, although there are examples of longer-lasting affairs.

As a result of single parenting, abandonment, or death, black and mulatta women were often the heads of their families. Indeed, the typical family unit of black slaves consisted of a mother and her children. Regardless of the ratio of adult men to adult women, the female-centered family was frequently found among slave and free people of color. Creole slaves showed an even greater tendency than African-born women to live in households with their children but without any husband present. Wherever there was a large slave population in colonial Latin America, there was a high incidence of family units headed by women. Female slaves also created synthetic households, frequently living with other women slaves in the cities, or serving as cooks and housekeepers for younger slave men on plantations.

The rate of illegitimacy among slaves was higher than for any other group in colonial society. In colonial Vila Rica, for example, while 52 percent of all births were illegitimate, among slave women this number rose to 98 percent. These rates of illegitimacy served to strengthen white society's vision of slave women as morally weak and sexually lax.

In general, contrary to their masters' expectations, female slaves exhibited low fertility. The average female slave bore fewer than four children during her lifetime. This low number of births probably resulted from a combination of demographic constraints and decisions made by slaves. Demographic factors included sexual imbalance in those areas receiving large numbers of African-born slaves, poor nutrition, late age at menarche, exhausting labor, protracted lactation, and early age of the mother at the time of her death. There is also a strong suggestion that female slaves used herbs as abortifacts. In addition, low birthrates were possibly also the result of infrequent sexual contact because of living arrangements, unstable unions, and widespread sexually transmitted diseases.

Low fertility was accompanied by high infant mortality. One out of every three children died before the end of his or her first year of life. Some historians have also suggested that slave mothers practiced infanticide. Slave populations also exhibited a high proportion of stillbirths and high rates of child mortality. Adult mortality was also high, but was lower for women than men. Perhaps slave women lived longer than men because they naturally had stronger constitutions and were used to doing less dangerous work.

Children born to black or mulatto women, whether legitimate or illegitimate, automatically assumed their mother's status. A slave's child thus became a slave and the property of his or her mother's master. Slave children began to work at an early age; girls aided their mothers in domestic tasks or served as *mulaques* (young servants) of their master's children. They could also be sold at a young age, such as the ten-year-old slave girl, Beatriz Criolla, bought to accompany a nun in a convent. (Those slave children who entered convent service at a young age, however, did have the possibility of picking up some rudimentary schooling.) Most slave children were reared by their mothers, and it was common practice for these children to be sold along with their mothers, not their fathers. Slave children were often freed along with their mothers by a master who at times was also their illegitimate father. Although some white fathers, usually single men, could and did benefit their black concubines and mulatta daughters by granting them small dowries, legal recognition of paternity was rare.

Regardless of their treatment, urban slaves had several advantages over their rural sisters. They participated in larger and more varied social networks and enjoyed a richer social life, which might range from religious cofradías to secular dances. Female slaves sent out to work selling services or goods enjoyed limited independence and the opportunity to socialize outside the control of their masters. Furthermore, domestic service, licit and illicit savings earned in day jobs, and intimate personal relations could each be used by industrious, determined female slaves eventually to win freedom.

Throughout colonial Latin America women enjoyed a clear advantage in gaining manumission. Among those receiving a *carta de libertad*, the percentage of women in the group ranged from 67.7 percent in seventeenth-century Lima to 58.8 percent in late-eighteenth-century Buenos Aires. This marked preference for freeing women operated in both urban and rural areas. Freedom could be gained through an owner's grant during his or her lifetime, as a provision in an owner's will, or through self-purchase. As a result of continual female manumission by the eighteenth century in many regions of Latin America, free women of color made up the fastest growing segment of the colored population.

Birthplace and race were also important variables in the probability of being freed; female slaves born in America and mulattas earned freedom in a greater proportion than their actual numbers. Furthermore, women born in the master's household or inherited by the master's children also enjoyed an advantage in the winning of freedom, possibly the result of a longer and more personal relationship between master and slave. Whereas age clearly affected the patterns of manumission for males (males were overwhelmingly freed as children), women slaves were freed at all ages.

My use of the term "master" should not obscure the fact that women composed a sizable segment of those who manumitted slaves. In absolute numbers women freed fewer slaves than men, in part because they owned fewer slaves. Nonetheless, between one-third and two-fifths of all slaves being manumitted belonged to women, usually single and widowed female heads of household. Female slave owners were far more likely than men to free slaves in their wills. In the manumission papers, women also frequently expressed what has been called "surrogate maternity," mentioning a special relationship with a certain slave because he or she had been "born in their household," "born in their arms," or "raised in their bed."

Owners often granted delayed manumission, freeing a female slave only after certain preconditions had been met. Eight-year-old Juana Bañol was freed by her mistress provided she first worked as a servant in a Lima convent and then served at least four years as a lay sister in the same institution. A slave might be freed only after she had served her master's widow for an additional time, or only after the widow's death. Furthermore, changing the conditions of freedom always lay in the hands of the slave owners and could be subjected to their whims. One seventeenth-century Bahian woman decided to cancel a female slave's promised freedom "because of her ingratitude and coldness towards me."[4] Some masters and mistresses, however, freed young female slaves with detailed instructions about their care and education.

Manumission granted in an owner's will, regardless of the terms, was never foolproof, as attested to by the amount of litigation occasioned by this process. Historians have also suggested that freeing an old slave was hardly a favor. Francisco Baldovinos, a Buenos Aires merchant who drew up his will in 1810, explained that he was not freeing his mulatta slave, María Paula, "so as not to expose her to hard work and an

---

[4] Will of Maria Leão, Salvador, 1 October 1656, Archives of the Santa Casa de Misericórdia, Salvador de Bahía, vol. 41, folios 46–47, cited in A. J. R. Russell-Wood, *The Black Man in Slavery and Freedom in Colonial Brazil* (New York: St. Martin's Press, 1982), 40.

old age full of misery." Instead he stipulated that "I order my heirs to attend to all her needs as I have always done because of her good service."[5]

Another route to freedom was self-purchase. Interestingly, self-purchase was the most common way of gaining freedom among both male and female slaves; it was also the mechanism used repeatedly by slave women to buy the freedom of their children. The frequency of female self-purchase attests to the determination of these women as well as to their ingenuity in saving the sums required to buy freedom.

In addition, throughout Latin America slave women could and did take advantage of legislation that forced their owners to declare publicly their sale price and sell them to anyone willing to meet the price. They also attempted to use the same mechanism to prevent their own sale to undesirable owners or distant places. A few women were able to purchase freedom for themselves and, once free, amass the necessary capital to buy their children out of bondage. Lastly, often working in concert with other slaves and freed people, slave women pooled their funds to buy each other out of slavery.

Freedom, however acquired, could often be tenuous, especially for young black and mulatta women who lacked the official documentation validating their freedom. Free women were often tricked into slavery; in one case, Gertrudis de Escobar, a free young mulatta woman living in mid-seventeenth-century Mexico, was sold into slavery by her own aunt and cousins.

Once free, women of color continued in many of the same occupations as slave women, working as servants, washerwomen, and vendors of prepared foods. Some women eventually became informal bankers, lending sums of money, sometimes up to one hundred pesos, to members of the African American community. Free women of color also owned modest inns, as well as provision stores, taverns, and pulperías selling everything from food and drink to clothing, tools, and work implements. In some regions such as the mining districts of Brazil, these women were often suspected of trading contraband goods, harboring fugitive slaves, and supplying runaway slave communities.

[5] Codicilo de don Francisco Baldovinos, Archivo General de la Nación (Argentina), Registro de Escribano 6, 1810, folios 199–202, quoted in Susan M. Socolow, *The Merchants of Buenos Aires, 1778–1810: Family and Commerce* (Cambridge: Cambridge University Press, 1978), 218.

Free women of color were also involved in prostitution as a result of what European observers insisted was their "moral turpitude." But Vilhena, writing of late-eighteenth-century Brazil, blamed the large number of prostitutes in Bahia on the fact that "the most miserable little mulatto girl would more easily work in a brothel than serve a duchess,"[6] suggesting that prostitution provided some degree of freedom of action, which domestic service did not. In general, free women of color, especially mulattas, were viewed as highly sensual temptresses who could be dangerous because they threatened the social order and morality. (See Document 3.)

The more successful free black women were able to purchase small plots of land, houses, and slaves. Still others amassed considerable property. Catalina de Zorita, a free black women living in mid-sixteenth-century Lima, owned a bakery staffed by ten slaves. Magdalena de la Paz, a free mulatta, sold wine, lard, cheese, and other provisions throughout the Viceroyalty of Peru using shipmasters and muleteers as her agents.

Regardless of their legal status, Spanish and Portuguese authorities constantly kept people of color under surveillance. Government attempts to legislate social order and morality often focused on slave and free women. Concerned about social control and crime (especially prostitution and theft), authorities often responded by limiting the geographical mobility of urban black women. Men and women of color were also frequently charged with vagrancy, drunkenness, and lascivious dancing, which was seen as leading to a host of problems, including brawling, knifings, and robbery.

Beginning in 1571, and repeated several times during the next two and one-half centuries, colonial government also enacted sumptuary legislation aimed at free black and mulatto women, forbidding them the use of silk, pearls, gold, mantillas, or fine stuffs. Dressing above one's station was socially dangerous, and the ostensible goal of these laws was to enforce social markers and maintain social hierarchy. But the laws were often justified by citing the "lascivious dress" and the lack of "modest" attire of black and mulatta women. Periodically decrees called for slave women to wear clothing that conformed to canons of Christian decency, expressing the hope that covering "nudity" would improve morality.

[6] Archivo Público do Estado da Bahia, Livros de Ordens régias, vol. 88. folios 209–211v, quoted in Russell-Wood, *The Black Man in Slavery and Freedom in Colonial Brazil*, 64.

Over and over, these decrees reflected a fear that lavish dress made women of color irresistible to "decent" men. Furthermore, any woman of color who could afford these luxuries was presumed to be enjoying the fruits of her illicit behavior. Only mulatta women married to Spaniards were sometimes excused from this legislation. While clearly intended to keep women of color in a subservient social position, sumptuary laws were haphazardly enforced. Although from time to time freed women of color were forced to turn over all their jewels and finery to the civil authorities, freed women were probably treated better than freed men. By the seventeenth century, for example, free women of color were specifically exempted from the tribute tax.

Although women were perceived as being less violent and easier to handle by their very nature, there are examples of acts of resistance by female slaves. Black women were reputed to have an extensive knowledge of poisons, and masters and mistresses lived in fear of falling victim to this terrifying art. Running away was another form of resistance. Although women slaves were less likely than their male counterparts to flee, one historian has calculated that approximately 25 percent of all runaways were female. One female slave in seventeenth-century Lima "jumped over the walls of her master's home" to flee; another woman slave sent to Lima to serve her master's two daughters, who were entering a convent, escaped from the cloister to marry by dressing in men's clothing and disguising herself as a member of a construction crew.[7]

Running from slavery could be a sporadic and repeated phenomenon or a permanent attempt at freedom. For some slaves, absenting themselves without permission was a quiet declaration of their independence and personality. Antonina, a twenty-one-year-old black slave, was described as "having the defect of being a street person, that is she leaves the house to walk about or she stays out whenever she's sent to do something in the street." Some women runaways used temporary flight as a strategy to negotiate for better treatment from their owners. The thirty-year-old mulatta María Josefa who fled her master's house in 1800 made it clear that she had left "because she was being mistreated and not because she had any vice." If a female slave was alone, she tended not to run as far as did men, instead seeking refuge

[7] Both cases are from the Archivo Arzobispal de Lima, Causas de negros (*Dr. Francisco Calvo de Sandoval v. licenciado Juan de Bonifacio; Juan Ochoa de Aranda v. Doña María de Prado*) and are cited in Frederick P. Bowser, *The African Slave in Colonial Peru, 1524–1650* (Stanford: Stanford University Press, 1974), 189.

with friends nearby. For this reason the communities of runaways that existed in many rural regions (*mocambos*) had relatively few women and were forced to abduct them from nearby areas.

Once Christianized, blacks, unlike Indians, were subject to the Inquisition. Holy Office records provide multiple examples of slave and free women charged with witchcraft, fortune telling, and other superstitious practices. Much of the testimony reflects the survival of African folk culture in America. While the limitations of bondage often made it impossible to maintain the purity of that culture, slave and free women were able to either syncretize or amalgamate African beliefs and usages into the mainstream Hispanic world. As a result of this syncretization, in popular religious beliefs Christian saints began to acquire African attributes, while in everyday household practices, African ingredients and cooking methods became part of a creole culture.

Women of color also adapted Mediterranean Christian practices, especially those that could be used to improve their condition. For example, *compadrazgo*, the naming of surrogate parents at the time of a child's baptism, was an Iberian godparent system that established a special relationship between the child and his or her sponsors, and between the natural parent or parents of a child and the honorary ones. This tradition was embraced by the population of African descent and used to extend family bonds. Whereas slave women were sometimes limited from freely choosing their offsprings' godparents, free women of color used compadrazgo to create powerful bonds of mutual obligation between themselves and other free black and mulatta women.

Another Mediterranean Christian institution adopted by slaves and free people of color was the religious confraternity or cofradía. In colonial Latin America these religious groups tended to follow racial lines with segregated confraternities serving Spaniards, Indians, and blacks. In general there was a tendency for blacks and mulattos to be segregated in confraternities by their African ethnic group of origin. Each cofradía was devoted to a different saint, and members sponsored special masses and festivities in honor of that saint. Membership also brought status within the community. When men and women belonged to the same cofradía, women occasionally served as *mayordomas* (or *môrdomas*), in charge of providing social services for sodality members stricken by sickness or poverty. Women of color were especially active in cofradías that were sex segregated. The Church of Nuestra Señora de los Desamparados in Lima, for example, had a cofradía made up black and mulatto women who met for devotions every Wednesday and for communion every fourth Sunday. Although black cofradías were sponsored by the Catholic Church, the authorities were often suspicious of these groups, believing that they served as a cover for planning crime or even rebellion. Cofradías were also suspected of serving as a cover for slaves who claimed to be using funds collected from solidarity members to buy their freedom; disgruntled slave owners believed the slaves were using stolen money.

Slave women far outnumbered slave men in the cities, but this was not at all the case in rural districts. Nonetheless, women still composed a sizable part of the rural slave population. A typical plantation might have two or three male slaves for every female, although the sex ratio varied according to the type and size of the plantation. Slave women were divided between the many assigned to field labor and the few used as domestic servants. In the field, women labored alongside male slaves, working at the same backbreaking tasks. There was little or no gender differentiation in work assigned to slaves on the large plantations. Women and men both worked in the "great gang," planting, hoeing, and harvesting sugarcane, cacao, and indigo. On some plantations the gangs that undertook heavy planting, cleaning, cultivation, and harvest of crops often had as many female as male laborers. Other plantations divided field labor along gender lines, reserving the heavier tasks, such as downing trees and moving large rocks, for men and the weeding and cane cutting for both sexes. Like men, female slaves often worked an eighteen-hour day. Only pregnant women and those suckling infant children were given lighter agricultural tasks, such as tending the chicken coops, growing garden provisions, and cleaning canals. For women, this pattern represented little change from the use of female labor in African agriculture.

On sugar plantations female slaves not only worked in the fields but were an important part of the sugaring process. They could be found grinding cane, cutting wood, and feeding the fire. Women probably did most of the dangerous milling tasks, and were used in various steps of the purging process. In addition, rebellious female slaves were punished by being assigned some of the more disagreeable tasks, such as driving the draft animals that powered the sugar mill or working in the boiling room. But the more highly skilled jobs usually associated with processing the crop were reserved for men. Slave women, for example, were never trained to be sugar masters, coopers, or carpenters and were usually not associated with the skilled work of the boiling house. Unlike slave men, slave women were not found in managerial, artisanal, or transport activities.

In domestic service there was an even greater gender-based task allocation. Female house slaves were overwhelmingly used to clean, wash, sew, and birth and tend children. Usually young women were introduced into the main house as servants or housekeepers and later moved on to the more specialized jobs of seamstresses, midwives, wet nurses, and washerwomen. Only the assignment of cook was given to either men or women. In general, all slaves employed in the main house were better housed, dressed, and nourished than those used for field labor.

Gender tended to be ignored when it came to punishing disobedient or rebellious slaves. Women received the same harsh physical punishment as men. Difficult slave women were routinely flogged; the more obstinate were fitted with leg irons and chains. Slave women who ran away three times or were absent for more than two months from a plantation could be punished with removal of both breasts. When rumors of an impending slave rebellion caused plantation owners alarm, women were feared as much as men.

Not all rural slaves lived on plantations. Female slaves were also used as nonplantation labor. Black and mulatto women could be found on estancias and haciendas where they cooked and cleaned. At the end of the sixteenth century, for example, five female slaves (three born in Africa and two in America) worked as cooks on Cortes's Tehuantepec hacienda. Female slaves, often ill-treated and exposed to harsh working and living conditions, also labored in tanneries and rural obrajes.

In either rural or urban settings, slave women, both black and mulatta, were the most disadvantaged of all women. Deprived of their freedom and lacking effective protection from abuse, they were used in a wide variety of difficult physical tasks, ranging from planting and cutting cane to working as laundresses. Viewed by European society as lacking in honor, they were often the victim of the unwanted sexual advances of their masters or other men. In theory slave women had certain legal rights guaranteed by church and crown. But for the majority their treatment depended less on what learned jurists or churchmen had theorized than on the generosity and humanity of their masters and mistresses. Knowledge of the law and the wherewithal to defend one's limited rights were also important, although judges usually disregarded the testimony of slaves. Mostly slave women counted on themselves, resisting their masters' arbitrary decisions, earning or buying their freedom, and choosing their sexual partners.

Once slaves were freed from servitude, their physical conditions could often be as bad or worse than before. Free women of color continued to labor in many of the same occupations in which they had worked as slaves, eking out a meager living. They were frequently single-parent heads of their households, forced to survive on poor diets and live in poor housing.

CHAPTER 10

WOMEN AND SOCIAL DEVIANCE: CRIME, WITCHCRAFT, AND REBELLION

> Being a close friend of Lusiana and my husband just having given me a slap in the face, I ran into Lusiana in the bathing room where she asked me if I wanted a remedy to take away my husband's drinking vice. I said I did and the next day she called me over to her house and told me to give my husband cemetery dirt to drink, that with this you tamed men, that in this way she had hers very well tamed.[1]

A society's definition of normal female behavior is often best viewed by examining those individuals considered to be socially and culturally atypical or "deviant." The study of the socially different also illuminates power relationships and the relative control that one group in society held over other groups. In colonial Latin America, "deviance" as reflected in criminal records, Inquisition trials, and personal papers ranges from the story of crime and punishment to cases of sorcery, riots and political uprisings, and examples of personal rebellion.

Women appear frequently in the criminal records of the courts of colonial Latin America, although given their numbers in these societies, they were less likely to appear in court than men. With few exceptions women were involved in interpersonal rather than economic or political crimes. Women's lesser involvement in all but domestic crime reflects the fact that women led more sheltered lives, did not hold

---

[1] From the testimony of Gertrudis Antonia del Castillo San Antonio Tlaxomulco, Mexico, 1716, in Archivo General de la Nación, Mexico, Ramo Inquisición 878, folio 401, cited in Ruth Behar, "Sex and Sin, Witchcraft and the Devil in Late-Colonial Mexico," *American Ethnologist*, 14:1 (February 1987), 40.

political or religious office, and did not have primary responsibility for contact with outsiders.

Women also tended to be the victims rather than the perpetrators of or accomplices to a crime. One-third of all homicide and assault victims in both central Mexico and in the Mixteca Alta, for example, were women. Far less frequent was the appearance of women criminals. Women rarely killed or stabbed or maimed; in Mexico they composed only 3 percent of homicide offenders and 7 percent of assault offenders. A study of criminal cases in eighteenth-century Buenos Aires shows that in only one out of ten cases involving women were they accused of committing a violent crime. This small number of female assailants is perhaps a reflection of colonial female culture: women were trained to use gossip and verbal abuse rather than physical aggression to vent their anger. Moreover, when women did commit crimes, they tended to be punished more leniently than men.

By far the most common crimes against women were physical abuse and wife beating, followed in frequency by rape, kidnapping, and murder. The victims of these reported crimes were usually poor women, living in either cities or in rural areas. There is no way to measure the amount of violence directed at women of middle and upper social groups, not because it did not occur but because these cases were seldom brought to the attention of the colonial justice system. Crime against women was usually committed by family, friends, acquaintances, or neighbors. Indeed, female victims were overwhelmingly the wives or sex partners of their assailants. Rarely was any type of crime against women committed by a stranger. (See Document 11.) The localized nature of crime reflected the familiar parameters of the feminine world. In addition, most crime against women was committed in the home, again suggesting a limited social milieu for women. Most reported crimes were committed by people of similar social backgrounds as the victims, an indication of the lack of social mobility and the class boundaries women faced in colonial society.

Crimes against women can be divided into two categories: domestic disturbances and sexual offenses. The first category included beating, stabbing, and attempted homicide. In these cases, daughters, wives, and mistresses were the victims of a father's, husband's, or lover's anger. Male anger was often fired by unseemly conduct on the part of a woman, especially her failure to conform to the norms of expected female sexual behavior. Women who worked – especially those who worked for other men, tending their houses, washing their clothing –

easily became the victims of their husbands' jealous rage. Men also used violence to protect their rights over female family members even when there was no indication of misconduct.

Most domestic disturbance involved husbands and wives. Married women, in a socially sanctioned subordinate position, were an easy target for their husbands' frustrations. Furthermore, a husband had the right to control and punish his wife. Women, on the other hand, might taunt their husbands about their failure to meet their economic obligations, their drunkenness, or their profligate behavior, but they often complained at great risk to life and limb. For example, when María Teresa, a poor Indian women living in the Morelos region of Mexico, chastized her husband for failing to find work and instead spending the day drinking cheap rum, he responded by first destroying her kitchen and then inflicting a fatal blow to her head with a rock.

Gender-related disputes – arguments between husbands and wives or between lovers over issues related to social behavior, economic support, or sexual jealousy – were probably the cause of a great deal of the criminal violence in colonial society. Family members and neighbors expected a degree of violence in relations between the sexes and generally ignored everyday incidences of wife or mistress beating. Again and again testimony in these cases demonstrates the high degree of physical abuse that was tolerated by some women, often over long periods of time. One such woman was María Antonia Josefa de Aguilar, who had been severely beaten by her husband for years with the full knowledge of her family and friends. Only when the physical abuse of a woman became so blatant and extreme as to threaten her life did custom and public morality force neighbors to step into domestic disturbances to protect the endangered woman. Frequently women complained that they were being abused by the very men whose duty it was to defend them, thus betraying the idealized societal norm that saw a man's duty as protecting his female kin.

Spousal abuse of women was especially pronounced in rural zones, among the lower classes, and in Indian communities. Rural women not only lived in relative isolation but were also limited in the culturally accepted solutions to the problem of abuse. A woman could flee to her family seeking protection from abuse but was usually counseled to return to her husband. Women who had left their village to live with their husbands, or had moved with their spouses in search of work, were especially at risk of being the victims of aggression, for they had no close-by father, brother, or other kinsman to protect them. Such was the case of María Gertrudis, the wife of the irascible Francisco Gerómino, who had migrated with him to the hacienda San Gaspar. Over the years María had suffered repeated scoldings, beatings with a stick, and threats with a knife; she eventually died as a result of a deep stab wound inflicted by her enraged husband.

Furthermore, abused wives had few alternatives to continued mistreatment. It was impossible to terminate a marriage legally, and abandoning one's husband, although a solution used by more than one woman, was socially condemned. Permanent separation was granted in extraordinary cases of physical abuse, such as the case of an eight-month pregnant Indian woman in rural Cuzco who was tied up and nearly beaten to death by a husband who then fled with his lover. Because remarriage was impossible, a "divorced" woman was even more vulnerable than an abused wife.

Even when harsh physical abuse was reported, judges tended to be lenient when dealing with these cases. Much of their questioning was concerned with the character of the woman involved, for if there was any stain on her reputation, her husband's conduct, no matter how inhumane, was absolved. The right of a husband to discipline a wife suspected of unseemly conduct (*mala conducta*) applied to all men regardless of race or legal condition; a slave could beat his wife, although she belonged to another master. The court's insistence on the need to document a female victim's good conduct, and the corollary that any treatment was justified to correct a bad woman, were also applied to cases involving wife murder. A wife's misconduct was the universal defense.

Men were not the only colonial abusers. Young married women were also frequently subjected to violence from their mothers-in-law, who joined with their sons to exact female subjugation. Josefa Rosalia, a widow living in Mexico City in the 1780s, for example, counseled her daughter-in-law, María Ignacia Zapata, to bend to her husband's will. When the young woman failed to obey, her mother-in-law, acting in concert with her son Albino, took part in beating his wife. Perhaps the older woman, a widow dependent on her son's protection and good-will, believed that siding with him was her only salvation, but the repeated cases of mother-in-law abuse of daughters-in-law suggests that age and family seniority gave older women power over younger, defenseless women. Since it was quite common among the poorer classes of colonial society for a newly married couple to live with a widowed mother, many young women no doubt found themselves in a situation of double physical jeopardy.

A hierarchy of race, class, and age also allowed one woman to abuse another. Spanish women beat slaves, free people of color, indias, and mestizas for supposed misbehavior. For example, a fourteen-year-old free mulatta women, working as a servant for a nun in the Queen of Heaven monastery in Mexico City, was thrashed by both the nun and an Indian servant woman, using shoes and heavy keys, for some minor infraction. Slave women were also mistreated by their fellow servants and older slave women.

Perhaps the most infamous woman in colonial Latin America was the seventeenth-century Chilean encomendera and slave owner doña Catalina de los Ríos y Lisperguer. A sadist who was protected by her membership in the local elite, "La Quintrala" was responsible for the death of at least thirty-nine people, including her own father, one of her lovers, and several female servants and slaves. Those she did not kill she brutally tortured. According to the official report, "Doña Catalina used to punish every day . . . for many years past, and sometimes two or three times . . . married and unmarried female Indians, stripping them stark naked, tying them to stakes or ladders with their hands about their heads, or suspending them head downwards, or with their hands tied, and laid out on the ground; they were beaten until they bled and choked profusely. . . . On one occasion, when she had flogged the mulatta Herrera, she had her suspended head downwards in a basin of live coals and chiles, from which she very nearly died of suffocation. . . . She also used to burn their mouths with [boiling] milk, eggs, and live coals, putting these inside and closing their lips. She hurt their eyes by putting chiles in them, pinching them, and slapping them with stinging-nettles."[2] It is interesting to note that many of her most sadistic crimes were committed in the relative privacy of her estate.

Although she was first denounced by the bishop of Santiago in 1634, La Quintrala was able to avoid trial for twenty-six years because her family was linked to many of the judges of the local high court (audiencia). Skillfully using her family and social connections, her social class and wealth, and her sex, she manipulated the judicial system throughout her life. Although eventually convicted of several heinous

---

[2] Charles Boxer, *Women in Iberian Expansion Overseas, 1415–1815: Some Facts, Fancies and Personalities* (New York: Oxford University Press, 1975), 46–47.

crimes, La Quintrala was never punished, for she died under house arrest while awaiting the results of her appeal to a higher court back in Spain. She was buried in a Santiago church, dressed in the habit of a nun and given full honors, as befitting a woman of her social stature.

The second major group of offenses that victimized women were sexual offenses, including rape and kidnapping. Again these crimes tended to be committed by men from within the same social world as the victim – neighbors, acquaintances, or kin, fictive and real. Although lust was frequently the motivating force, these crimes were usually not random crimes of passion but crimes in which the victim was well chosen by the assailant. Often the rape of a married woman was just one step in a personal dispute between the assailant and the woman's husband. Arguments between men that had started over land, personal insults (*palabras injuriosas*), and affronts to a man's honor escalated to involve his wife. In other words, the married woman was assaulted as much because she was an object of desire, as she was the means by which to attack her husband and his honor. It was the man whose honor had been jeopardized, and it was the man who sought legal redress.

Single women were also the victims of rape, kidnapping, and other violent crimes. Young girls, between the ages of five and seventeen years old were also rape victims. Although occasionally a member of a "good" family was abused, in general the girls and single women who appear in the criminal records were poor whites, mixed-bloods, or slaves. Like women of all ages they were more likely to be attacked if they were alone at home, running around the town or city doing errands, or working in the fields. Again the victims often knew their aggressors, who were more often than not from a similar social and racial background. Although we have no way of knowing how many of these crimes were never reported to the local authorities, some parents did step forward, denouncing this "enormous crime" and demanding justice in the form of prison, monetary payment, or marriage. Colonial judges seem to have been especially worried that young victims of rape would be tempted to become prostitutes when they grew older, contaminated by the fact that they had already "sinned."

In cases involving the rape of a single woman, the burden of proof was placed on the victim, and punishment was rarely meted out to the offender. Punishment was more likely to be exacted in those cases where a woman had a male guardian – husband, brother, or father – helping her in court. Criminals were punished more to assuage the masculine sense of honor and shame than to repay a woman for harm done her. The only cases of rape that greatly upset local magistrates were those of child rape, cases in which the victim was less than fifteen years old. Even here, though, as in all cases of rape of an unmarried woman, the burden of proof was on the female, and complete physical entry had to be proved before the charges were felt to merit serious punishment. But the rape of a female child was seen as being far less heinous than the rape of a male child, because sodomy, unlike any intercourse with females, was abhorrent, unnatural, contrary to God's law, and, therefore warranted the most severe punishment.

Another group of victims of violent sexual crimes comprised unprotected women, viewed as fair game for sexual advances. Women, even temporarily, without husband, father, or brothers, were treated as ownerless property, waiting to be claimed through male sexual prowess. If a woman invited a man into her house, even in broad daylight, rape was justified, as it was if a woman failed to lock her door at night or had shown any form of friendship to her assailant. In the countryside, women alone were even more frequent victims of rape and violence than in the city, although in some rural areas kidnapping and rape of unmarried girls were part of the local courtship pattern, especially among more marginal social sectors.

The countryside was dangerous territory for women, especially in those regions and times of year when men were required to be absent from their homes. Although soldiers, muleteers, shepherds, and hunters might go to great lengths to protect their women from losing their virtue and thus staining the family's honor, leaving their wives alone often meant exposing them to the actions of predatory males. Even when the head of the household was present, activities such as planting and harvesting, which required the participation of all household members, could create situations in which a woman might be attacked, thus threatening her family's honor.

Rural women, at least in some parts of Latin America, were also at risk to be captured by Indian raiding parties. In the Río de la Plata and Chile, women were taken prisoners along the long Indian frontier throughout the colonial period, with only brief periods of relative peace. Raids on frontier settlements, farms, and ranches (*estancias*) continued well into the nineteenth century. As late as 1833, 235 female captives lived among Indian tribes. In Brazil and part of Spanish America runaway slave communities (*mocambos*) also raided for women, cattle, and food.

Although not always directly reflected in criminal records, there were always women who transgressed the accepted social and moral code. Their treatment varied greatly by social class. Those groups with pretensions to higher social status were most vigilant in preventing their women from involvement in sinful liaisons and in quickly pun-ishing the wayward women. Adultery among the upper and middle class was viewed as a personal matter, and the sinning wife was packed off to either the local house of religious retreat or the girls' orphanage until she mended her ways. All testimony points to the ease with which upper- and middle-class men could use extralegal mechanisms to send their wayward wives or daughters to these houses of correction, or place them under the care of outstanding churchmen. Only rarely did adul-tery among the *gente decente* become public knowledge, for this form of punishment maintained adultery as a private crime.

Court records suggest that, unlike their elite counterparts, lower-class women exercised a surprising degree of sexual freedom and were involved in sexual relations of their own volition. Illicit unions of all types – adultery, concubinage, and incest – were widely tolerated for long periods of time. The high incidence of illegitimate births attests to the widespread acceptance of both casual and long-lasting relations. Concu-binage, especially between upper-class men and women of economically or socially "inferior" groups, could go on for twenty or more years and was often public knowledge. Among the common people irregular unions were not only generally accepted, but, much to the despair of civil and church authorities, in isolated rural areas couples often refused to obey repeated warnings to stop. Even imprisonment, which usually lasted about three months, did little to deter determined couples.

From time to time churchmen undertook determined campaigns to improve sexual morality. Such was the case of a thirteen-year investi-gation (*visita*) begun by the bishop of Caracas in 1771. As the crusad-ing Bishop Mariano Martí crisscrossed the region, he discovered more than twelve hundred cases of fornication, concubinage, premarital sex, and adultery. While some couples quickly normalized their unions, others found themselves unable to do so. José Herrera, a mulatto bach-elor who was living in a long-term consensual union with his relative, María Aparicio, was prevented from marrying when the bishop refused his request for a dispensation in order to marry. The bishop justified his stand by arguing that granting a dispensation would encourage sinful conduct among kin.

While Bishop Martí focused on the seductive nature of the women of his dioceses, implicit in much of the legal writings and court testimony concerning women, regardless of their social class, was the belief that women were weak and, by their very nature, disorderly, prone to sexual excesses, and irrational in their sexual behavior. Paradoxically this attitude served women in certain situations. Regardless of the woman's cooperation in forming an adulterous union, for example, the tempestuous female was not as guilty as her lover; rather the crime of adultery was perceived by society as being committed by one man against another man's wife. Of course, her husband still reserved this right to kill his wife and her lover if they were found *inflagrante delito*. In fact, homicide as the result of a woman's adultery was not considered premeditated and was therefore never punished with death.

Women transgressors were also visible in the records of another powerful institution, the Holy Office of the Inquisition, an agency created to preserve Roman Catholic orthodoxy. As early as the sixteenth century, a few women were called up before the Inquisition on charges of being "secret Jews." Among the more socially prominent were doña Francisca de Carbajal and her four daughters, who were eventually burned at the stake in Mexico City as Judaizers. Although she herself practiced the forbidden religion, doña Francisca, like many other women called before the Holy Office, was probably apprehended because of her familial relationship to men who were considered to be the prime culprits.

The vast majority of women called before the Inquisition were *curanderas* (folk healers), practitioners of traditional medicine, or *hechiceras* (or *feiticerias*), women adept at casting spells. Whereas the former were seen as using magic and potions to cure, the latter invoked magic and spells to do harm. Although the Inquisition prosecuted both groups of women for deviating from the dogma of free will, in Spain and in America these folk healers and witches were usually viewed by the authorities as being motivated by ignorance. Blasphemy was still another crime for which the Inquisition judged a fair number of women; in general, for first-time offenders, blasphemy was punished by the public humiliation of being paraded through the streets of the city.

Although both men and women were accused of being curanderos and hechiceros, women were far more likely than men to be so identified and called before the Holy Office. Of seventy-one individuals who appeared before the Inquisition in Mexico between 1613 and 1806, for example, forty-seven (66 percent) were women. Both male and female curanderos used a mixture of European, African, and Indian folk beliefs to practice their occult arts, but men tended to use a more aggressive magic, which often employed astrology or palmistry. Women were most frequently charged with using their power to heal the sick, induce illness, and practice love magic or sexual witchcraft. Some witches were also accused of flying, changing into animal and other human shapes, paying homage to a male goat, and making pacts with the devil. But women were rarely prosecuted for being involved in major dealings with the devil.

Both female witches and female clients were primarily involved in love magic, although women slaves also used magic to control the anger of their mistresses. The goal of most female magic was the seduction and conquest of a man. Hoping to enhance their sexual allure, women probably first tried Roman Catholic saints (such as Saint Anthony in Brazil) credited with special powers over love and marriage. When that failed they turned to love magic, seeking out female specialists in magic and spells. Sexual witchcraft, it was believed, could solve romantic problems by enhancing one's sexuality and furthering amorous overtures. Female clients also came to curanderas to solve sexual problems, especially their husband's or lover's unfaithfulness. Depending on the situation love magic could be used to determine a man's amorous intentions, obtain a man's love, recover the attention of a neglectful lover, or control a husband prone to excessive violence.

Love magic clearly threatened the social order, for its goal was to tie a man to a woman, making him weak, unable to resist or exercise his free will. Most feared by men was the supposed ability of witches to cause male impotence through magical ligatures, causing a man to be incapable of having sexual intercourse with anyone other than his wife or lover. The use of magical ligature reflected the importance of winning and retaining a man, perhaps because men were crucial in warding off poverty and social marginalization. Of course, the use of love magic also attests to the sexuality and passion of colonial women.

In the eyes of the church, witchcraft and magic were sins, especially when they touched on the arena of human sexuality. The power of witches clearly made them dangerous because they knew how to reverse normal male-female relations. These women were especially disruptive for they could change male behavior, do physical harm by rendering a man impotent or sterile, or cause illness or even death to an ex-lover. But compared with heresy, the Inquisition's major concern, witchcraft was a relatively minor problem. It was included in the general category of superstition and usually dealt with leniently. Usually women found guilty of sorcery were publicly shamed by being paraded through the streets of the city and wearing the *sanbenito* (penitential cloak) for a period of time. Perhaps because it was treated so benignly, witchcraft continued to flourish in colonial society, and women continued to fear and respect the power of witches.

Perhaps the most famous outbreak of *hechiceria y brujeria* occurred in seventeenth-century New Spain. Denunciations for these crimes grew markedly between 1605 and 1630, reaching a peak in 1614–1615 when several young women from Celaya and Querétaro were brought before the Holy Office to testify about their involvement in magical cures, spells, divination, and sexual witchcraft. Single, married, and widowed, these young women ranged from socially prominent Spaniards to a handful of mestizas, mulattas, and indias. Concerned primarily with controlling their husbands, keeping their own love affairs secret, determining whether their men were faithful, or trying to bring men back, the Celaya testimonies show how women of differing social and racial backgrounds might band together in a female conspiracy to control male actions. Over and over again, Inquisition records give us glimpses of networks of women from all castes and classes who shared information about how a woman could deal with a recalcitrant, violent, or unfaithful man.

Female practitioners of this magic were often older nonwhite women, frequently widows past childbearing age. Those accused of sexual witchcraft were usually marginal women who lived alone and thus provoked their neighbor's suspicions and fears. A review of Inquisition records suggests that their power derived from their sexual, racial, and social "otherness." Midwives were especially open to charges that they were also practitioners of love magic, for it was commonly believed that midwives had magical remedies, including those capable of inducing abortion. (At least eleven of the Celaya women accused of being curanderas were also listed as midwives.) Clearly women who delved into the mysteries of the female body were especially suspect of involvement in the occult.

While many of the practitioners of sexual witchcraft were of Indian, black, or mixed-blood, their clientele ranged from elite urban women to poor rural ones, reflecting a wide range of ages, legal statuses, and racial groups. Many women who resorted to witchcraft were at first torn between using this magic and defying Catholic proper behavior. What all these women had in common was a belief in the efficacy of magic to control people and events that were normally outside of their influence.

Food was the most common medium for witchcraft – a natural medium with which women could work, given their domestic role. At the end of the seventeenth century, Francisca de los Angeles, a mulatta married to a mestizo shoemaker in Querétaro, told how her cousin Clara de Miranda had advised her "to change her husband's behavior and turn him into a simpleton . . . [by taking] a few of the fat worms . . . that can be found under the earth," and, once dried and turned into powder, serve them to him in food and drink. Frequently a women's pubic hair or menstrual blood was stirred into the food, a reflection of the mystery of women's physiology and sexual power. A common recipe used to tame a man involved mixing menstrual blood in his drink. Other female fluids such as the water that had been used to wash female genitalia were also useful. The aforementioned Clara de Miranda advised another women to make her husband care for her by preparing his chocolate with the water she had used to cleanse herself after having intercourse with him. All these fluids were, of course, tied to a deep-rooted fear of women as polluters and a belief in the power of contamination of the female body and female fluids, although sexual magic could also involve semen or other powerful ingredients. Feiticerias such as Antonia Fernandes in late-sixteenth-century Bahia recommended that women give a drink with semen in it to assure their man's affection. Lusiana, mentioned at the beginning of this chapter, believed in the efficacy of soil from the local cemetery.

Practitioners of love magic also used special powders often concocted from mystical herbs that were dusted on people's clothing, as well as charms, amulets, or trinkets secretly sewn into garments. In Mexico hummingbirds frequently figured in both powders and charms as did the use of corn kernels to predict the future of a love affair; both practices clearly had Aztec roots. In Brazil objects of African origin such as a crow's head and feathers, eyes of a swallow, and soil taken from cemeteries were believed capable of inducing love.

Witchcraft could sometimes take on political overtones, as in the case of an old Guachichil woman accused of being a witch, who attempted to use her power to stir up her people against Spanish authorities. Like all who encouraged rebellion against the crown, the woman was hung. There was also the ever present fear that black and mestiza women were plotting revolt, a reflection of racial and sexual paranoia that was rarely substantiated. In 1658, for example, a black woman was indicted by the Santiago Cabildo for having arrowheads in her possession. Women of color were also suspected of plotting against their masters with varying degrees of success. Here again punishment was harsh. When a seventeenth-century free mulatta was found guilty of poisoning her mistress by lacing her fried eggs with mercury chloride, the servant was hung even though her mistress survived.

While women were closely linked by witchcraft, they did not take a leading role in the frequent urban tumults, although they could be found among the crowd that joined in the fray once a riot began. Colonial disturbances were usually occasioned by tax increases rather than food shortages and therefore had little direct influence on women and the domestic sphere. Furthermore, women were rarely the victims of riots. Crowds took pains to attack property, not people, and were especially solicitous of women and children. During the 1765 riots that swept through Quito, for example, rioters ransacked the house of a Spanish merchant, destroying his belongings, but allowing his wife and child to escape unharmed.

Rural riots usually had more active female involvement. Women participated in local attacks against officials in a series of uprisings in southern Mexico in 1660s. Eyewitness descriptions speak of hundreds of women, often outnumbering men, in uprisings in Oaxaca. Indeed female action in rural riots was a long-standing tradition, and women took a leading role in the numerous local rebellions that punctuated rural community life in colonial Spanish America. Women led riots in Tlapanoya, Hidalgo (1690), and Amanalco, Mexico (1792), as well as the uprising in Otuzco in the Viceroyalty of Peru (1758). At least one-fourth of the uprisings in eighteenth-century Mexico involved female leadership.

Women were charged with defending the home, and mobs of women, armed with spears, kitchen knives, or rocks were ready to respond to what they perceived as threats to their communities or way of life. Women also tended to be more aggressive and insulting toward the authorities sent to put down local uprisings. In 1798, for example, a group of seventy-three Mayan women living in the town of Santa María Nebaj seized the local church, holding the priest, a doctor, and his medical team hostage. The women were protesting a change in burial customs, which had resulted from the high mortality of a typhus epidemic ravaging the region. Bearing the disinterred bodies of the recently deceased, they demanded that the dead again be buried in the church, and that age-old rituals be observed.

Riots sometimes were led by local Indian noblewomen. The Zozo-quiapan uprising of 1805 led by Felipa Escudero is such a case. But many others were led by peasant women, such as Mariana, described as a tall scar-faced women from the town of Santa Lucia who in 1719 led a group of men and women in preventing Spanish officials who had come to mark the town's boundaries from doing their work. She not only cut the measuring rope but also engaged in hand-to-hand combat with one of the Spaniards and led a rock-throwing barrage that forced the Spaniards to retreat.

Occasionally rebellion was expressed more indirectly through local charismatic religious movements; at times women played a critical role as self-anointed religious leaders. In Tulancingo (Hidalgo) in 1769, a woman venerated as the Virgin of Guadalupe preached the second coming of the Messiah. In a few cases the mystical experiences of these women did lead to uprisings. In 1712, María López, a thirteen-year-old Indian girl from Cancuc (Yucatan), claimed to have been visited by the Virgin Mary. The Virgin's message was that the Spanish God had died and an Indian redeemer had come. María's vision sparked the Tzeltal Rebellion in which, according to some sources, she took an active role, participating in the ordination of Indian priests and order-ing the execution of a local friar. Interestingly, María's followers were challenged by another Indian woman who claimed that the Virgin had also appeared to her.

Women also had an active role in the widespread uprisings that marked the age of Andean Insurrection (1742–1782). The first of these rebellions, the messianic movement to liberate Indians and mestizos led by Juan Santos Atahualpa "Apu-Inca" (Inca Lord) from 1742 to 1752, contained a separate fighting unit of some fifty women, led by Doña Ana, a *zamba* (mixed Indian-black) from Tarma.

The next major rebellion, the Tupac Amaru revolt (1780–1783), demonstrates the role of women even more clearly. In the movement led by José Gabriel Tupac Amaru, women played an active role in sup-plying the rebels with ammunition and overseeing finances. Micaela Bastides, the mestiza wife of the rebel leader, served as commandant of the rebel stronghold while her husband took to the field; she soon took on the added posts of commissar of war and paymaster general. Addressed by her followers as "Señora Gobernadora," Micaela exercised authority over recruitment and supply, requisitioning goods to feed the troops, controlling banditry and looting, and supervising the manufac-ture of arms. A forceful woman, Bastides was also a pragmatic realist who did not hesitate to give advice on political and military strategy to her husband. In a famous letter, she rebuked her husband for delaying the siege of Cuzco and provided tactical advice, pointing out that hungry soldiers would soon desert "because as you will have noticed they act mainly out of self-interest."[3]

A battlefield commander, commended by her enemies for her horsemanship and bravery, Michaela was not the only female participant in the Great Rebellion. Tomasu Titu Condemayta, the wealthy *cacica* (chief) of Arcos, provided silver and supplies and commanded a group of women who defended the Pilpinto pass for over a month. María Esquivel, wife of a Spanish obraje owner and gunsmith who participated in the rebellion, was described as "supervising a mulatto melting bullets."[4] Indeed, thirty-two women were among the seventy-three people eventually brought to trial.

Spanish observers of the Andean uprisings were startled by the level of ferocity displayed by these Indian and mestiza women. A member of the Arequipa militia wrote that "he had never witnessed such obstinacy and desperate defense as that of the Indian women . . . they can be seen with rifles raised at their breast and not only do they not ask to be pardoned, but they never cease to throw rocks and do injury to the troops."[5] Others noted that these women were "supermasculine" and capable of great cruelty.[6] Gregoria Apasa, the sister of Julian Apasa Tupac Catari, was described "as bloody a butcher as her brother."[7]

Nonetheless, the women who took an active role in the culture of resistance were faithful to the traditional gender roles ascribed to them by both Andean and Spanish culture. Both cultures underlined the importance of family ties. Marriage created family alliances, and a woman was expected to support her husband and his family. The Andean female rebels who defended their customs, rituals, and communities by taking an active role in rebellions were also tied through marriage or kinship to the rebels; they were, in the main, the wives and

---

[3] Scarlett O'Phelan Goday, *Rebellions and Revolts in Eighteenth Century Peru and Upper Peru* (Cologne: Bohlau, 1985), 240.

[4] Ibid., 231.

[5] "Diario y operaciones de la columna de Arequipa . . . Abril de 1782," in Melchor de Paz y Guini, *Guerra separatista: rebeliones de indios en Sur América: La sublevación de Tupas Amaru, crónica*, ed. Luis Antonio Eguiguren (Lima, 1952), 243, quoted in Leon G. Campbell, "Women and the Great Rebellion in Peru, 1780–1783," *The Americas*, 42:2 (1985), 186.

[6] Campbell, "Women and the Great Rebellion," 170.

[7] Ibid., 186.

sisters of the leading rebel caciques. Women also seemed to have provided the kinship links between many of the leaders of the uprising. At their trials, these women and their lawyers defended their actions by claiming they were only obeying their husbands. This defense, while probably containing a great deal of truth, did not prevent them from being found guilty of lese majesty and other lesser crimes and punished by execution, imprisonment, or exile.

In addition to women participating in group uprisings, there are some rather stunning examples of individual women, who with differing degrees of success, defied social conventions. Perhaps the most unusual case in colonial Latin America was that of doña Catalina de Erauso, better known as "the ensign nun" (la monja alférez). Erauso, who left a written record of her exploits, was born in Spain in 1592 and sent to a convent at age four. Although some scholars are beginning to question the veracity of her account, according to Catalina at age fifteen, as she prepared to take final vows, she was sexually abused by an older nun. Fleeing the convent dressed as a man, she spent two years traveling around Spain in her newfound disguise, and then sailed to the New World. Catalina ended up in Peru, where she continued her cross-dressing, successfully passed herself off as a man, joined the Spanish army, and engaged in several heroic exploits, including the Araucanian Wars. Although she eventually ran afoul of the authorities and was discovered to be a woman, Erauso returned to Europe and managed to convince the pope to grant her a dispensation so she could continue to wear men's clothing; in addition, the crown agreed to provide her with a pension. Still cross-dressing, she returned to the New World, where she worked as a muleteer and began traveling between Mexico City and Veracruz. She prospered, in spite of some run-ins with the law over her propensity to challenge rivals to a duel, and died from natural causes in Mexico at the age of fifty-eight.

Although still in the small minority, there are other examples of less dramatic personal rebellions by headstrong young girls willing to defy their parents and social conventions and marry for love. In colonial Mexico approximately three young women per year joined their fiancés in ecclesiastical courts to contest their parents' opposition to their marriages. Although this number would drop to one case per year after marriage oppositions were moved to secular courts in the late eighteenth century, a handful of young women still refused to bow to social and parental pressures. Mariquita Sánchez, the daughter of a prominent

Buenos Aires merchant, whose acid description of marriage among the elite appears in Chapter 6, opposed her parent's choice of a marriage candidate for more than four years and eventually wed the young man of her own choice.

Other extraordinary women who defied social conventions to "do their own thing" include Micaela Villegas (La Perricholi), a young and beautiful limeña actress, described by one historian as "flirtatious, sensual, impudent and vivaciously immoral,"[8] who became the lover of the aging viceroy Manuel de Amat and a local social arbiter. Still another women intent on defying social convention was María Ana Perichon (La Perichona), wife of Tomás O'Gorman, who began a rather public affair with a fellow Frenchman, the twice-widowed viceroy of Buenos Aires, Santiago de Liniers. La Perichona was eventually exiled to her ranch because of her scandalous behavior.

In spite of these cases, all forms of personal rebellion were especially frowned upon for women. Drinking to excess, for example, was always much more socially objectionable for women than it was for men. Although lower-class and peasant women were occasionally accused of abusing alcohol, in theory a "decent" woman's consumption was restricted to ceremonial occasions. Furthermore, a woman's periodical drunkenness was viewed in the most negative terms, whereas that of her husband was considered to be normal social behavior. Indeed, part of the wifely role for lower-class women was to maintain their sobriety while their husbands got drunk. Wives suspected of drinking without their husband's consent were severely punished.

In conclusion, violence was a fact of everyday life for many women, especially the poor and unprotected. Standards of masculinity combined with a subculture of violence to make women the victims of men and other women, usually kinfolk. Although violence against women varied from group to group, it was universally accepted. Nonetheless, women used magic, specifically love magic, to alter their condition of victim and gain the upper hand in their relationships with their husbands and lovers. This supposed power that women controlled made them feared by civil and religious authorities as well as by the men who were the objects of their "cures" and spells.

A few extraordinary women managed to break the bounds of social

---

[8] Luis Alberto Sánchez, *La Perricholi* (Lima: Universidad Nacional Mayor de San Marcos, 1963), quoted in ibid., 164.

and gender convention, but they usually did so at great risk to themselves and their families. At the same time, women seemed to have a natural right to participate in specific types of political demonstrations, as long as their actions did not get out of hand. When they did, when local riots became regional uprisings, women suffered the same fate as their male counterparts.

CHAPTER 11

WOMEN AND ENLIGHTENMENT

REFORM

From the youngest age all [the women of Buenos Aires] are instructed in the essential principles of our wonderful religion; and joining the endowments of their spirit with those of their heart, the ease of learning with the dedication to know more everyday through a wise education, they make such rapid progress that they possess, not only the principles of their native language, but they also know how to create, read, and write with admirable dominion, exactitude and correctness. And in addition to dogma, the mysteries, and the basic tenets of Christian morality, some of them repeat the most well known passages of both Testaments, [as well as] the history, progress, and actual state of our religion. Some know how to discuss the climate, government, religion, laws, character, and customs of many European nations; and there are even some who have been instructed in French and English and can produce a moderate translation.[1]

The eighteenth century, first in the Iberian Peninsula and then in Latin America, was a century of reform. Influenced by the French *philosophes*, a new generation of Spanish and Latin American writers began to spread innovative ideas about the nature of knowledge, rational thinking, and economic advancement. At the same time Iberian governments moved to tighten their control over the inhabitants of the colonies and, in the case of Spanish America, to regulate what they viewed to be social disorder. How did these changes affect colonial women and their position in society?

[1] This article, "Elogio a las porteñas," authored by Narciso Fellovio Canton, who identified himself as "an indifferent philosopher, a native of Spain and a resident of Buenos Aires," appeared in the *Telégrafo Mercantil*, 2:20 (18 October 1801).

Throughout Latin America, spurred by Enlightenment thought and a desire to improve the economic potential of the colonies, the condition of women gradually emerged as a public issue. By the last decades of the eighteenth century, creole intellectuals, following peninsular thinkers such as Feijóo, began to publish pieces that questioned the status of women in society, and suggested change. To the best of our knowledge all of these authors were men. Nonetheless their writings, primarily newspaper articles, reflect a new awareness among the intellectual elite of the role of women in Latin American society. Foremost in these writings about women was a concern with improving women's inferior social position through education.

An interest in woman's education was not altogether new. Shortly after the conquest of Mexico, the Catholic Church had concentrated on educating noble Indian women in Spanish Christian ways. In order to prepare Indian women to be Christian wives and mothers, Indian girls were initially allowed to sit in the patios of the Franciscan schools, memorizing the lessons of the priests. By 1529 a Spanish woman began a *casa-hogar* in Texcoco, providing basic instruction to Spanish and Indian girls. Soon after a group of beatas arrived in Mexico under the auspices of the first bishop of Mexico. He supported the creation of a boarding school for noble Indian girls, but a disagreement over whether the school was to be directly under church control soon developed, and by 1545 the beata-run school for girls was abandoned.

Although these early efforts eventually failed, some rudimentary education, usually reserved for a select handful of girls, was always available in colonial convents. In groups of two and three, girl students shared living quarters with the nun who served as their teacher, were educated in schools run by female teachers (*amigas*), or learned at home. Most male thinkers believed that teaching a girl to read was useful because she could pray and read books of religious devotion but writing was superfluous or even dangerous for women. In addition, the nuns or lay teachers who provided instruction were usually only minimally educated themselves. Nonetheless the most formidable female intellectual of colonial Mexico, Sor Juana Inéz de la Cruz, managed to learn to read and write in Spanish and Latin in an *escuela de amigas* in her hometown of Amecameca. No colonial woman ever attended a secondary school or university.

Schooling for women was usually practical and utilitarian, rather than abstract, because women were believed to have little need of formal knowledge. Only those girls who showed an "inclination" were taught to read, and few ever went beyond basic literacy (*primeras letras*). The rest were instructed in cooking, sewing, spinning, weaving, embroidery, and music. For two hundred years the ideal education for an elite woman throughout Latin America was the "domestic arts" with (perhaps) a bit of reading and writing. According to one historian, in seventeenth century Brazil an elite woman's education consisted of learning to sew and embroider, prepare tasty delicacies, read her prayers and hymns, and manage a few household slaves.

Feminine education was not only limited, it was rare. Only 10 percent of the elite Indian women seeking entry as novitiates in the eighteenth-century Mexico City convent of Corpus Christi had any formal schooling. Most women, including elite Spanish women, were illiterate. Some women, although they had been taught to read or at least to sign their names, forgot these skills in later life because they did not use them. Those who were able to sign their names did so in a slow and clumsy fashion, tracing a signature rather than writing with fluency. Even those who could read and write fairly well were usually very superficially educated.

There were always a few exceptions to the general rule of female illiteracy and subsequent lack of participation in the cultural life of the colonies. In seventeenth-century Lima at least one literary society, the Academia Anártida, counted a few notable women among its members. There was a sprinkling of baroque women poets, both religious and lay, and women appeared in theatrical performances, although they were usually dressed as men.

The late eighteenth century witnessed a change in the prevailing philosophy and practice of female education. Along with a greater acceptance of some formal education for the daughters of the elite, as well as a handful of other Spanish women and an occasional noble Indian girl, came growth of the idea that women had some intellectual aptitude. Educating women, it was believed, would make them better wives and mothers, thus indirectly helping to improve society by tapping feminine potential. Education would also help women over-come a list of what were viewed as women's most common defects: sus-ceptibility to disease, exaggerated sensitivity, weakness of character, overly lively emotions, extravagance, and ostentation. But there was no universal agreement as to exactly what this female education should consist of.

Most Enlightenment authors were primarily concerned with

educating upper-class women, whose lives they tended to picture as
ones of extreme sloth. Female lethargy was seen as a serious problem,
and one that these thinkers were ready to remedy. It was also considered important to educate less fortunate Spanish women, thus making
them more attractive marital candidates or preparing them for future
employment as teachers of young girls. Only a few thinkers counseled
the development of practical skills that would make women economically active, for the majority of reformers did not believe that upper-
class women should actually work. Rather they stressed the need for
women to be virtuous in thought and behavior.

The purpose of an elite women's education was to make her better
able to attend to her household and guide her children, to teach her
some social graces, and to give her enough skills to prevent her from
falling into idleness. The goal of even the most forward-looking female
education was to produce more competent wives and mothers. Women
were educated to be more effective helpmates, not to make any public
display of their knowledge, and manners were more important than
intellectual brilliance in the making of a perfect woman. In fact, in
spite of Enlightenment reform, any and all advanced education continued to be denied to women.

Convinced by Enlightenment thinkers of the social benefits that
would result, both crown and church slowly came to endorse the creation of schools for women, although the crown usually supported
non-convent education. New schools were founded, and preexisting
institutions such as convents and beaterios were encouraged to add or
enhance the educational services provided for young women. In 1753
La Enseñanza, a new French religious order devoted exclusively to
female education, founded its first school in Mexico City; in the following years others were begun in several Spanish American cities.

There was also a movement to create a series of lay schools for "poor
but honest" women. Among the most famous of these was the Colegio
de las Vizcaínas in Mexico City, founded by a group of wealthy merchants in 1732 but allowed to begin functioning (because of a juris-
dictional dispute) only in 1767. By the beginning of the nineteenth
century, local economic societies (Sociedades Económicas de Amigos
del Pais) charged by royal decree with overseeing public education were
also encouraged to create schools for orphan girls. The most successful
was the Casa de Educandas in Havana, which by 1794 cared for and
educated twenty-seven "white, poor orphans," between the ages of
seven and ten. The casa's curriculum consisted of religion, reading,

sewing, sweeping, laundering, and cooking. The net result of the founding of these and other new schools was a modest increase in women's access to education. Although more schooling for women became increasingly available in large urban centers, smaller cities, towns, and rural areas continued to provide little to no educational opportunities for women.

In cities across Spanish America, schools such as those founded by La Enseñanza increasingly took an interest in educating both the daughters of the elite as well as *hijas del pueblo*, provided that the latter were legitimate and of pure Spanish blood. Like the schools run by La Enseñanza, most colonial schools for women served two bodies of students, boarders and day students. There was a clear social division between more prestigious *internas*, daughters of the local elite, and needy *externas*, and they were often physically separated within the school. Poor girls attended classes for free, whereas the wealthy paid for their lessons, room, and board. Even orphanages also began to take in day students, whose parents paid a monthly fee for the privilege of having their daughters educated separately from the inmates of the institution. By the standards of the time, female education was expensive. In Mexico City, for example, it cost seventy pesos per year, or two-thirds of the annual salary of a manual worker, to send a young woman to school.

As education outside of the confines of their home became more acceptable for the daughters of the elite, the mission and the clientele of some schools changed dramatically. The Colegio de Nuestra Señora de la Caridad in Mexico City (usually referred to as "el colegio de las niñas") had been founded and supported by a cofradía since the mid-sixteenth century for the education of poor but honorable mixed-blood daughters of conquistadors and their descendants. By the middle of the seventeenth century it had become a school for the daughters of the city's elite. The school now provided an education modeled on that received by "the principal ladies of Spain and the best Christian women" to daughters of the most distinguished Spanish and creole merchants, bureaucrats, and mineowners.

On the whole there was no startling change in the subjects deemed proper for young women to study. The curriculum, reflecting the goal of producing better wives and mothers, continued to emphasize domestic arts ("ornate handwork, . . . embroidering with silk and gold thread, stocking making, lacemaking, and making buttons edged in lace; sewing shirts, slips and mantillas, mending, spinning thread, . . . and repairing holes in stockings"), Christian doctrine, and some reading, writing, and arithmetic. Women were also encouraged to become interested in the arts. There were some exceptions such as the female *colegio* set up for privileged young women in Buenos Aires that required literacy for entrance and included physical education, music, and the teaching of "decency" as well as embroidery in its curriculum. Perhaps it was the graduates of this school so lauded for the breadth of their knowledge by the "indifferent philosopher" whose positive assessment of female accomplishments is quoted at the beginning of this chapter.

Although Bourbon reformers could not envision elite women working, they encouraged nonelite women to enter the work force as "productive" members of society. Women of course were to work in jobs considered appropriate to their sex; in addition to those crafts long deemed appropriate for women (weaving, sewing) manufactory work was considered to be particularly "appropriate" for women. In a royal decree issued in 1799, women and girls were urged "to engage in all labors and manufactures compatible with their strength and the decorum of their sex, regardless of guild ordinances and governmental regulations to the contrary."[2]

Just as education and work strove to end female "idleness," newspaper articles provided advice on qualities that a man should look for when choosing a wife. Prospective grooms were cautioned to seek a wife from among economic as well as social equals. Writers stressed that a good marriage was based on financial security, and defined a good wife as one who helped her husband attain this state. Men were counseled to avoid women who might lead their marriage into financial ruin, avoiding extravagant women even if they came with a sizable dowry.

Education and the new vision of the elite mother and wife were not the only spheres in which the Enlightenment influenced women. Some outstanding elite women began to sponsor literary salons where local literary lights displayed their erudition to a select few. Among the most well known was doña Manuela Sanz de Santamaría of Bogotá, whose weekly *tertulias* (social gatherings) explored science, literature, and more frivolous passing fashions. A few elite women tried their hand at writing poetry, essays, and satire. Doña Manuela, for example, published an article in the *Papel periódico de Santafé de Bogotá* entitled

---

[2] Consultation of Viceroy Azanza to the Council of the Indies reproduced in Richard Konetzke, *Colección de documentos para la historia de la formación social de Hispanoamérica, 1493–1810* (Madrid: Consejo Superior de Investigaciones Científicas, 1953–62), 5:767–769.

"Reflections of a Philosophical Lady on an Important Point of Public Education."

Even more important than being a good wife, women were encouraged to be good mothers. Over and over women were told that motherhood was the most serious task confronting women. The Enlightenment interest in science and medicine eventually led to a discussion of women's health or at least those aspects of women's health that directly affected their children. Journal articles were especially concerned with pregnancy, prenatal care, and care of the newborn infant. Women were encouraged to turn to medical doctors and applied science to improve their and their children's health. Wet nurses were denounced as ignorant practitioners responsible for a large degree of infant mortality, and mothers were encouraged to breast-feed their own children. Increasingly women were also envisioned as the first-line educators of their children and admonished not to spoil their children.

In their campaign to reduce pregnancy complications and infant morality, writers attacked midwives, calling them curanderas and accusing them of superstitious and barbarous practices. The mid-eighteenth-century royal *protomedicato* of Madrid worried about the quality of attention given to pregnant women and considered examining and licensing midwives, although the august doctor clearly believed that delivering children was woman's work. Instructions drawn up in 1759 addressed both the theory and the practice of midwifery and recommended that all women delivering children have some basic anatomical knowledge. The protomedicato also advised that midwives be literate, young, vigilant, careful, merciful, temperate, able to keep secrets, in robust health, and have strong, well-developed hands.

Eventually the crown turned its attention to the state of obstetrics in America, but although American protomedicatos were armed with the power to require midwives to have four years of training with a licensed master, they showed little inclination to enact any change in the practice of midwifery. Although doctors and other Enlightenment writers repeatedly commented on the dismal state of obstetrics in Mexico and Peru, accusing midwives of being unprincipled, ignorant of prenatal care, and totally untrained, reform made little headway in America. Nonetheless, beginning in the 1770s, there was a revival of interest in Caesarean births spurred by Viceroy Bucareli of Mexico, who began to encourage the practice. Not until 1804, however, was a royal cédula issued for America detailing how midwives were to perform this surgical intervention. The issuing of these instructions was not motivated by an interest in female health as much as by theological concerns for the unborn child, and a desire to increase the number of the faithful.

Because so much of a woman's health was associated with reproduction and her "shameful parts," other important issues were ignored. Women, especially slave women, had long been victims of sexual sadism. Certain folk beliefs, such as the Brazilian belief that sexual intercourse with a black virgin entering the age of puberty cured syphilis and gonorrhea, were detrimental to women's health. In addition, abortion seems to have been widely used by poor and slave women who chose not to bear children into poverty and enslavement. Syphilis, a disease endemic in all social classes, further endangered women's lives. Endemic venereal disease (euphemistically called "sickness") continued to be a major health problem, although it was consistently ignored.

The Enlightenment in Latin America brought more than educational changes or improvements in health. The Spanish crown was also concerned with problems of order, and as a result several of their eighteenth-century reforms bordered on social engineering. From the middle of the century on, the crown enacted a series of new policies reflecting a growing interest in controlling colonial society. The general tendency was to increase government control over arenas that had traditionally been church-controlled. Included in this widening of royal control was a new concern about marriage.

The crown had long regulated the marriages of two specific groups in society: regular army officers and high-court (*audiencia*) judges. From the seventeenth century, in an attempt to provide disinterested governance by separating judicial and military officers from local society, both groups were required to obtain royal permission to marry. But in practice the crown had rarely denied permission to its royal servants; over and over again military men and Audiencia judges received the required permission and married local women.

In the eighteenth century, a renewed interested in the marriage of those representing the royal government was broadened by economic and new social concerns. Because of the relatively low wages paid to army officers and the growing costs of maintaining a wife and family in a "decent state," the crown began to see marriage as an economic burden for military men. Furthermore, the Bourbon rulers were especially sensitive to social disorder, often understood as the result of marriage between social, economic, or racial unequals. To combat both problems, military ordinances enacted in the 1760s required that the bride have a social status equal to that of the groom and set minimum dowry requirements before permission to marry would be granted. At the same time, the creation of pension funds to provide benefits for the widows and children of deceased officers and bureaucrats provided the crown with a powerful weapon to enforce the new regulations. Only those officers who complied with the new marriage regulations qualified for the protection afforded by these funds.

Pension monies institutionalized already existing protection, which had traditionally been granted the most needy widows of government employees on a case-by-case basis. Although the pensions followed a sliding scale depending on the rank of one's late father, and made no allowance for the size of the family left behind, the regulations did favor female children. Daughters of military men and bureaucrats were allowed to draw a government pension until they married or entered a convent regardless of their ages, while sons were cut off at age eighteen.

The Bourbon desire to lessen creole influence in government also led to a royal order, issued in 1779, requiring that government officials in America zealously enforce preexisting marriage legislation. The king, Charles III, also added all government officials employed directly or indirectly by the royal exchequer (*real hacienda*) to the list of those who needed royal permission to marry. Although this new legislation would be weakened in succeeding years, the need to request special permission before marriage created an additional set of hurdles that could affect young men and women.

As the crown intensified its control, there were growing delays and refusals, which tended to jeopardize the honor of too willing young women. Doña Toribia María Guerra Mier, for example, a young heiress from a prominent family in Valledupar, New Granada, became engaged to marry don Lorenzo de Parga, a Spanish military officer, sometime around 1779. The couple began sexual relations while waiting for the official permission to marry. Before the permission arrived, war broke out and don Lorenzo was transferred to Cartagena, leaving his intended and their illegitimate daughter behind. Until her death eight years later, Doña Toribia remained a spinster, lacking both the legal security of marriage and the economic support for her child.

Government interest in marriage now went beyond affecting the marriage possibilities of civil and military officers. The state had always believed that, in order to protect a family's honor, marriage should be between social equals. By the eighteenth century, the reforming kings of Spain became increasingly convinced of the need to control the choice of spouse to maintain the social system. In 1778, citing his desire to "contain the lack of order that has slowly been introduced into society,"[3] Charles III issued a royal edict on marriage for his American colonies. Parental permission, never before required under canon law, now became an absolute requisite for marriage. Any person marrying despite parental opposition could be immediately disinherited. In addition, the jurisdiction over marriage was moved from ecclesiastical to civil courts.

Although parents were enjoined not to block their children's marriage because of frivolous reasons, the new law permitted parents to deny the necessary permission on the basis of "inequality." The local magistrates soon interpreted inequality to refer to race, social background (including illegitimacy), wealth, and moral behavior. These new impediments were added to the more traditional ones (such as already being married or wanting to marry a close blood relation) that the Catholic Church had used to decide who could marry whom. Furthermore, in America the Royal Pragmática was specifically targeted to protect elite Spaniards; "mulattos, blacks, mestizos and members of other similar mixed races" were specifically excluded from the new regulations.

Couples wishing to marry in spite of parental objections were now placed in the difficult situation of bringing a legal suit against their parents. In essence they were forced to prove that their parents were preventing the marriage without a valid justification – that there was no inequality between the prospective bride and groom. Magdalena Somalo, for example, went to court when her parents, arguing that "the groom-to-be is from an unknown family," objected to her plans to marry Santiago Costa.[4] In 1794 the Buenos Aires merchant Manuel Martinez de Ochagavia prevented the marriage of his son, Feliciano, to Maria

[3] Konetzke, *Colección de documentos para la historia de la formación social de Hispanoamérica*, 3:438–442.

[4] Archivo de la Provincia de Buenos Aires, Somalo contra Somalo, 7-5-17-25, 7-5-17-26, and 7-5-17-60, quoted in Susan M. Socolow, "Acceptable Partners: Marriage Choice in Colonial Argentina, 1778–1810," in Asunción Lavrin, *Sexuality and Marriage in Colonial Latin America* (Lincoln: University of Nebraska Press, 1989), 233.

Elgueta, the mother of "several of his children," on grounds of moral inequality.[5]

In addition to arming parents who wished to protect their daughters against a socially inopportune marriage, the eighteenth-century regulations also showed an increasing interest in protecting "poor but honest" women. In several of the cities of Spanish America the town council and religious authorities began to propose special institutions to house needy widows. There was also an interest in helping wayward women correct the errors of their "mala vida"; again the remedy suggested was the creation of an institution to house and reeducate these "lost souls."

The Bourbon kings also tried to clean up, control, and refashion their citizens as useful, productive, obedient servants. Included in this new vision of humanity was a puritanical attempt to encourage good morals and to control sexual mores and civil behavior, including, for example, drinking and gambling. Paradoxically this control proved ever more elusive as urban poverty grew faster than any reform that could be instituted in colonial Latin America. Increased migration from rural districts to the cities, a migration that was heavily female, probably worsened the living conditions of many women, forcing them to combine legal and illegal, moral and immoral activities in order to survive.

The late eighteenth century also saw a growth in the idea of personal happiness, and the beginnings of a change of values. Although a few women had always rebelled against their husbands' abuse of authority, the number of divorces grew in places as separate as Brazil and Mexico. Overwhelmingly it was women who sought divorce, justifying their actions by claiming they had been subjected to great cruelty or physical abuse by their husbands or had been made to endure unusual hardships. Repeated and public adultery was also grounds for divorce, although adultery was rarely the principal cause cited. In Brazil more couples also began to seek mutual separation because of incompatibility.

Early-nineteenth-century political and economic crises in Spain, while not directly a result of the Bourbon reforms, also affected religious women in Spanish America. Because of disastrous political, economic, and military policies, the crown found itself bankrupt by the

---

[5] Archivo General de la Nación Argentina, Ochagavia contra Ochagavia, Tribunales, Legajo E-6, Expediente 12, IX-40-9-2. This case is cited in Socolow, "Acceptable Partners," 220.

end of the century, and increasingly turned to its American colonies for emergency funds. The most far-reaching of these special "loans" was enacted in the 1804 law of Consolidación de Vales Reales, a law that dictated the forced sale of clerical real estate to provide capital to the Spanish crown.

For the first time ever, the assets of convents as well as the dowries and reservas of their nuns were directly threatened. Between 1805 and 1809, while managing to avoid any substantial loss of real property, the convents of New Spain turned over approximately 850,000 pesos in liquid capital to the crown. This translated directly into a major reduction in the amount of capital that convents had at their disposal for investments.

As the political and economic conditions continued to deteriorate in much of Spanish America during the second decade of the nineteenth century, convents also found their urban rental properties threatened. In Mexico and Peru the income from rental property suffered a two-pronged decline. On the one hand rental property was subject to new taxes, which ran as high as 10 percent, while on the other hand the worsening of economic conditions forced many of the convents' tenants to default on their rent. Chaotic economic conditions threatened more than urban income; interest and principal on other convent investments, chiefly loans, liens (*depósitos*), and pious deeds (*obras pías*) also fell off markedly, just as the royal government began to extract forced loans. Lastly the political turbulence of the decade was reflected in a decrease in the numbers of new nuns entering the convent, and a corresponding decline in new capital injected in the form of professing dowries. In general the convents of Spanish America found themselves in a weaker economic position by the early years of independence than had been the case twenty years earlier.

In certain regions of Latin America, women became involved in the wars of independence, which ended Spanish control of Latin America. A handful of women had sponsored and attended tertulias where ideas of independence had originally been discussed, but few women were directly involved in the events leading up to the declarations of independence. As the wars of independence began, elite women could be found acting as supporters, nurses, spies, and couriers for both the rebel and loyalist factions. Other women followed the troops throughout the years of military campaigns, preparing food, nursing the wounded, burying the dead, and providing companionship. Many of these women were drawn into independence because of close personal ties to men involved in the conflict.

There are isolated examples of women who went as far as bearing arms. At least three women, for example, fought at Pichincha in 1822, the final battle of Ecuadorian independence. Interestingly they and other women who literally went to war usually assumed masculine dress and names. Nicolasa Jurado, one of the Pinchincha warriors, was discovered to be a woman only after she was wounded in the battle. Simon Bolívar, the leader of independence movements in northern South America, referred to these fighters as "Amazons" and extolled their valor. In spite of the participation of women, at no time did they act as a group, or suggest any change in the position or role of women.

The eighteenth century was a time of change in the Spanish and Portuguese colonies. While these changes affected the perception of women, they did not produce dramatic change in women's lives. Rather, Enlightenment ideas and policies resulted in moderate adjustments: improved though still limited education for elite women; increased parental control over marriage; and, paradoxically, growing resistance to enduring marital abuse. But the vast majority of these changes affected only elite women of European descent. The perception and treatment of women of other racial groups and social classes changed little.

Conclusion

The role of women in colonial Latin American society was markedly different than that of men. Men were supposed to be intelligent, active, independent; women were usually portrayed as silly, passive, dependent creatures. Men were charged with protecting their family's honor and fortune whereas women could endanger them through sexual misbehavior. Men could freely come and go, but women's physical movement was closely scrutinized. In other words, gender mattered.

Colonial Latin American women lived in a patriarchal society, a world in which men occupied positions of authority and power. In general men had rights over women that they did not have over other men, and women did not have over themselves. Men also defined acceptable female conduct, and controlled the justice system, which punished those who overstepped the established boundaries of acceptable behavior. But even here there was always some room for negotiation, for protecting a women who had failed to adhere to the rules of the game. The culture of patriarchy was never as absolute in reality as it was in theory.

But race and class also mattered, both in determining what was expected from any woman and in defining the possible roles open to her. The parameters of acceptable female conduct and activities were closely tied to her social class and racial category. Elite white women were to be chaste and under the direct supervision of their male kin. In theory these women, prized for their purity, were to be protected, cloistered, chaperoned, and never left alone in the company of men who were not their close kin. White women, both those of the elite and those who aspired to join its ranks, were usually under great social pressure to conform to the stereotype of female passivity and dependence.

This ideal for women, this "social construct," was so all-pervasive that residents and visitors alike failed to see a far more complicated social reality. For example, although artisan-class women, regardless of their race, should only work alongside their husbands and fathers, this was not always possible. As a result, they were freer to search for other employment and, depending on the social, racial, and economic position of the head their family, were held to a looser code of sexual conduct. Women of color and plebeian white women could little afford the luxury of economic dependence. Forced by necessity to work to survive, these women were poor but free to move about and interact with others. Slave women were by definition required to work; they were also seen as sexually available and without any binding male protection.

Age, marital conditions, local economic conditions, and the demographic balance between men and women also affected women's condition. White elite girls and adolescents were no doubt the most sheltered. On the whole marriage and childbearing continued to limit these women, although there are isolated cases of well-born women who rebelled against the socially accepted norm. In some cases widowhood or advancing age brought economic power and some independence to individual women. Age and widowhood functioned quite differently for poor women, who usually found themselves left with few resources outside of their physical labor. They often became more impoverished with advancing years. The same was true of ex-slaves who were freed when they were past their most productive years.

Geographical location – whether they lived in the city or in the countryside – also affected women's possibilities and their social position. Indian women who migrated to cities were faced with a far more complex world, but they also had the possibility to achieve some degree of economic independence if not wealth. Those who continued to live in rural indigenous communities were more circumscribed in their choices and their physical independence. The same was true of slave women who were subject to greater control of their movement on rural plantations than were their urban sisters. Furthermore, although women were in the majority in many urban centers, in a few towns along the frontier they were a scarce commodity. This tended to give them a degree of independence and power.

Like men, women identified closely with their respective race and class. On the whole there was little expression of gender solidarity. Elite (white) women punished female domestic slaves with sadistic cruelty. Female slaves and other servants stole from their mistresses, or spread malicious gossip about them. Indian and black women fought over control of local market stalls. Women complained about other women's behavior and testified against each other in court. Nonetheless, we have occasional glimpses of empathy and depth of feeling between women of different social and racial groups, especially between those who lived under the same roof – often as mistress and slave or mistress and servant. In addition, there was a range of cross-class, all-female spheres or social networks in colonial Latin America. Women were linked together through their socializing in the street, in their homes and in church, by commercial dealings, by relating together over food or children. These affective ties were reflected in small loans in life and testamentary gifts in death.

To the degree that colonial women exercised power, much of it was informal and tended to take place within the homes. Women of all racial and social groups spent much of their lives in the home, either their own or that of their mistresses. Although women were not secluded (except for those in convents), most of their tasks were tied to caring for children, preparing food, and maintaining the household. Only women of middle and lower social groups left their homes to work, but many of the tasks they performed were extensions of the work done at home. Because the Iberian culture saw physical work as socially degrading, and believed that women moving about freely were morally suspect, work brought few social or economic rewards.

Although there was a slight shift in the view of women and a new interest in improving their education as a result of the Enlightenment, society continued to see women's roles in terms of color and social position. While some women participated in riots, uprisings, and revolts, they never addressed any issues relating specifically to the female gender nor did they demand any improvement in the feminine condition. Early-nineteenth-century independence movements would do little to change the power, position, or perception of women. Only with the increasing economic development and social ferment of the late nineteenth century would women in Latin America begin to question their colonial traditions.

DOCUMENTS

1. Letter of Maria de Carranza, wife of a textile mill owner, in Puebla, to her brother Hernando de Soto in Seville, 1589.

Desired and beloved brother of my heart:

I have never had a reply to the many letters I have written you, except one, and it gave me great joy to know of the health of yourself and my sister-in-law and my nephews, whom I hope our Lord someday lets me see, as I desire. My husband Diego Sanchez Guadalupe was no less happy than I, though for him as well as for me, after our having so desired it, and having put so much into sending to call you here, it would be a greater happiness to see you; yet you want to stay there in that poverty and need which people suffer in Spain. I ask you for the love of God to spare me such pain from your absence, and yourself such necessity, when I have the means to give you relief. Do be sure to come quickly now, and don't make your children endure hunger and necessity. I would have sent money for your trip, but since I have had no reply to my letters, I didn't dare. Go to Ronda and collect the rent from my houses, and if you wish to, mortgage them and take four or five years' income in advance; I leave it to your discretion. And invest all except what you need for travel in fine cloths, in Rouen and Dutch linens; be sure you do it yourself, and don't trust it to others.

Be aware that anyone who brings children must come very well prepared; six hundredweight of hardtack will be enough, but better have over that than under, and make it yourself, since you know how. And buy four cured hams from Ronda, and four cheeses; twelve pounds of rice; chickpeas and beans, rather too much than too little; all the spices; vinegar and olive oil, four jugs of each; jerked beef and mutton, plenty of it and well dressed; and as much linen and woolen clothing for you to wear as you can bring, because here it is very expensive.

Do everything in your power to bring along with you two masters of weaving coarse woolens and carding, for they will profit us greatly, and also a candlemaker, who should be an examined journeyman and good at his trade. Buy their provisions and make a contract with them from the day they sail, and I fulfill whatever you agree to; I will pay their passage and any debts they have when they arrive. And you can do all this much better than I could. Your brother-in-law Diego Sanchez Guadalupe, to whom you owe more than to me, shares my desires; to make me happy he would have gone there himself, and I tempted to let him for the sake of you and my sister-in-law and my nephews, but in order not to be left here alone and because he is an older man, I didn't let him go.

Tell the sister of my soul to consider this letter hers; how is it that her heart doesn't melt like mine for us to see each other? I understand that she is the reason you haven't come, yet she is the one who loses and has lost in not enjoying a land where food is plenteous and she can give me a good old age. I ask here, since it is in her own favor, to come quickly and make my old age happy with her arrival and that of my longed-for nephews.

Cristobal de Velasco, my brother-in-law, was here, and I gave him hospitality which he enjoyed considerably, but then he went to Panama and left me disconsolate in his absence, and I will not be satisfied until he comes back. Our Lord fulfill my desires, so that you can find relief, and I happiness.

I greet Aunt Ana de Ribera and Aunt Ana Ruiz, and when you come here, leave them where you can send them some presents, money and other things to help them, because we owe it to them, since they are sisters of our mother. Diego Sanchez Guadalupe is not writing because he is tired of sending letters and peevish that you don't answer, so he only gave permission for me to write. Maybe I will have more luck than he has had. I am sorry that so much is necessary for your own redemption.

I will send you power to collect on the property in Ronda or sell it, and I do not send it now because I am now sure it will reach your hands, for I think that if my letters had arrived, I would already have had some letter from you to enjoy. And if you decide not to come with this fleet because you aren't outfitted yet, write me, and give the letter to

Francisco Lopez de Olmos to be directed to the house of Alonso de
Casas in Puebla. Trusting our Lord will give me this happiness, I and
mine continue in our hope, and we greet my sister-in-law and my
beloved nephews. And as to my beloved daughter Mencia Gomez, I
have reserved a very rich marriage for her. May God arrange it for his
holy service as I wish. From Puebla, 2nd of October, 1589.

Maria de Carranza

James Lockhart and Enrique Otte, *Letters and People of the Spanish
Indies: Sixteenth Century* (Cambridge: Cambridge University Press,
1976), 135–138.

2. Grant of an encomienda by Pedro de Valdivia, the conqueror of
Chile, to his mistress, doña Inés Suárez, 1544.

You, doña Inés Suárez, came with me to these provinces to serve his
Majesty there, undergoing toil and fatigue as much because of the
length of our overland journey as for some encounters which we had
with Indians, and hunger and other hardships suffered before arriving
where we founded the city of Santiago de Chile. These things were difficult for the men to survive, and so much more so for a woman as del-
icate as you. In addition to this, when the Indians rose up and besieged
this city, and were almost about to carry it off, your good efforts and
work was part of the reason that they were not successful, for all the
Christians in the city were fighting so hard against the enemy that they
forgot about the Indian chiefs who were imprisoned which was the
main reason that the Indians had come to force their release. And you,
stealing your courage, ordered that the chiefs be killed, which was the
reason that most of the Indians stopped fighting and left the city when
they saw that their leaders were dead. And it is certain that if they had
not died and had instead been freed, there would not be one Spaniard
alive in the entire city today, and Spaniards throughout the land would
only be able to survive with much effort. And after the death of the
chiefs, with masculine verve you went out to enhearten the Christians
who were still fighting, curing the wounded and inspiring the healthy,
giving them all encouraging words, which was one of the reasons that,
with your words in their ears, they went to where a large number of
Indians were usually encamped and defeated them, and then the said

Indians came to this city and they took whatever you had without leaving you any clothing nor anything else, and you lost a large amount of gold and silver.

C. R. Boxer, *Women in Iberian Expansion Overseas, 1415–1815: Some Facts, Fancies and Personalities* (New York: Oxford University Press, 1975), 113–114.

3. An English Jesuit describes the women of Mexico City.

To the by-word touching the beauty of the women I must add the liberty they enjoy for gaming, which is such that the day and night is too short for them to end a primera when once it is begun; nay, gaming is so common to them that they invite gentlemen to their houses for no other end. To myself it happened that passing along the streets in company with a friar that came with me that year from Spain, a gentlewoman of great birth, knowing us to be chaperons (so they call the first year those that come from Spain), from her window called unto us, and after two or three slight questions concerning Spain asked us if we would come in and play with her a game of primera.

Both men and women are excessive in their apparel, using more silks than stuffs and cloth. Precious stones and pearls further much this their vain ostentation. A hat-band and rose made of diamonds in a gentleman's hat is common, and a hat-band of pearls is ordinary in a tradesman. Nay, a blackamoor or tawny young maid and slave will make hard shift, but she will be in fashion with her neck-chain and bracelets of pearls, and her ear-bobs of some considerable jewels. The attire of this baser sort of people of blackamoors and mulattoes (which are of a mixed nature, of Spaniards and blackamoors) is so light, and their carriage so enticing, that many Spaniards even of the better sort (who are too prone to venery) disdain their wives for them.

Their clothing is a petticoat of silk or cloth with many silver or golden laces, with a very broad double ribbon of some light color with long silver or golden tags hanging down before, the whole length of their petticoat to the ground, and the like behind. Their waistcoats are made like bodices, with skirts, laced likewise with gold or silver, without sleeves, and a girdle about their body of great price stuck with pearls and knots of gold (if they be any way well esteemed of). Their sleeves are broad and open at the end, of holland or fine China linen, wrought some with colored silks, some with silk and gold, some with silk and silver, hanging down almost unto the ground. The locks of their heads are covered with some wrought colf, and over it another of network of silk bound with a fair silk, or silver, or golden ribbon which crosseth the upper part of their forehead, and hath commonly worked out in letters some light and foolish love posy. Their bare, black, and tawny breasts are covered with bobs hanging from their chains of pearls.

When they go abroad, they use a white mantle of lawn or cambric rounded with a broad lace, which some put over their heads, the breadth reaching only to their middle behind, that their girdle and ribbons may be seen, and the two ends before reaching to the ground almost. Others cast their mantles only upon their shoulders, and swaggerers-like, cast the one end over the left shoulder that they may the better jog the right arm, and shew their broad sleeve as they walk along. Others instead of this mantle use some rich silk petticoat to hang upon their left shoulder, while with their right arm they support the lower part of it, more like roaring boys than honest civil maids. Their shoes are high and of many soles, the outside whereof of the profaner sort are plated with a list of silver, which is fastened with small nails of broad silver heads. Most of these are or have been slaves, though love have set them loose, at liberty to enslave souls to sin and Satan. And there are so many of this kind, both men and women, grown to a height of pride and vanity, that many times the Spaniards have feared they would rise up and mutiny against them. The looseness of their lives and public scandals committed by them and the better sort of the Spaniards were such that I have heard those who have professed more religion and fear of God say often they verily thought God would destroy that city, and give up the country into the power of some other nation.

Sin and wickedness abound in Mexico, yet there are no more devout people in the world toward the Church and clergy. In their lifetime they strive to exceed one another in their gifts to the cloisters of nuns and friars. Some erect altars to their best devoted saints, worth many thousand thousand ducats; others present crowns of gold to the pictures of Mary, others, lamps; others, golden chains; others build cloisters at their own charge; others repair them; others at their death leave to them two or three thousand ducats for an annual stipend.

Among these great benefactors to the churches of that city I should wrong my history if I should forget one that lived in my time, called Alonso Cuellar, who was reported to have a closet to his house laid with bars of gold instead of bricks, though indeed it was not so, but only reported for his abundant riches and store of bars of gold which he had in one chest standing in a closet distant from another, where he had a chest full of wedges of silver.

This man alone built a nunnery for Franciscan nuns, which stood him in above thirty thousand ducats, and he left for the maintenance of the nuns two thousand ducats yearly, with obligation of some Masses to be said in the church every year for his soul after his decease.

It is ordinary for the friars to visit the devoted nuns, and to spend whole days with them, hearing their music, feeding on their sweetmeats, and for this purpose they have many chambers which they call locutorios, to talk in, with wooden bars between the nuns and them, and in these chambers are tables for the friars to dine at, and while they dine the nuns recreate them with their voices. Gentlemen and citizens give their daughters to be brought up in these nunneries, where they are taught to make all sorts of conserves and preserves, all sorts of needlework, all sorts of music, which is so exquisite in that city that I dare be bold to say that the people are drawn to their churches more for the delight of the music than for any delight in the service of God. More, they teach these young children to act like players; and to entice the people to their churches, they make these children act short dialogues in their choirs, richly attiring them with men's and women's apparel, especially upon Midsummer Day, and the eight days before their Christmas. These are so gallantly performed that there have been many factious strifes and single combats – some were in my time – for defending which of these nunneries most excelled in music and in the training up of children. No delights are wanting in that city abroad in the world, nor in their churches, which should be the house of God, and the soul's, not the senses' delight.

The gallants of this city shew themselves some on horseback, and most in coaches, daily about four of the clock in the afternoon in a pleasant shady field called la Alameda, full of trees and walks, somewhat like unto our Moorfields, where do meet as constantly as the merchants upon our exchange about two thousand coaches, full of gallants, ladies, and citizens, to see and to be seen, to court and to be courted. The gentlemen have their train of blackamoor slaves, gallant liveries, heavy with gold and silver lace, with silk stockings on their black legs, and roses on their feet, and swords by their sides. The ladies also carry their train by their coach's side of such jet-like damsels as before have been mentioned for their light apparel, who with their bravery and white mantles over them seem to be, as the Spaniard saith, "mosca en leche," a fly in milk. . . .

At this meeting are carried about many sorts of sweetmeats and papers of comfits to be sold, and for relish a cup of cool water, which is cried about in curious glasses, to cool the blood of those love-hot gallants. But many times these meetings sweetened with conserves and comfits have sour sauce at the end, for jealousy will not suffer a lady to be courted, no, nor sometimes to be spoken to, but puts fury into the violent hand to draw a sword or dagger and to stab or murder whom he was jealous of.

J. Eric S. Thompson, ed., *Thomas Gage's Travels in the New World* (Norman: University of Oklahoma Press, 1958), 68–74.

4. Last requests of Juana Guancapamba, 1767.

In the name of God Amen. I, Juana Guancapamba, sick of body but sane of mind, draw up these requests to ease my soul, and when God our Lord is ready to take me from this life, that my body be buried in the parish of San Sebastian, next to the Holy Water font, and that the priest accompany my body with the cross on high and that two masses be said for me, one a sung mass and the other a mass recited with my body present. . . .

And I hereby leave half a plot of land, which I own and inherited from my sister, Isabel Criolla, deceased, to be sold to pay for my funeral. . . .

I owe 12 reales to Madalena, the Indian pulpera [storeowner] in Espinosa and I here order that this be paid.

I owe 4 reales to Marica. I order it be paid.

That half a real be given as charity to Saint Sebastian.

That another half real be given to the Virgin of Gracia.

And that if any money be left over, it be saved for me, to be used for the prayers on the anniversary of my death.

I have served as steward [Priosta] of the Confraternity of San Sebastian for ten years. . . .

I am a member of the Confraternity of the glorious San Salvador. I ask that they accompany my body [in the funeral] with their banner.

I have been a member of the Confraternity of the Virgen de los Remedios. I ask and beseech the officers that they accompany my body with their banner and candles.

I have been a member of the Confraternity of the glorious Saint Nicolas. I ask the officers that they accompany my body as is their regular custom.

I have been a member of the Confraternity of the Virgin del Rosario and I ask that they accompany my body as is their regular custom.

Miguel Guapriana and his wife owe me 2 reales.

Magdalena Cortes owes me 1 real. I ask that it be collected.

And the wife of Ornillo owes me 1 real.

Anton Cuerdar owes me half a real.

And the Obanda woman owes me half a real. I ask that it be collected.

And Juan Sanchez owes me one real. I ask that it be collected.

I don't remember owing anything else to anyone nor having anyone else owing me. If anything else come forward, pay it.

I leave three small old pots and two jars and two hens and six Guinea pigs. All this may my son Francisco Elias have and enjoy with my blessing.

The house in which I have lived for the last 60 years belongs to Francisco Chas, for it belonged to his parents. I have no interest in it as it is publicly known.

This account to serve as a last will and testament was drawn up on 13 May 1657, in the presence of Jacinto Mendez Ramos, notary and Domingo Guarniso. Witnessed by Francisco Mendez Ramos.

Archivo Nacional de Historia, Quito, Tierras, 1765, caja 85, cited in Alfonso Anda Aguirre, *Indios y negros bajo el dominio español en Loja* (Quito: Ediciones Abya-Yala 1993), 69–71.

5. Letter from the Countess de Galve to the Duchess del Infantado y Pastrana, Marchioness del Cenete. Mexico City, 28 May 1693.

Most excellent lady,

My lady, sister-in-law, and lifelong friend, in the last packet boat I wrote you and now I do so again because of the great pleasure I take in it and also for the news I wish to have of your health. I shall be happy if it is as good as I wish and if it is the same with my brother-in-law and nephews, whose hands I kiss. My husband places himself at your feet. I remain to serve you in everything, though very ill, because the recurrence of my illness has caused me headaches to severe that I am prevented from writing in my own hand. You will therefore excuse its being written in someone else's hand. Now, I shall go on to tell you that I am sending the money, as you have ordered me, by don Pablo Vizarrón. You can rely on him whenever you want to send something. I am very pleased to have successfully served you, and by what you tell me about my not sending you something that may break.

For this reason, no pottery is coming. I am only sending you an image of [the Virgin of] Guadalupe, painted from the original, since you are so devoted to the Lady, and some chocolate. I shall be happy if it is to your liking. With that, you will not notice that the fans I am sending you are not very good. Since the boat from China did not come this year, nothing was to be found. You will thus pardon the insignificance of the gift. When I come, I shall try to bring some of the best.

I wish the day had already arrived when we might see one another in that court. In the meantime, do not fail to order me, since you know I am very much yours. May Our Lord protect you, my lady and sister-in-law, the many years I wish. Mexico City. 28 May 1693.

My love, here is the list from the raffles, if it would please you to entertain yourself reading it and so that you will know that I am a businesswoman. The money I asked for is being used for the cacao so that don Pablo Viazarrón can sell it and send you an accounting. Because he is my husband's agent and a very reputable man, I sent it to him, saying that he should do what you order him to. I shall be pleased if you like this arrangement, since that is my wish. I am as always, and there is nothing new here. Everything is quiet.

Most excellent lady, your sister-in-law and surest friend kisses your hands.

Gelvira

Most excellent lady duchess, the Duchess del Infantado y Pastrana, Marchioness del Cenete, my lady, sister-in-law and friend,

Record of the pieces of crystal sent to be sold with the highest prices at which they could be appraised, which serve as a guide for the raffle (although with some variation)

A small worked cup decorated with red and green enamel, appraised at 80 pesos.

Another cup with a tiny decoration at the tip of its base, appraised at 74 pesos.

A small, smooth crystal shield with a gilt base and handles, appraised at 64 pesos.

A small, worked dicebox without any decoration, appraised at 120 pesos.

Another dicebox with a lid and handles, with some decoration, appraised at 100 pesos.

A goblet from Carmona [Spain] with base, appraised at 200 pesos.

A water jug with gilt handle and base with some inlaid pearls and rubies, appraised at 100 pesos.

A round flask with gilt, black enamel mouth, appraised at 12 pesos.

Another, more flat-nosed crystal flask, appraised at 10 pesos.

A crystal cask without a lid, appraised at 10 pesos.

Another little crystal cask with a lid to one side, appraised at 10 pesos.

Three small crystal cases without decoration, appraised at 23 pesos each, which comes to 72 pesos.

A round, flat-nosed, decorated crystal box, appraised at 14 pesos.

A long, decorated crystal box, appraised at 12 pesos.

Inside the box, another small worked crystal box with small black enamel metal springs and four turquoises, appraised at 26 pesos.

Another decorated crystal box in the form of a heart, appraised at 16 pesos.

A tiny crystal chestnut, appraised at 12 pesos.

Two small crystal casks with taps, appraised at 20 pesos.

A crystal globe, appraised at 14 pesos.

A blue, decorated crystal box, appraised at 10 pesos.

A crystal egg-shaped card with merlon-shaped decoration on which a San Antonio is painted, appraised at 40 pesos.

A pair of drop earrings in the form of eagles with rubies, appraised at 260 pesos.

Another crystal box in the form of a star, appraised at 16 pesos.

An aventurine cask with tap, appraised at 8 pesos.

A small aventurine ark with filigree metal springs, appraised at 10 pesos.

A small aventurine cask, with top decorated with blue enamel and two little chains, appraised at 20 pesos.

The pieces of crystal and aventurine are worth (so it seems) 1,330 pesos according to the appraisal. What resulted from the raffle was 1,479 pesos, so that the amount was increased by 139 pesos above the appraisal.

Meredith D. Dodge and Rick Hendricks, eds., *Two Hearts, One Soul: The Correspondence of the Condesa de Galve, 1688–96* (Albuquerque: University of New Mexico Press, 1993), 139–143.

6. Letter from the Countess de Galve, vicereine of Mexico to her brother, the marquis de Távara. Mexico City, 5 June 1696.

My brother and love of my life and heart:

On the occasion of my husband's dispatching this packet boat, I tell you how excited I am to have received two letters from you. The most recent is from 28 June. Because you are well, all else is less important. I deeply regret that you are still stuck in that remote corner. I trust in God that we will all soon be able to hold our heads high.

God has seen fit for us to see one another with this fleet. I assure that I am mad with joy. Through the way is difficult and very dangerous, I have no fear; rather my desire is to get on with it. I believe our departure from here will be around the first of May and from Veracruz around the middle of June.

I trust in God that we shall see one another this year. For this reason, I do not plan to write at length. We are very hurried, as much to dispatch this packet boat as to make the preparations for our journey. We shall see each other and speak of the nine years here that we have not seen one another.

Here I want to say that the death of Brigida [de España, a chambermaid] is a shame. She married, and not to my satisfaction. She gave birth to a girl and died during childbirth. I have the child in my home and am struggling to understand her. She is more than a year old, and I have to carry her nursing. She is as ugly as can be, but very much the joker.

There is nothing new here to tell you about. If there is, it will be when my husband leaves office. I shall carry this news to you there, but what I shall not take is my maidservants.

There is a great rush to marry. One young woman you do not know married, as did one from my chamber. Two others are about to marry. One is doña Manuela [Rojo, a lady-in-waiting in the Galve household], and I greatly regret it because she will remain here. When we see each other, we shall speak of many things. I ask God that we achieve this. May his majesty protect you for me, love of my life, as is so necessary to me.

She who loves you most and is yours until death.

Meredith D. Dodge and Rick Hendricks, eds., *Two Hearts, One Soul: The Correspondence of the Condesa de Galve, 1688–96* (Albuquerque: University of New Mexico Press, 1993), 156–157.

7. *Teresa de Aldao y Rendón v. Carlos Ortiz de Rozas* for having reneged on his promise to marry her, Buenos Aires, 1746.

How is it that Carlos Ortiz de Rozas spoke the same or similar words [a promise to marry her] when before beginning to court her he knew from various people that a captain of this garrison had previously taken her honor [had sexual relations with her], having given her his word and paper [that is after promising to marry her by oral and written promise]. At the same time Ortiz also knew, because of the complaint filed by her mother or someone else in her family before don Domingo Ortiz de Rozas who was then governor of this province, that don Juan Bautista Agüero, don Pedro Cueli, and Basilio de Pesoa had been exiled from the city because at an unseemly time of night they were found in the house of don Jacinto Aldao. Therefore the defendant should not have given his word of marriage to such a worldly woman, nor should his reputation have permitted it, for in proposing marriage to her he would be obligated, as a man of honor, to fulfill his promise."

Archivo de la Curia Ecclesiatica (Buenos Aires), Legajo 17, Expediente 25, Autos seguidos por D. Jazinto de Aldao en causa de Da. Francisca de Aldao, su hija contra el capitán D. Carlos Jasinto de Rosas, sobre la palabra de casamiento y demas . . ., reproduced in Raul A. Molina, *Historia de los divorcios en el período hispánico* (Buenos Aires: Fuentes históricas y genealógicas argentinas, 1985), 161.

8. Accounts of Carmen Bajo Convent, Quito, 1749–1753.

Money received by the prioress:

Income from annuities [*censos*]	9,812 p 2 r
Weekly money from the haciendas	3,290 p
Gentlemen who have paid for the honor of marching in a procession with the key to the Holy Sacrament:	
Don Bartolomé Pinto	200 p
Don Juan Antonio de Ochoa	100 p
Don Clemente Sánchez	100 p
Payment for expenses of 3 noviates	300 p
A gift from the bishop	113 p
Loan from judge don José Quintana	2,666 p 5 r
A gift from the judge for an ornament	707 p 6 r

During the past four years the administrator of the haciendas has turned over the following funds:

From the sale of old cows	9 p 3 r
From the sale of 7 fanegas [c. 1.5 bushels] of beans and oats	9 p 7 r
One arroba [c. 25 pounds] of sugar	4 p
One arroba of rice	
From the sale of 9 fanegas of oats	11 p
4 arrobas of sugar for the festival of Our Lady of Carmen at 4 pesos per arroba	16 p
Another arroba of sugar	4 p
In milk	9 p 3 r
Another 4 arrobas of sugar	16 p
Plus another 5 arrobas of sugar	20 p
40 pesos in silver	40 p
One hundredweight of rice	
1 arroba of fish	

Brought from the haciendas:

90 fanegas of corn from Caspigazi
225 large bags of potatoes from Caspigazi
925 mule-loads of charcoal

36 fanegas of beans
5 fanegas of beans
3 fanegas of common vetch [alverja]
490 cheeses from Aychapicho
605 large bags of potatoes from Aychapicho
2 fanagas of sweet-pea flour
2 fanegas of oats
14 fanegas of wheat flour

Expenses 1749–1753:

Rations for the nuns for 4 years	8,567 p 5 r
Black sackcloth for each nun's habit	550 p
Fine flannel for 4 tunics for each nun	321 p 5 r
Flannel	163 p 6 r
Printed cotton cloth	160 p 7 r
Three and a half pieces of cambric from Cambrai for veils	42 p
Coarse shirting for the servants	64 p 5 r
Rope-soled shoes	146 p
Salary and tips for the servants	157 p 2 r
Payment to 3 sacristans	153 p
Salary to the washerwomen	60 p
For the barber	48 p
For the harp maker	48 p
To the pharmacy for the purchase of 4 bottles of almond oil	411 p
Other pharmacy charges	140 p 4 r
4 feast days [fiestas] in honor of Our Lady of Carmen	336 p 2 r
4 feast days in honor of Saint Joseph	206 p 2 r
4 feast days in honor of Saint Teresa	304 p 5 r
Money given to beggars	48 p
4 plenary indulgences [jubileos] for the 40 Hours	95 p 1 r
4 plenary indulgences for the Holy Trinity	24 p
Holy Week expenses	140 p
Masses and musicians when the Virgen of Quinche and the Virgen of Guápulo were here	19 p

Bulls for the servants	14 p
Benzoin, civet and other supplies to make cakes or lozenges	170 p
Gifts to the gentleman who marched with the key, to the priests for the talks during Advent, Lent, and religious spiritual exercises	80 p
For the burial of Sister Juana de Dios and the masses in honor of her family and benefactors	121 p
The chaplain's salary	1,880 p
48 mules	828 p
Wax	2,153 p 3 r
Wine	26 p
1 misal	30 p
Gold and silver thread, silk, embroideries, and other material to make flowers and other odds and ends to make scapularies and ribbons	120 p
Repairs made by various artisans	145 p
1 serving bowl of china and some Talavera plates	12 p 6 r
Adornments for an image	12 p
Payment for the wreath of Our Lady of Carmen and the diadem of Saint Joseph	34 p
Sale of the old mostrance to don Bernabé Enríquez and with that silver 4 silver eagles and their coats of arms and 4 small pitchers were made	400 p
Total	18,243 p 5 r

Archivo del Carmen Bajo, Quito, Cuentas de la Madre Francisca María de la Madre de Dios y San Miguel, 1749–1753, legajo 17, reproduced in María del Carmen Luna Tobar, *Historia del Convento del Carmen Bajo* (Quito: Agencia Española de Cooperación Internacional, 1997), 88–91.

9. Letter of Victoria Antonia de Pesoa to her husband, the merchant Fernando Maseira, absent in Paraguay for three years, Buenos Aires, 1754.

My dearest husband Fernando de Maseira,

Dear husband my soul will be most happy if this letter finds you in perfect health. Your son and I are here to serve you although we always feel the weight of your absence. As the years of your absence grow longer, so too does this sentiment. I am only sustained by the hope that God who gives us life give me that we will soon see each other again, and that this will be soon. I didn't send you a letter in the boat because I wasn't sure when it was leaving. I rather send this to you with the priest Don Simón, who will also tell you about everything that has befallen me here. If it hadn't been for Don Juan Arias, we would have lost our house and our servants, for everything was about to be auctioned off. Don Juan Arias has been like a father to me, and I live giving thanks to him. He and my brothers hid our stuff. Doña Sabina has finally been repaid, and you shouldn't worry any more. I will send you the shirts in the next boat if you send me money with which to buy Brittany linen. Don't forget that I have five people to dress, that counting myself we are six, and that we also have to eat. Joaquín sends you word of his little mulatto slave named José Gaspar who was born on 24 December 1753, and who is more beautiful than Manuel. I'm sending you the measurements for the doors and windows that you asked for; you can read the little pieces of paper in which each one is wrapped and will understand where each one is. And try to return as soon as posssible because we are now a large group of people and we have no house to live it. And Joaquín is not learning to read, although I have him in school because I am in the country as much as I'm in town. And about your request that I prevent my father from working on the corner property that you sold him, I haven't done it so that he doesn't think I'm ungrateful, for they are going to begin to build and because we have enough room. My father is fine, although suffering with the shame of my brother's, Fernando, being in jail. Don Bartolo Galban will tell you all the details.

Everyone here at home is fine and we all send you our regards and hope that God protects you for many years. Buenos Aires. 25 January 1754.

Your wife who esteems you and would like to see you.

                                        Vitoria Antonia de Pesoa

[In the margin]

Stop fooling yourself for no one gives us anything free of charge. Don Bartolo has given me nothing for free.

Carlos Mayo and Amalia Lotrubesse de Diaz, *Cartas de una mujer porteña (siglo XVIII)* (La Pampa, Argentina: Universidad Nacional de la Pampa, 1983), 14.

10. Letter of doña Manuela Camacho y Pinto to her lover Don Manuel Bustillo, Cochabamba, 1789.

My most beloved friend of my soul, delight of my sorrow, I received your letter this morning, my love, brought by José Manuel, in which you speak of your health and the hardship that you are suffering. Don't be silly. Don't allow yourself to die or to come to grief over such trifling difficulties. I, who am a woman, could do that, but I haven't and I'm as fresh as a lettuce because it's nothing to me, so great is the love I have for you. I have no other desire but to love you more and more and that you be true to me. So, my love, don't become despondent or worry. They're not going to take me to be tortured and even if they do, they can't accuse me of murdering anyone or of falsifying money, but only that I love you. Yes I love you and I'm true to you and you must have courage and be strong in your love for me and do more to endure all this as I'm doing. And have patience because the day will come, my love, when everything will be better. . . . I don't trust Losada or Maldonado or little Diego because they are all in league with each other, and you shouldn't trust anyone either because the friend who seems to be the most loyal is your enemy. . . . And so I commend you to God, my joy, my heart, my soul, my consolation, and my most beloved master. I commend you to God with whom I remain. I ask that you be guarded many years so that you can comfort me and that we be given the delight that we want as soon as possible. Your true lover wants to be with you and to kiss you. Manuela Camacho loves Manuel Bustillo until death. . . . Goodbye my love.

Archivo General de la Nación (Argentina), Criminales, Legajo 33, Número 6, IX-32-4-5, cited in Susan Migden Socolow, *The Bureaucrats of Buenos Aires, 1769–1810: Amor al Real Servicio* (Durham: Duke University Press, 1987), 200–221.

11. Deposition given by Maria Santos Narvona against Nicolás Bazán, 1798.

Nicolás Bazán, having been accused by Atanasio Pasos of abusing his wife, María Santos Narvona, the latter declares that "... while her husband was absent in the settlement of Nonogasta, Nicolás Bazán came into her house and said to her 'come mount up behind me, let's go to the woods,' and she answered him 'I don't want to go with you, for I am not your wife nor your lover, and if I was when I was single, I no longer am,' and Bazán answered, 'who took this right away from me?' and she responded, 'God and my husband Atanacio'; and then Bazán repeated, 'Didn't I tell you that we were going to mount, because now you're getting me angry, for you did it before and you'll it again'; and she answered 'I already told you that I don't want to,' and hearing this Bazán became furious and he gave her a good slap, telling her again, 'Mount, because I'm now very angry,' and she again repeated that she wasn't going to do it because he wasn't her husband, and she slid off the horse, although he grabbed her by the hair, and having gotten away from him with much effort, she hid behind a loom for weaving hemp, and he came after her, chasing her, with her running around the said loom in order to escape from him because he was after her with a knife in his hands trying to stab her in order to overtake her and rape her, and seeing herself under such a violent attack, she fled toward the kitchen, but he beat her to the door and he grabbed her by the arm, dragged her out of the house up to his horse, and forced her to mount, although she still resisted, taunting him by asking when they would marry, and he told her that she had better mount up because if she didn't do it right now he would take her out and tie her up where everyone would see her; under this threat she got on the horse while he held onto her arm so that he could drag her along, but then a woman who is her neighbor came out, and Bazán went away, and later thinking that she was free of any danger, she went out to the vineyard to gather firewood [with] two children, and when the said Bazán realized that she had gone to the vineyard adjoining the property of Felipe Castro, jumping over a fence which he had and coming upon her, he grabbed her by the arm and said to her that if you don't want to mount up behind me, I'll make you walk to the woods, where you are going to repay me for the times that you betrayed me when you were single, and she answered 'I don't owe you anything,' and then Reducindo Carabajal screamed 'here comes the Alcalde and the priest,' and he answered, 'It doesn't matter to me for I do whatever I like,' and, saying this, he took her into the woods close to the vineyard, and he told her that he was going to cut off her head or her ears and, her hair, and, saying that, he took out this knife, grabbed her by the hair and, trying to cut it off, twisted the wrist of the child who was with her and, in addition to these violent acts, he wounded her on her shoulder with a small slash, telling her that he was giving her an example of what he could do, and to this she repeated that she was not his wife nor his lover, and if she had been his lover before, she wasn't anymore, and in spite of his threats, she escaped and beat him to her house, and back in her house she shouted that because of that devil I've wasted the whole afternoon, but after a while the said Bazán returned to her house, and he said to her 'If you don't do what I want, I'm going to take you out in front of everyone and force you to mount on that duck and they continued to have words until the said Bazán went on his way still threatening her with cutting her ears.'"

Archivo General de la Nación Argentina, Sala IX, Tribunales, Leg. 180, Exp. 28, fs. 2, cited in Eduardo R. Saguier, "Las contradicciones entre el fuero militar y el poder político en el Virreinato del Río de la Plata," *European Review of Latin American and Caribbean Studies*, 56 (June 1994), 72–73.

SUGGESTED FURTHER READING

GENERAL

Silvia Marina Arrom, "Historia de la mujer y de la familia latinoamericanas," *Historia mexicana*, 2 (1992), 379–418.

Pilar Gonzalbo Aizpuru, ed., *Familias novohispanas: Siglos XVI al XIX* (Mexico: El Colegio de México, 1991).

Pilar Gonzalbo Aizpuru, *Las mujeres en la Nueva España: Educación y vida cotidiana* (México: El Colegio de México, 1987).

June E. Hahner, *Women in Latin American History: Their Lives and Views* (Los Angeles: UCLA Latin American Center, 1976).

Elizabeth Anne Kuznesof, "The Construction of Gender in Colonial Latin America," *Colonial Latin American Review*, 1:1–2 (1992), 253–270.

Asunción Lavrin, ed., *Latin American Women: Historical Perspectives* (Westport, Conn.: Greenwood Press, 1978).

Asunción Lavrin, "*Lo femenino*: Women in Colonial Historical Sources," in Francisco Javier Cevallos-Candau et al., eds., *Coded Encounters: Writing, Gender and Ethnicity in Colonial Latin America* (Amherst: University of Massachusetts Press, 1994), 153–176.

Asunción Lavrin, "Women in Spanish American Colonial Society," in Leslie Bethell, ed., *The Cambridge History of Latin America* (Cambridge: Cambridge University Press, 1984), 2:321–355.

Asunción Lavrin and Edith Couturier, "Las mujeres tienen la palabra: Otras voces en la historia colonial de México," *Historia mexicana*, 31:2 (October–December 1981), 278–313.

Laura A. Lewis, "The 'Weakness' of Women and the Feminization of the Indians in Colonial Mexico," *Colonial Latin American Review*, 5:1 (1996), 73–94.

Colin M. MacLachlan and Jaime E. Rodríguez, *The Forging of the Cosmic Race: A Reinterpretation of Colonial Mexico* (Berkeley: University of California Press, 1980).

Josefina Muriel, *Las mujeres de Hispanoamérica: Epoca colonial* (Madrid: Mapfre, 1992).

Ann M. Pescatello, *Power and Pawn: The Female in Iberian Families, Societies and Cultures* (Westport, Conn.: Greenwood Press, 1976).

Maria Odelia Silva Dias, *Power and Everyday Life: The Lives of Working Women in Nineteenth-Century Brazil* (New Brunswick, N.J.: Rutgers University Press, 1995).

IBERIAN WOMEN

León Carlos Alvárez Santalo, *Marginación social y mentalidad en Andalucia occidental: Expósitos en Sevilla (1613–1910)* (Seville: Consejería de Cultura de la Junta de Andalucía, 1980).

Renato Barahona, "Coercion, Sexuality and the Law in Early Modern Spain (1550–1750)" (unpublished paper, 1996).

Renato Barahona, "Courtship, Seduction and Abandonment in Early Modern Spain: The Example of Vizcaya, 1500–1700," in Alain Saint-Saëns, ed., *Sex and Love in Golden Age Spain* (New Orleans: University Press of the South, 1996), 43–55.

Renato Barahona, "Mujeres vazcas, sexualidad y ley en la época moderna (siglos XVI y XVII), in Alain Saint-Saëns, ed., *Historia silenciada de la mujer: La mujer española desde la época medieval hasta la contemporánea* (Madrid: Editorial Complutense, 1996), 79–94.

Jodi Bilinkoff, "Charisma and Controversy: The Case of María de Santa Domingo," in Magdalena S. Sánchez and Alain Saint-Saëns, eds., *Spanish Women in the Golden Age: Images and Realities* (Westport, Conn.: Greenwood Press, 1996), 23–35.

Woodrow Borah and Sherburne Cook, "Marriage and Legitimacy in Mexican Culture: Mexico and California," *California Law Review*, 54:2 (1966), 946–1008.

JoEllen M. Campbell, "Women and Factionalism in the Court of Charles II of Spain," in Magdalena S. Sánchez and Alain Saint-Saëns, eds., *Spanish Women in the Golden Age: Images and Realities* (Westport, Conn.: Greenwood Press, 1996), 109–124.

Ricardo Córdoba de la Llave, "Las relaciones extraconyugales en la sociedad castellana bajomedieval," *Anuario de estudios medievales*, 16 (1986), 571–619.

Alfonso de Cossío y Corral, "El régimen económico del matrimonio en las legislaciones americanas," *Anuario de estudios americanos*, 6 (1949), 501–554.

Edith Couturier, "Women and the Family in Eighteenth-Century Mexico: Law and Practice," *Journal of Family History*, 10:3 (Fall 1985), 294–304.

Heath Dillard, *Daughters of the Reconquest: Women in Castilian Town Society, 1100–1300* (Cambridge: Cambridge University Press, 1984).

André Fernández, "The Repression of Sexual Behavior by the Aragonese Inquisition between 1560 and 1700," *Journal of the History of Sexuality*, 7:4 (April 1997), 469–501.

Enrique Gacto Fernández, "La filiación ílegítima en la historia del derecho español," *Anuario de historia del derecho español*, 41 (1971), 899–944.

Enrique Gacto Fernández, *La filiación no legítima en el derecho histórico español* (Seville: Universidad Hispalense y Universidad de Sevilla, 1969).

Juan García González, "El incumplimiento de las promesas de matrimonio en la historia del derecho español," *Anuario de historia del derecho español*, 23 (1953), 611–642.

Stephen H. Haliczer, "Sexuality and Repression in Counter-Reformation Spain," in Alain Saint-Saëns, ed., *Sex and Love in Golden Age Spain* (New Orleans: University Press of the South, 1996), 81–93.

Eugene H. Korth and Della M. Flusche, "Dowry and Inheritance in Colonial Spanish America: Peninsular Law and Chilean Practice," *The Americas*, 43:4 (April 1987), 395–410.

Linda Lewin, "Natural and Spurious Children in Brazilian Inheritance Law from Colony to Empire: A Methodological Essay," *The Americas*, 48:3 (January 1992), 351–396.

Guillermo F. Margadant, "La familia en el derecho novohispano," in Pilar Gonzalbo Aizpuru, ed., *Familias novohispanas: Siglos XVI al XIX* (Mexico: El Colegio de México, 1991), 27–56.

Carmen Martín Gaite, *Love Customs in Eighteenth-Century Spain* (Berkeley: University of California Press, 1991).

Africa Martínez Medina, *Espacios privados de la mujer en el siglo XVIII* (Madrid: horas y HORAS, 1995).

Geraldine McKendrick and Angus MacKay, "Visionaries and Affective Spirituality during the First Half of the Sixteenth Century," in Anne J. Cruz and Mary Elizabeth Perry, eds., *Culture and Control in Counter-Reformation Spain* (Minneapolis: University of Minnesota Press, 1992), 93–124.

Renée Levine Melammed, "Women in (post-1492) Spanish Crypto-Jewish Society," *Judaism*, 41:2 (Spring 1992), 156–168.

Teresa Ortiz, "From Hegemony to Subordination: Midwives in Early Modern Spain," in Hilary Marland, ed., *The Art of Midwifery: Early Modern Midwives in Europe* (London: Routledge, 1993), 95–114.

José María Ots Capdequí, "Bosquejo histórico de los derechos de la mujer casada en la legislación de Indias," *Revista general de legislación y jurisprudencia*, 132 (1918), 162–182.

Mary Elizabeth Perry, "Behind the Veil: Moriscas and the Politics of Resistance and Survival," in Magdalena S. Sánchez and Alain Saint-Saëns, eds., *Spanish Women in the Golden Age: Images and Realities* (Westport, Conn.: Greenwood Press, 1996), 37–53.

Mary Elizabeth Perry, *Gender and Disorder in Early Modern Seville* (Princeton: Princeton University Press, 1990).

Mary Elizabeth Perry, "Magdalens and Jezebels in Counter-Reformation Spain," in Anne J. Cruz and Mary Elizabeth Perry, eds., *Culture and Control in Counter-Reformation Spain* (Minneapolis: University of Minnesota Press, 1992), 124–144.

Ruth Pike, *Aristocrats and Traders: Sevillian Society in the Sixteenth Century* (Ithaca: Cornell University Press, 1972).

Rosalind Z. Rock, "'Pido y Suplico': Women and the Law in Spanish New Mexico," *New Mexican Historical Review*, 65 (April 1990), 137–144.

Alain Saint-Saëns, "A Case of Gendered Rejection: The Hermitess in Golden Age Spain," in Magdalena S. Sánchez and Alain Saint-Saëns, eds., *Spanish Women in the Golden Age: Images and Realities* (Westport, Conn.: Greenwood Press, 1996), 55–65.

Alain Saint-Saëns, "'It is not a Sin!': Making Love according to the Spaniards in Early Modern Spain," in Alain Saint-Saëns, ed., *Sex and Love in Golden Age Spain* (New Orleans: University Press of the South, 1996), 11–26.

Alain Saint-Saëns, ed., *Sex and Love in Golden Age Spain* (New Orleans: University Press of the South, 1996).

Magdalena S. Sánchez, "Pious and Political Images of a Habsburg Woman at the Court of Philip III (1598–1621)," in Magdalena S. Sánchez and Alain Saint-Saëns, eds., *Spanish Women in the Golden Age: Images and Realities* (Westport, Conn.: Greenwood Press, 1996), 91–107.

María Helena Sánchez Ortega, "Sorcery and Eroticism in Love Magic," in Anne J. Cruz and Mary Elizabeth Perry, eds., *Cultural Encounters: The Impact of the Inquisition in Spain and the New World* (Berkeley: University of California Press, 1991), 58–92.

María Helena Sánchez Ortega, "Woman as Source of 'Evil' in Counter-Reformation Spain," in Anne J. Cruz and Mary Elizabeth Perry, eds., *Culture and Control in Counter-Reformation Spain* (Minneapolis: University of Minnesota Press, 1992), 196–215.

Stuart B. Schwartz, "Pecar en las Colonias: Mentalidades populares, Inquisición, y actitudes hacia la fornicación simple en España, Portugal y las colonias americanas," *Cuadernos de historia moderna*, 18 (1997), 53–67.

Marta V. Vicente, "Images and Realities of Work: Women and Guilds in Early Modern Barcelona," in Magdalena S. Sánchez and Alain Saint-Saëns, eds., *Spanish Women in the Golden Age: Images and Realities* (Westport, Conn.: Greenwood Press, 1996), 128–139.

IBERIAN WOMEN IN AMERICA

Ida Altman, "Emigrants and Society: An Approach to the Background of Colonial Spanish America," *Comparative Studies in Society and History*, 30:1 (January 1988), 170–190.

Ida Altman, *Emigrants and Society: Extremadura and Spanish America in the Sixteenth Century* (Berkeley: University of California Press, 1989).

Analola Burges, "La mujer pobladora en los origenes americanos," *Anuario de estudios americanos*, 29 (1972), 389–444.

Alexandra Parma Cook and Noble David Cook, *Good Faith and Truthful Ignorance: A Case of Transatlantic Bigamy* (Durham, N.C.: Duke University Press, 1991).

Lucia Gálvez, *Mujeres de la conquista* (Buenos Aires: Planeta, 1990).

James Lockhart, *Spanish Peru, 1532–1560: A Social History* (Madison: University of Wisconsin Press, 1968).

Luis Martin, *Daughters of the Conquistadores: Women of the Viceroyalty of Peru* (Dallas: Southern Methodist University Press, 1983).

Ann M. Pescatello, "Ladies and Whores in Colonial Brazil," *Caribbean Review*, 5:2 (April–June 1973), 26–30.

Teresa Piossek Prebisch, *Las conquistadoras: Presencia de la mujer española en América durante el siglo XVI* (self-published, 1989).

Barbara Potthast, "Imagen y realidad de la participación de la mujer española en la conquista rioplatense," in Pedro M. Piñero Ramírez and Christian Wentzlaff-Eggebert, eds., *Sevilla en el imperio de Carlos V: Encrucijada entre dos mundos y dos épocas* (Sevilla: Universidad de Sevilla, 1991), 199–206.

A. J. R. Russell-Wood, "Women and Society in Colonial Brazil," *Journal of Latin American Studies*, 9 (1977), 1–34.

Evelyn Stevens, "Marianismo," in Ann M. Pescatello, *Female and Male in Latin America: Essays* (Pittsburgh: University of Pittsburgh Press, 1973), 89–101.

David J. Weber, *The Spanish Frontier in North America* (New Haven: Yale University Press, 1992).

Before Columbus

Ferdinand Anton, *Woman in Pre-Columbian America* (New York: Abner Schram, 1973).

David Birmingham, *Trade and Conflict in Angola: The Mbundu and Their Neighbours and the Influence of the Portuguese, 1483–1790* (Oxford: Clarendon Press, 1966).

Pedro Carrasco, "Royal Marriages in Ancient Mexico," in H. R. Harvey and Hanns J. Prem, eds., *Explorations in Ethnohistory: Indians of Central Mexico in the Sixteenth Century* (Albuquerque: University of New Mexico Press, 1984), 41–81.

Inga Clendinnen, *Aztecs: An Interpretation* (Cambridge: Cambridge University Press, 1991).

Nancy Farriss, *Maya Society under Colonial Rule: The Collective Enterprise of Sur-*

vival (Princeton: Princeton University Press, 1984).

Adam Jones, "Female Slave-Owners on the Gold Coast: Just a Matter of Money?" in Stephan Palmié, ed., *Slave Cultures and the Cultures of Slavery* (Knoxville: University of Tennessee Press, 1995), 100–111.

Susan Kellogg, "Aztec Inheritance in Sixteenth-Century Mexico City: Colonial Patterns, Prehispanic Influences," *Ethnohistory*, 33:3 (1986), 313–330.

Susan Kellogg, "Cognatic Kinship and Religion: Women in Aztec Society," in J. Kathryn Josserand and Karen Dakin, eds., *Smoke and Mist: Mesoamerican Studies in Memory of Thelma D. Sullivan* (Oxford: BAR International Series, 1998), 666–681.

Cecelia F. Klein, "Fighting with Femininity: Gender and War in Aztec Mexico," in Richard C. Trexler, ed., *Gender Rhetorics: Postures of Dominance and Submission in History* (Binghamton, N.Y.: Medieval and Renaissance Texts and Studies, 1994), 107–146.

Alfredo López Austin, *Cuerpo humano e ideologia: Las concepciones de los antiguos Nahuas*, 2 vols. (Mexico: Universidad Nacional Autónima de Mexico, 1984).

Robert McCaa, "Child Marriage and Complex Families among the Nahuas of Ancient Mexico," *Latin American Population History Bulletin*, 26 (Fall 1994), 2–11.

Yoland Murphy and Robert F. Murphy, *Women of the Forest*, 2nd ed. (New York: Columbia University Press, 1985).

June Nash, "The Aztecs and the Ideology of Male Dominance," *Signs*, 4:2 (1978), 349–362.

Noemí Quezada, "Creencias tradicionales sobre embarazo y parto," *Anales de antropología* (Mexico), 14 (1977), 307–326.

Noemí Quezada, "Métodos anticonceptivos y abortivos tradicionales," *Anales de antropología* (Mexico), 12 (1975), 223–242.

Claire Robertson, "Africa into the Americas?: Slavery and Women, the Family, and the Gender Division of Labor," in Darlene Clark Hines and Barry Gaspar, eds., *More than Chattel: Black Women and Slavery in the Americas* (Bloomington: Indiana University Press, 1996), 3–40.

Claire C. Robertson and Martin A. Klein, eds., *Women and Slavery in Africa* (Madison: University of Wisconsin Press, 1983).

Brenda Rosenbaum, *With Our Heads Bowed: The Dynamics of Gender in a Maya Community* (Albany: Institute for Mesamerican Studies of the State University of New York, 1993).

María Rostworowski de Diaz Canseco, *La mujer en la época prehispánica* (Lima: Instituto de Estudios Peruanos, 1988).

Frank Salomon and George L. Urioste, trans., *The Huarochirí Manuscript: A Testament of Ancient and Colonial Andean Religion* (Austin: University of Texas Press, 1991).

Linda Schele and Mary Ellen Miller, *The Blood of Kings: Dynasty and Ritual in Maya Art* (Fort Worth: Kimbell Art Museum, 1986).

Susan Schroeder, "The First American Valentine: Nahua Courtship and Other Aspects of Family Structuring in Mesoamerica," *Journal of Family History*, 23:4 (October 1998), 341–354.

Irene Silverblatt, *Moon, Sun and Witches: Gender Ideologies and Class in Inca and Colonial Peru* (Princeton: Princeton University Press, 1987).

John Thornton, *Africa and Africans in the Making of the Atlantic World, 1400–1680* (Cambridge: Cambridge University Press, 1992).

CONQUEST AND COLONIZATION

Arthur J. O. Anderson, "Aztec Wives," in Susan Schroeder, Stephanie Wood, and Robert Haskett, eds., *Indian Women of Early Mexico* (Norman: University of Oklahoma Press, 1997), 55–85.

Elinor Burkett, "In Dubious Sisterhood: Class and Sex in Spanish Colonial America," *Latin American Perspectives*, 4:1–2 (1977), 18–26.

Eleonor Burkett, "Indian Women and White Society: The Case of Sixteenth-Century Peru," in Asunción Lavrin, ed., *Latin American Women: Historical Perspectives* (Westport, Conn.: Greenwood Press, 1978), 101–128.

Louise M. Burkhart, "Mexica Women on the Home Front: Housework and Religion in Aztec Mexico," in Susan Schroeder, Stephanie Wood, and Robert Haskett, eds., *Indian Women of Early Mexico* (Norman: University of Oklahoma Press, 1997), 25–54.

Chantal Caillavet, "La artesanía textil en la época colonial: El rol de la producción doméstica en el norte de la Audiencia de Quito," *Cultura* (Quito), 8 (1986), 521–530.

José Cardiel, *Las misiones del Paraguay* (Madrid: Historia 16, 1989).

Pedro Carrasco, "Indian-Spanish Marriages in the First Century of the Colony," in Susan Schroeder, Stephanie Wood, and Robert Haskett, eds., *Indian Women of Early Mexico* (Norman: University of Oklahoma Press, 1997), 87–103.

Pedro Carrasco, "Matrimonios hispano-indios en el primer siglo de la Colonia," in Simposio de Historia de las Mentalidades, *Familia y poder en Nueva España* (Mexico: Instituto Nacional de Antropología e Historia, 1991), 11–21.

Inga Clendinnen, "Yucatec Maya Women and the Spanish Conquest: Role and Ritual in Historical Reconstruction," *Journal of Social History*, 15 (Spring 1982), 427–442.

Sarah L. Cline, "Land Tenure and Land Inheritance in Late Sixteenth-Century Culhuacan," in H. R. Harvey and Hanns J. Prem, eds., *Explorations in Ethnohistory: Indians of Central Mexico in the Sixteenth Century* (Albuquerque: University of New Mexico Press, 1984), 277–309.

Sarah L. Cline, "The Spiritual Conquest Reexamined: Baptism and Christian Marriage in Early Sixteenth-Century Mexico," *Hispanic American Historical Review*, 73:3 (August 1993), 453–480.

Nicholas P. Cushner, *Farm and Factory: The Jesuits and the Development of Agrarian Capitalism in Colonial Quito, 1600–1767* (Albany, N.Y.: SUNY Press, 1982).

Susan M. Deeds, "Double Jeopardy: Indian Women in Jesuit Missions of Nueva Vizcaya," in Susan Schroeder, Stephanie Wood, and Robert Haskett, eds., *Indian Women of Early Mexico* (Norman: University of Oklahoma Press, 1977), 255–272.

Oliver Dunn and James E. Kelley, Jr., eds., *The Diario of Christopher Columbus's First Voyage to America, 1492–1493* (Norman: University of Oklahoma Press, 1989).

Gabriel Guarda Geywitz, "Los cautivos en la guerra de Arauco," *Boletín de la Academia Chilena de la Historia*, 54 (1987), 93–157.

Pilar Gonzalbo Aizpuru, *Historia de la educación en la época colonial: El mundo indígena* (Mexico: El Colegio de México, 1990).

Kevin Gosner, "Women, Rebellion, and the Moral Economy of Maya Peasants in Colonial Mexico," in Susan Schroeder, Stephanie Wood, and Robert Haskett, eds., *Indian Women of Early Mexico* (Norman: University of Oklahoma Press, 1977), 217–230.

Ramón A. Gutiérrez, "A Gendered History of the Conquest of America: A View from New Mexico," in Richard C. Trexler, ed., *Gender Rhetorics: Postures of Dominance and Submission in History* (Binghamton, N.Y.: Medieval and Renaissance Texts and Studies, 1994), 47–63.

Robert Haskett, "Activist or Adulteress? The Life and Struggle of Doña Josefa María of Tepoztlán," in Susan Schroeder, Stephanie Wood, and Robert Haskett, eds., *Indian Women of Early Mexico* (Norman: University of Oklahoma Press, 1997), 145–163.

John Hemming, *Red Gold: The Conquest of the Brazilian Indians, 1500–1760* (Cambridge: Harvard University Press, 1978).

Julia Hirschberg, "Social Experiment in New Spain: A Prosopographical Study of the Early Settlement at Puebla de los Angeles, 1531–1534," *Hispanic American Historical Review*, 59:1 (February 1979), 1–33.

Diane Elizabeth Hopkins, "Ritual, Sodality and Cargo among Andean Women: A Diachronic Perspective," in Albert Meyers and Diane Elizabeth Hopkins, *Manipulating the Saints: Religious Brotherhoods and Social Integration in Postconquest Latin America* (Hamburg: Wayasbah, 1988), 175–195.

Marta Espejo-Ponce Hunt and Matthew Restall, "Work, Marriage, and Status: Maya Women of Colonial Yucatan," in Susan Schroeder, Stephanie Wood, and Robert Haskett, eds., *Indian Women of Early Mexico* (Norman: University of Oklahoma Press, 1977), 231–252.

Catherine J. Julien, "Colonial Perspectives on the Chiriguaná (1528–1574)," in María Susana Cipolletti, ed., *Resistencia y adaptación nativas en las tierras bajas latinoaméricanas* (Quito: Ediciones Abya-Yaya, 1997), 17–76.

Mary Karasch, "Damiana da Cunha: Catechist and *Sertanista*," in David C. Sweet and Gary B. Nash, eds., *Struggle and Survival in Colonial America* (Berkeley: University of California Press, 1981), 102–120.

Susan Kellogg, "From Parallel and Equivalent to Separate but Unequal: Tenochca Mexica Women, 1500–1700," in Susan Schroeder, Stephanie Wood, and Robert Haskett, eds., *Indian Women of Early Mexico* (Norman: University of Oklahoma Press, 1977), 123–143.

Susan Kellogg, "Kinship and Social Organization in Early Colonial Tenochtitlán," in Ronald Spores, ed., *Ethnohistory: Supplement to the Handbook of Middle American Indians* (Austin: University of Texas Press, 1986), 103–121.

Susan Kellogg, *Law and the Transformation of Aztec Culture, 1500–1700* (Norman: University of Oklahoma Press, 1995).

Susan Kellogg, "The Social Organization of Households among the Tenochca Mexico before and after Conquest," in Robert S. Santley and Kenneth G. Hirth, eds., *Prehispanic Domestic Units in Western Mesoamerica: Studies of the Household, Compound, and Residence* (Boca Raton: CRC Press, 1993), 207–224.

Jacques Lafaye, *Quetzalcóatl and Guadalupe: The Formation of Mexican National Consciousness, 1531–1813* (Chicago: University of Chicago Press, 1974).

Luis A. León, "La mujer indígena en el régimen laboral incáico y colonial del reino y de la real audiencia de Quito," *América indígena*, 35 (November 1973), 539–558.

Peggy Liss, *Mexico under Spain, 1521–1556: Society and the Origins of Nationality* (Chicago: University of Chicago Press, 1975).

James Lockhart, *The Nahuas after Conquest: A Social and Cultural History of the Indians of Central Mexico, Sixteenth through Eighteenth Centuries* (Stanford: Stanford University Press, 1992).

June Nash, "Aztec Women: The Transition from Status to Class to Empire and Colony," in Mona Etienne and Eleonore Leacock, eds., *Women and Colonization: Anthropological Perspectives* (New York: Praeger, 1980), 134–148.

Leslie S. Offutt, "Women's Voices from the Frontier: San Estevan de Nueva Tlaxcala in the Late Eighteenth Century," in Susan Schroeder, Stephanie Wood, and Robert Haskett, eds., *Indian Women of Early Mexico* (Norman: University of Oklahoma Press, 1977), 273–289.

Roberto Quevedo, "La mestiza Doña Isabel Venegas," *Historia Paraguaya*, 20 (1983), 189–219.

María Rostworowski de Diaz Canseco, *Doña Francisca Pizarro: Una ilustre mestiza, 1534–1598* (Lima: Instituto de Estudios Peruanos, 1989).

Frank Salomon, "Indian Women of Early Colonial Quito as Seen through

Their Testaments," *The Americas*, 44:3 (January 1988), 325–341.

Susan Schroeder, Stephanie Wood, and Robert Haskett, eds., *Indian Women of Early Mexico* (Norman: University of Oklahoma Press, 1997).

William L. Sherman, *Forced Native Labor in Sixteenth-Century Central America* (Lincoln: University of Nebraska Press, 1979).

Irene Silverblatt, "'The Universe has turned inside out . . . There is no justice for us here': Andean Women under Spanish Rule," in Mona Etienne and Eleonore Leacock, eds., *Women and Colonization: Anthropological Perspectives* (New York: Praeger, 1980), 149–185.

Susan Migden Socolow, "Spanish Captives in Indian Society: Cultural Contact along the Argentine Frontier, 1600–1835," *Hispanic American Historical Review*, 72:1 (February 1992), 73–99.

Lisa Mary Sousa, "Women and Crime in Colonial Oaxaca: Evidence of Complementary Gender Roles in Mixtec and Zapotec Societies," in Susan Schroeder, Stephanie Wood, and Robert Haskett, eds., *Indian Women of Early Mexico* (Norman: University of Oklahoma Press, 1977), 199–214.

Ronald Spores, "Mixteca *Cacicas*: Status, Wealth, and the Political Accommodation of Native Elite Women in Early Colonial Oaxaca," in Susan Schroeder, Stephanie Wood, and Robert Haskett, eds., *Indian Women of Early Mexico* (Norman: University of Oklahoma Press, 1977), 185–197.

Ward Stavig, *Amor y violencia sexual: Valores indígenas en la sociedad colonial* (Lima: Instituto de Estudios Peruanos and University of South Florida, 1996).

Ward Stavig, "'Living in Offense of Our Lord': Indigenous Sexual Values and Marital Life in the Colonial Crucible," *Hispanic American Historical Review*, 75:4 (November 1995), 597–622.

Verena Stolcke, "Conquered Women," *Report on the Americas*, 24:5 (February 1991), 23–28.

Verena Stolcke, "Mujeres invadidas: La sangre de la conquista de America," in Stolcke, ed., *Mujeres invadidas: La sangre de la conquista de América* (Madrid: horas y HORAS, 1993), 29–45.

David G. Sweet, "Francisca: Indian Slave," in David G. Sweet and Gary B. Nash, eds., *Struggle and Survival in Colonial America* (Berkeley: University of California Press, 1981), 274–291.

Stephanie Wood, "Matters of Life at Death: Nahuatl Testaments of Rural Women, 1589–1801," in Susan Schroeder, Stephanie Wood, and Robert Haskett, eds., *Indian Women of Early Mexico* (Norman: University of Oklahoma Press, 1997), 165–182.

Ann Zulawski, "Social Differentiation, Gender, and Ethnicity: Urban Indian Women in Colonial Bolivia, 1640–1725," *Latin American Research Review*, 25:2 (1990), 93–114.

Ann Zulawski, *"They Eat from Their Labor": Work and Social Change in Colonial Bolivia* (Pittsburgh: University of Pittsburgh Press, 1995).

Women and Slavery

Solange Alberro, "Juan de Morga and Gertrudis de Escobar: Rebellious Slaves," in David G. Sweet and Gary B. Nash, eds., *Struggle and Survival in Colonial America* (Berkeley: University of California Press, 1981), 165–188.

Hilary McD. Beckles, *Natural Rebels: A Social History of Enslaved Black Women in Barbados* (New Brunswick, N.J.: Rutgers University Press, 1989).

Frederick P. Bowser, *The African Slave in Colonial Peru, 1524–1650* (Stanford: Stanford University Press, 1974).

Frederick P. Bowser, "The Free Person of Color in Mexico City and Lima: Manumission and Opportunity, 1580–1650," in Stanley L. Engerman and Eugene D. Genovese, *Race and Slavery in the Western Hemisphere: Quantitative Studies* (Princeton: Princeton University Press, 1975), 331–368.

Barbara Bush, *Slave Women in Caribbean Society, 1650–1838* (Bloomington: Indiana University Press, 1989).

Patrick Carroll, *Blacks in Colonial Veracruz* (Austin: University of Texas Press, 1991).

Dora Estela Celton, "Fecundidad de las esclavas en la Córdoba colonial," *Revista de la Junta Provincial Histórica* (Córdoba), 15 (1993), 29–48.

R. Douglas Cope, *The Limits of Racial Domination: Plebian Society in Colonial Mexico City, 1660–1720* (Madison: University of Wisconsin Press, 1994).

María Elena Cortés J., "El matrimonio y la familia negra en las legislaciones civil y eclesiástica coloniales: Siglos XVI–XIX," in Seminario de Historia de las Mentalidades, *El placer de pecar y el afán de normar* (Mexico: Instituto Nacional de Antropología e Historia, 1987), 217–248.

Philip D. Curtin, *The Atlantic Slave Trade: A Census* (Madison: University of Wisconsin Press, 1969).

Della M. Flusche and Eugene H. Korth, *Forgotten Females: Women of African and Indian Descent in Colonial Chile, 1535–1800* (Detroit: Blaine Ethridge, 1983).

Arlette Gautier, "Les esclaves femmes aux Antilles françaises, 1635–1848," *Historical Reflections/Réflexions Historiques*, 10:3 (Fall 1983), 409–451.

Marta B. Goldberg and Silvia C. Mallo, "La población africana en Buenos Aires y su campaña: Formas de vida y de subsistencia," *Temas de Africa* (Buenos Aires), 2 (1993), 15–69.

Kimberly S. Hanger, *Bounded Lives, Bounded Places: Free Black Society in Colonial New Orleans, 1769–1803* (Durham, N.C.: Duke Uuniversity Press, 1997).

Kimberly S. Hanger, "'Free Like You': Free Black Women's Resistance to Racial and Gender Inequities in Spanish New Orleans, 1769–1803" (unpublished paper, 1996).

B. W. Higman, "African and Creole Slave Family Patterns in Trinidad," *Journal of Family History*, 3:2 (Summer 1978), 163–180.

Christine Hünefeldt, *Paying the Price of Freedom: Family and Labor among Lima's Slaves, 1800–1854* (Berkeley: University of California Press, 1994).

Lyman L. Johnson, "Manumission in Colonial Buenos Aires, 1776–1810," *Hispanic American Historical Review*, 59:2 (May 1979), 258–279.

Herbert S. Klein, "Blacks," in Louisa S. Hoberman and Susan M. Socolow, eds., *The Countryside in Colonial Latin America* (Albuquerque: University of New Mexico Press, 1996), 167–186.

Edgar F. Love, "Marriage Patterns of Persons of African Descent in a Colonial Mexico City Parish," *Hispanic American Historical Review*, 51:1 (February 1971), 79–91.

Alida C. Metcalf, "Searching for the Slave Family in Colonial Brazil: A Reconstruction from São Paulo," *Journal of Family History*, 16:3 (1991), 283–297.

Rhoda E. Reddock, "Women and Slavery in the Caribbean: A Feminist Perspective," *Latin American Perspectives*, 12:1 (Winter 1985), 63–80.

Eduardo R. Saguier, "La fuga esclava como resistencia rutinaria y cotidiana en el Buenos Aires del siglo XVIII," *Revista de Humanidades y Ciencias Sociales* (Santa Cruz, Bolivia), 1:2 (December 1995), 115–184.

Stuart B. Schwartz, "The Manumission of Slaves in Colonial Brazil: Bahia, 1648–1745," *Hispanic American Historical Review*, 54:4 (November 1974), 603–635.

Stuart B. Schwartz, *Sugar Plantations in the Formation of Brazilian Society: Bahia, 1550–1835* (Cambridge: Cambridge University Press, 1985).

Fernando Winfield Capitaine, comp., *Esclavos en el Archivo Notarial de Xalapa, Veracruz, 1668–1699* (Jalapa: Universidad Veracruzana, 1984).

WOMEN, MARRIAGE, AND THE FAMILY

Kenneth J. Andrien, *Crisis and Decline: The Viceroyalty of Peru in the Seventeenth Century* (Albuquerque, 1985).

Carmen Arretx, Rolando Mellafe, and Jorge L. Somoza, *Demografía histórica en América latina: Fuentes y métodos* (San José, Costa Rica, 1983).

Silvia M. Arrom, "Marriage Patterns in Mexico City, 1811," *Journal of Family History*, 3:4 (Winter 1978), 376–391.

Jacques A. Barbier, "Elites and Cadres in Bourbon Chile," *Hispanic American Historical Review*, 52:3 (August 1972), 410–425.

Jacques A. Barbier, *Reform and Politics in Bourbon Chile, 1755–1796* (Ottawa: University of Ottawa Press, 1980).

Jackie R. Booker, *Veracruz Merchants, 1770–1829: A Mercantile Elite in Late Bourbon and Early Independent Mexico* (Boulder: Westview Press, 1993).

Peter Boyd-Bowman, *Indice geobiográfico de 40,000 pobladores españoles de*

América en el siglo XVI, vol. 1: *1493–1519* (Bogotá: Instituto Caro y Cuervo, 1964).

Richard Boyer, "Honor among Plebeians," in Lyman L. Johnson and Sonya Lipsett-Rivera, eds., *The Faces of Honor: Sex, Shame and Violence in Colonial Latin America* (Albuquerque: University of New Mexico Press, 1998), 152–178.

Richard Boyer, *Lives of the Bigamists: Marriage, Family, and Community in Colonial Mexico* (Albuquerque: University of New Mexico Press, 1995).

Richard Boyer, "Women, *La Mala Vida*, and the Politics of Marriage," in Asunción Lavrin, ed., *Sexuality and Marriage in Colonial Latin America* (Lincoln: University of Nebraska Press, 1989), 252–286.

David A. Brading, *Miners and Merchants in Bourbon Mexico, 1763–1810* (Cambridge: Cambridge University Press, 1971).

David A. Brading and Celia Wu, "Population Growth and Crisis: León, 1720–1860," *Journal of Latin American Studies*, 5:1 (May 1973), 1–36.

Thomas Calvo, "Matrimonio, iglesia y sociedad en el occidente de México: Zamora (siglos XVII a XIX)," in Pilar Gonzalbo Aizpuru, ed., *Familias novohispanas: Siglos XVI al XIX* (Mexico: El Colegio de México, 1991), 101–108.

Thomas Calvo, *La Nueva Galicia en los siglos XVI y XVII* (Guadalajara: El Colegio de Jalisco-CEMCA, 1989).

Thomas Calvo, "The Warmth of the Hearth: Seventeenth-Century Guadalajara Families," in Asunción Lavrin, ed., *Sexuality and Marriage in Colonial Latin America* (Lincoln: University of Nebraska Press, 1989), 287–312.

Marcelo Carmagnani, "Demografía y sociedad: La estructura social de los centros mineros del norte de México, 1600–1720," *Historia mexicana*, 21:3 (January–March 1972), 442–444.

Carmen Castañeda, "La formación de la pareja y el matrimonio," in Pilar Gonzalbo Aizpuru, ed., *Familias novohispanas: Siglos XVI al XIX* (Mexico: El Colegio de México, 1991), 73–90.

Kátia da Costa Bezerra, "'Pernambuco illustrado pelo sexo feminino': A condição feminina no relato de Dom Domingos Loreto Couto," *Colonial Latin American Review*, 6:1 (1997), 59–69.

Edith Couturier, "The Letters of the Countess of Miravalle and the Question of Colonial Women's Biography" (unpublished paper, 1994).

Keith A. Davies, *Landowners in Colonial Peru* (Austin: University of Texas Press, 1984).

Gonzalo de Doblas, "Memoria histórica, geográfica, política y económica sobre la Provincia de Misiones de indios guaraníes," in Pedro de Angelis, ed., *Colección de obras y documentos relativos a la historia antigua y moderna de las provincias del Río de la Plata* (Buenos Aires: Plus Ultra, 1970), 5:32.

Guiomar Dueñas Vargas, *Los hijos del pecado: Ilegitimidad y vida familiar en la Santafé de Bogotá colonial* (Bogotá: Editorial Universidad Nacional, 1997).

Guiomar Dueñas Vargas, "Sociedad, familia y género en Santafé, Nueva Granada, a finales de la colonia," *Latin American Population History Bulletin*, 25 (Spring 1994), 2–22.

Dolores Enciso Rojas, "La legislación sobre el delito de bigamía y su aplicación en Nueva España," in Seminario de Historia de las Mentalidades, *El placer de pecar y el afán de normar* (Mexico: Instituto Nacional de Antropología e Historia, 1987), 249–294.

Dolores Enciso Rojas, "Tres matronas del siglo XVIII y su influencia en la vida conyugal de los hijos," in Simposio de Historia de las Mentalidades, *Familia y poder en Nueva España* (Mexico: Instituto Nacional de Antropología e Historia, 1991), 143–154.

María del Carmen Ferreyra, "El matrimonio en Córdoba durante el siglo XVII: Algunas referencias demográficas," *Cuadernos de Historia* (Córdoba), 1 (1994), 5–21.

Robert J. Ferry, *The Colonial Elite of Early Caracas: Formation and Crisis, 1567–1767* (Berkeley: University of California Press, 1989).

Alberto Flores Galindo and Magdalena Chocano, "Las Cargas del Sacramento," *Revista Andina*, 2:2 (December 1984), 403–434.

Ramón A. Gutiérrez, "Honor Ideology, Marriage Negotiation, and Class-Gender Domination in New Mexico, 1690–1846," *Latin American Perspectives*, 12:1 (Winter 1985), 81–104.

Robert Himmerich y Valencia, *The Encomenderos of New Spain, 1521–1555* (Austin: University of Texas Press, 1991).

Ann Hagerman Johnson, "The Impact of Market Agriculture on Family and Household Structure in Nineteenth-Century Chile," *Hispanic American Historical Review*, 58:4 (November 1978), 625–648.

Lyman L. Johnson and Sonya Lipsett-Rivera, eds., *The Faces of Honor: Sex, Shame and Violence in Colonial Latin America* (Albuquerque: University of New Mexico Press, 1998).

John L. Kessell, ed., *Remote beyond Compare: Letters of don Diego de Vargas to His Family from New Spain and New Mexico, 1675–1706* (Albuquerque, University of New Mexico Press, 1989).

John E. Kicza, *Colonial Entrepreneurs: Families and Business in Bourbon Mexico City* (Albuquerque: University of New Mexico Press, 1983).

Elizabeth Anne Kuznesof, "Household Composition and Headship as Related to Changes in Mode of Production: São Paulo, 1765 to 1836," *Comparative Studies in Society and History*, 22:1 (January 1980), 79–109.

Elizabeth Anne Kuznesof, "The Role of the Female-Headed Household in Brazilian Modernization: São Paulo, 1765 to 1836," *Journal of Social History*, 13 (Summer 1980), 589–613.

Doris M. Ladd, *The Mexican Nobility at Independence, 1780–1826* (Austin: University of Texas Press, 1976).

Frédérique Langue, "El círculo de las alianzas: Estructuras familiares y estrategias económicas de la élite mantuana (siglo XVIII)," *Boletín de la*

Academia Nacional de la Historia (Caracas), 78 (1995), 97–121.

Asunción Lavrin, ed., *Sexuality and Marriage in Colonial Latin America* (Lincoln: University of Nebraska Press, 1989).

Asunción Lavrin and Edith Couturier, "Dowries and Wills: A View of Women's Socioeconomic Role in Colonial Guadalajara and Puebla, 1640–1790," *Hispanic American Historical Review*, 59:2 (May 1979), 280–304.

Sonya Lipsett-Rivera, "A Slap in the Face of Honor," in Lyman L. Johnson and Sonya Lipsett-Rivera, eds., *The Faces of Honor: Sex, Shame and Violence in Colonial Latin America* (Albuquerque: University of New Mexico Press, 1998), 179–200.

Verena Martínez Alier, *Marriage, Class and Colour in Nineteenth-Century Cuba: A Study of Racial Attitudes and Sexual Values in a Slave Society* (Cambridge: Cambridge University Press, 1974).

Carlos A. Mayo, María A. Diez, and Carmen S. Cantera, "Amor, ausencia y destitución: El drama de Victoria Antonia de Pesoa," *Investigaciones y ensayos*, 43 (January–December 1993), 321–335.

Carlos A. Mayo and Amalia Lotrubesse de Díaz, *Cartas de una mujer porteña (Siglo XVIII)* (La Pampa: Universidad Nacional de la Pampa, 1983).

Claude Mazet, "Population et société a Lima aux XVIe et XVIIe siècles," *Cahiers des Amériques Latines*, 13–14 (1976), 51–100.

Robert McCaa, "Gustos de los padres, inclinaciones de los novios y reglas de una feria nupcial colonial: Parral, 1770–1814," *Historia mexicana*, 40:4 (April–June 1991), 579–614.

Robert McCaa, "Marriageways in Mexico and Spain, 1500–1900," *Continuity and Change*, 9:1 (May 1994), 11–43.

Robert McCaa, "Tratos nupciales: La constitución de uniones formales e informales en México y España, 1500–1900," in Pilar Gonzalbo Aizpuru and Cecilia Rabell Romero, eds., *Familia y vida privada en la historia de iberoamérica* (Mexico: El Colegio de México, 1996), 21–57.

Robert McCaa, "La viuda viva del Mexico borbónico: Sus voces, variedades y vejaciones," in Pilar Gonzalbo Aizpuru, ed., *Familias novohispanas: siglos XVI al XIX* (Mexico: El Colegio de México, 1991), 299–324.

Eni de Mesquita Samara, "Mulheres que 'fizeram a América,'" *Populações* (São Paulo), 3 (1996), 1–3.

Alida C. Metcalf, *Family and Frontier in Colonial Brazil: Santana de Parnaíba, 1580–1822* (Berkeley: University of California Press, 1992).

Muriel Nazarri, *Disappearance of the Dowry: Women, Families, and Social Change in São Paulo, Brazil, 1600–1900* (Stanford: Stanford University Press, 1991).

Muriel Nazarri, "Parents and Daughters: Change in the Practice of Dowry in São Paulo (1600–1770)," *Hispanic American Historical Review*, 70:4 (November 1990), 639–665.

Maria Beatriz Nizza da Silva, "Divorce in Colonial Brazil: The Case of São

Paulo," in Asunción Lavrin, ed., *Sexuality and Marriage in Colonial Latin America* (Lincoln: University of Nebraska Press, 1989), 313–340.

Sergio Ortega Noriega, "El discurso teológico de Santo Tomás de Aquino sobre el matrimonio, la familia y los comportamientos sexuales," in Seminario de Historia de las Mentalidades, *El placer de pecar y el afán de normar* (Mexico: Instituto Nacional de Antropología e Historia, 1987), 15–78.

Juan Javier Pescador, "La familia Fagoaga y los matrimonios en la ciudad de México en el siglo XVIII," in Pilar Gonzalbo Aizpuru, ed., *Familias novohispanas: Siglos XVI al XIX* (Mexico: El Colegio de México, 1991), 203–226.

Cecilia Andrea Rabell, "Estructuras de la población y características de los jefes de los grupos domésticos en la ciudad de Antequera (Oaxaca), 1777," in Pilar Gonzalbo Aizpuru, ed., *Familias novohispanas: Siglos XVI al XIX* (Mexico: El Colegio de México, 1991), 273–298.

Susan E. Ramírez, *Provincial Patriarchs: Land Tenure and the Economics of Power in Colonial Peru* (Albuquerque: University of New Mexico Press, 1986).

Donald Ramos, "City and Country: The Family in Minas Gerais, 1804–1838," *Journal of Family History*, 3:4 (Winter 1978), 361–375.

Donald Ramos, "Marriage and the Family in Colonial Vila Rica," *Hispanic American Historical Review*, 55:2 (May 1975), 200–225.

Donald Ramos, "Single and Married Women in Vila Rica, Brazil, 1754–1838," *Journal of Family History*, 16:3 (Fall 1991), 261–282.

Daisy Rípodas Ardana, "Una salteña, 'fiscala' del Consejo de Indias: Doña María Josefa de Asteguieta (1745–1779)," *Boletín del Instituto San Felipe y Santiago de Estudios Históricos de Salta*, 41 (1992), 47–56.

James S. Saeger, "Eighteenth-Century Guaycuruan Missions in Paraguay," in Susan E. Ramírez, ed., *Indian-Religious Relations in Colonial Spanish America* (Syracuse: Syracuse University Press, 1989), 55–86.

Bernd Schröter, "Acerca de la posición de la mujer en el contexto del matrimonio en una región fronteriza de la América hispánica a fines del período colonial: Resultados y desiderata," in Susana Menéndez and Barbara Potthast, eds., *Mujer y familia en América Latina, siglos XVIII–XX*, (Malaga: AHILA, 1996), 69–95.

John Frederick Schwaller, "La identidad sexual: Familia y mentalidades a fines del siglo XVI," in Pilar Gonzalbo Aizpuru, ed., *Familias novohispanas: Siglos XVI al XIX* (Mexico: El Colegio de México, 1991), 59–72.

Stuart B. Schwartz, *Sovereignty and Society in Colonial Brazil: The High Court of Bahia and Its Judges, 1609–1751* (Berkeley: University of California Press, 1973).

Patricia Seed, "The Church and the Patriarchal Family: Marriage Conflicts in Sixteenth- and Seventeenth-Century New Spain," *Journal of Family History*, 10:3 (Fall 1985), 284–293.

Patricia Seed, "Marriage Promises and the Value of a Women's Testimony in Colonial Mexico," *Signs*, 13:2 (1988), 252–276.

Patricia Seed, *To Love, Honor, and Obey in Colonial Mexico: Conflicts over Marriage Choice, 1574–1821* (Stanford: Stanford University Press, 1988).

Susan Migden Socolow, "Acceptable Partners: Marriage Choice in Colonial Argentina, 1778–1810," in Asunción Lavrin, ed., *Sexuality and Marriage in Colonial Latin America* (Lincoln: University of Nebraska Press, 1989), 209–246.

Susan Migden Socolow, *The Merchants of Buenos Aires, 1778–1810: Family and Commerce* (Cambridge: Cambridge University Press, 1978).

Michael M. Swann, "The Spatial Dimensions of a Social Process: Marriage and Mobility in Late Colonial Northern Mexico," in David J. Robinson, ed., *Social Fabric and Spatial Structure in Colonial Latin America* (Syracuse: Dellplain, 1979), 117–180.

Lourdes Villafuerte García, "El matrimonio como punto de partida para la formación de la familia: Ciudad de México, siglo XVII," in Pilar Gonzalbo Aizpuru, ed., *Familias novohispanas: Siglos XVI al XIX* (Mexico: El Colegio de México, 1991), 91–99.

SEXUALITY AND SIN

Solange Alberro, "El amancebamiento en los siglos XVI y XVII: Un medio eventual de medrar," in Simposio de Historia de las Mentalidades, *Familia y poder en Nueva España* (Mexico: Instituto Nacional de Antropología e Historia, 1991), 155–166.

Solange Alberro, "Beatriz de Padilla: Mistress and Mother," in David G. Sweet and Gary B. Nash, eds., *Struggle and Survival in Colonial America* (Berkeley: University of California Press, 1981), 247–256.

Solange Alberro, "El matrimonio, la sexualidad y la unidad doméstica entre los cripto judíos de la Nueva España, 1640–1650," in Seminario de Historia de las Mentalidades, *El placer de pecar y el afán de normar* (Mexico: Instituto Nacional de Antropología e Historia, 1987), 103–145.

Ana María Atondo Rodríguez, *El amor venal y la condición femenina en el México colonial* (Mexico: Instituto Nacional de Antropología e Historia, 1992).

Ana María Atondo Rodríguez, "Un caso de lenocinio en la ciudad de México en 1577," in Seminario de Historia de las Mentalidades, *El placer de pecar y el afán de normar* (Mexico: Instituto Nacional de Antropología e Historia, 1987), 81–101.

Osvaldo Barreneche, "'Esos Torpes Dezeos': Delitos y desviaciones sexuales en Buenos Aires, 1760–1810," *Estudios de historia colonial* (La Plata, Argentina), 13 (1993), 29–45.

Jorge René González Marmolejo, "Confesores y mujeres en el Obispado de Puebla, siglo XVIII," in Seminario de Historia de las Mentalidades, *El placer de pecar y el afán de normar* (Mexico: Instituto Nacional de Antropología e Historia, 1987), 147–166.

Ramón Gutiérrez, "From Honor to Love: Transformations of the Meaning of Sexuality in Colonial New Mexico," in Raymond Smith, *Kinship Ideology and Practice in Latin America* (Chapel Hill: University of North Carolina Press, 1984), 237–263.

Ramón A. Gutiérrez, *When Jesus Came, the Corn Mothers Went Away: Marriage, Sexuality, and Power in New Mexico, 1500–1846* (Stanford: Stanford University Press, 1991).

Frédérique Langue, "Las ansias del vivir y las normas del querer: Amores y 'mala vida' en Venezuela colonial," in Elías Pino Iturrieta, ed., *Quimeras de amor, honor y pecado en el siglo XVIII venezolano* (Caracas: Editorial Planeta, 1994), 35–64.

Asunción Lavrin, "Sexuality in Colonial Mexico: A Church Dilemma," in Asunción Lavrin, ed., *Sexuality and Marriage in Colonial Latin America* (Lincoln: University of Nebraska Press, 1989), 47–92.

Lana Lage da Gama Lima, "Aprisionando o Desejo: Confissão e Sexualidade," in Ronaldo Vainfas, ed., *História e Sexualidad no Brasil* (Rio de Janeiro: Edições Graal, 1986), 67–88.

Lana Lage da Gama Lima, "O padre e a moça: O crime de soliticação no Brasil no século XVIII," *Anais do Museu Paulista*, 35 (1986–1987), 15–29.

Lana Lage da Gama Lima, "O Santa Oficio e a moralização do clero no Brasil colonial," *Vozes* (Petrópolis), 83:6 (November–December 1989), 693–703.

Eliane Cristina Lopes, "A bastardia no São Paulo Setecentista," *Populações* (São Paulo), 2 (1995), 1–6.

Silvia Mallo, "Hombres, Mujeres y Honor: Injurias, calumnias y difamación en Buenos Aires (1770–1840)," *Estudios de historia colonial* (La Plata, Argentina), 13 (1993), 9–26.

María Emma Mannarelli, "Mujeres, ilegitimidad y jerarquías sociales en Lima colonial," in Martha Moscoso, ed., *Palabras del silencio: Las mujeres latinoamericanas y su historia* (Quito: Abya-Yala, 1995), 111–145.

María Emma Mannarelli, *Pecados públicos: La ilegitimidad en Lima, siglo XVII* (Lima: Ediciones Flora Tristan, 1993).

Carlos A. Mayo, "'Amistades ilicitas': Las relaciones extramatrimoniales en la campaña bonaerence, 1750–1810," *Cuadernos de historia regional*, 1:2 (April 1985), 3–9.

Laura de Mello e Souza, "O Padre e as Feiticeiras: Notas sobre a Sexualidade no Brasil Colonial," in Ronaldo Vainfas, ed., *História e Sexualidad no Brasil* (Rio de Janeiro: Edições Graal, 1986), 9–18.

Muriel Nazzari, "An Urgent Need to Conceal," in Lyman L. Johnson and Sonya Lipsett-Rivera, eds., *The Faces of Honor: Sex, Shame and Violence in Colonial Latin America* (Albuquerque: University of New Mexico Press, 1998), 103–126.

Maria Beatriz Nizza da Silva, "O problema dos expostos na capitania de São Paulo," *Revista de Historia Economica e Social*, 5 (1980), 95–104.

Elías Pino Iturrieta, ed., *Quimeras de amor, honor y pecado en el siglo XVIII venezolano* (Caracas: Editorial Planeta, 1994).

Renato Pinto Venâncio, "Nos Limites da Sagrada Família: Ilegitimidade e Casamento no Brasil Colonial," in Ronaldo Vainfas, ed., *História e Sexualidad no Brasil* (Rio de Janeiro: Edições Graal, 1986), 107–123.

Mary del Priore, "Deus Dá Licença ao Diabo: A Contravenção nas Festas Religiosas e Igrejas Paulistas no Século XVIII," in Ronaldo Vainfas, ed., *História e Sexualidad no Brasil* (Rio de Janeiro: Edições Graal, 1986) 89–106.

Pablo Rodríguez, *Seducción, amancebamiento y abandono en la colonia* (Bogotá: Fundación Simón y Lola Guberek, 1991).

Stuart B. Schwartz, "Pecar en las colonias. Mentalidades proulares, Inquisición y actitudes hacia la fornicación simple en España, Portugal y las colonias americanas," *Cuadernos de Historia Moderna*, 18 (1997), 51–67.

Seminario de Historia de las Mentalidades, *El placer de pecar y el afán de normar* (Mexico: Instituto Nacional de Antropología e Historia, 1987).

Joan Sherwood, *Poverty in Eighteenth-Century Spain: The Women and Children of the Inclusa* (Toronto: University of Toronto Press, 1988).

Marcela Suárez Escobar and Guadalupe Ríos de la Torre, "Un drama de la vida cotidiana: Los amores de ocasión," in Pilar Gonzalbo Aizpuru, ed., *Imágenes de lo cotidiano* (Mexico: UNAM, 1989), 131–171.

Ann Twinam, "Honor, Sexuality, and Illegitimacy in Colonial Spanish America," in Asunción Lavrin, ed., *Sexuality and Marriage in Colonial Latin America* (Lincoln: University of Nebraska Press, 1989), 118–155.

Ann Twinam, "The Negotiation of Honor," in Lyman L. Johnson and Sonya Lipsett-Rivera, eds., *The Faces of Honor: Sex, Shame and Violence in Colonial Latin America* (Albuquerque: University of New Mexico Press, 1998), 68–102.

Ann Twinam, *Public Lives, Private Secrets: Gender, Honor, Sexuality and Illegitimacy in Colonial Spanish America* (Stanford: Stanford University Press, 1999).

Ronaldo Vainfas, ed., *História e Sexualidad no Brasil* (Rio de Janeiro: Edições Graal, 1986).

Ronaldo Vainfas, "Sodomia, mulheres e inquisição: Notas sobre sexualidade e homossexualismo feminino no Brasil colonial," *Anais du Museu Paulista*, 35 (1986–1987), 233–249.

Ronaldo Vainfas, "A Teia da intriga: Delação e Moralidade na Sociedade Colonial," in Ronaldo Vainfas, ed., *História e Sexualidad no Brasil* (Rio de Janeiro: Edições Graal, 1986), 41–66.

Kathy Waldron, "The Sinners and the Bishop in Colonial Venezuela: The *Visita* of Bishop Mariano Martí, 1771–1784," in Asunción Lavrin, ed.,

Sexuality and Marriage in Colonial Latin America (Lincoln: University of Nebraska Press, 1989), 156–177.

WOMEN AND WEALTH

Edith Couturier, "The Letters of the Countess of Miravalle and the Question of Colonial Women's Biography" (unpublished paper, 1994).

Edith Couturier, "Una viuda aristócrata en la Nueva España del siglo XVIII: La Condesa de Miravalle," *Historia mexicana*, 41:3 (1992), 327–363.

Edith Couturier, "Women in a Noble Family: The Mexican Counts of Regla, 1750–1830," in Asunción Lavrin, ed., *Latin American Women: Historical Perspectives* (Westport, Conn.: Greenwood Press, 1978), 129–149.

François Joseph Depons, *Travels in part of South America, during the Years 1801, 1802, 1803 and 1804 containing a Description of the Captain-Generalship of Carraccas* (London: Richard Phillips, 1806).

Meredith D. Dodge and Rick Hendricks, *Two Hearts, One Soul: The Correspondence of the Condesa de Galve, 1699–96* (Albuquerque: University of New Mexico Press, 1993).

Clara López Beltrán, "La buena vecindad: Las mujeres de élite en la sociedad colonial del siglo XVII," *Colonial Latin American Review*, 5:2 (1996), 219–236.

Robert Ryal Miller, trans. and ed., *Chronicle of Colonial Lima: The Diary of Josephe and Francisco Mugaburu, 1640–1697* (Norman: University of Oklahoma Press, 1975).

Nelly R. Porro, J. Eloísa Astiz, and María Margarita Rospide, *Aspectos de la vida cotidiana en el Buenos Aires virreinal* (Buenos Aires: Universidad de Buenos Aires, 1982).

Nelly Raquel Porro Girardi and Estela Rosa Barbero, *Lo suntuario en la vida cotidana del Buenos Aires virreinal: de lo material a lo espiritual* (Buenos Aires: PRHISCO/Conicet, 1994).

Susan Migden Socolow, "Marriage, Birth, and Inheritance: The Merchants of Eighteenth Century Buenos Aires," *Hispanic American Historical Review*, 60:3 (August 1980), 387–406.

Ann Twinam, "Gender, Crime and Popular Culture: An Ecuadorian Murder Mystery" (unpublished paper, RMCLAS, 1996).

Sergio Vergara Quiroz, *Cartas de mujeres en Chile, 1630–1885* (Santiago de Chile: Editorial Andrés Bello, 1987).

WOMEN AND RELIGION

Solange Alberro, "Herejes, brujas y beatas: mujeres ante el Tribunal del Santo Oficio de la Inquisición en la Nueva España," in Carmen Ramos-

Escandón et al., eds., *Presencia y transparencia: La mujer en la historia de Mexico* (Mexico: El Colegio de México, 1987), 79–94.

Leila Mezan Algranti, *Honradas e devotas: Mulheres da colônia: Condição feminina nos conventos e recolhimentos do Sudeste do Brasil, 1750–1822* (Rio de Janeiro: Livraria José Olympio Editora, 1993).

Electa Arenal and Stacey Schlau, *Untold Sisters: Hispanic Nuns in Their Own Works* (Albuquerque: University of New Mexico Press, 1989).

Alicia Bazarte Martínez, *Las cofradías de españoles en la ciudad de México (1526–1860)* (Mexico: Universidad Autónoma Metropolitana, 1989).

Kathryn Burns, *Colonial Habits: Convents and the Spiritual Economy of Cuzco, Peru* (Durham, N.C.: Duke University Press, 1999).

Edith Couturier, "'For the Greater Service of God': Opulent Foundations and Women's Philanthropy in Colonial Mexico," in Kathleen D. McCarthy, ed., *Lady Bountiful Revisited: Women, Philanthropy, and Power* (New Brunswick, N.J.: Rutgers University Press, 1990), 119–141.

Ann Miriam Gallagher, "The Indian Nuns of Mexico City's *Monasterio* of Corpus Christi, 1724–1821," in Asunción Lavrin, ed., *Latin American Women: Historical Perspectives* (Westport, Conn.: Greenwood Press, 1978), 150–172.

Donald L. Gibbs, "The Economic Activities of Nuns, Friars and Their Conventos in Mid-Colonial Cuzco," *The Americas*, 45:3 (January 1989), 343–362.

Jacqueline Holler, "I, Elena de la Cruz . . ." (M.A. thesis, Simon Fraser University, 1989).

Asunción Lavrin, "El capital eclesiástico y las élites sociales en Nueva España a fines del siglo XVIII," *Mexican Studies/Estudios Mexicanos*, 1:1 (Winter 1985), 1–28.

Asunción Lavrin, "La congregación de San Pedro, una cofradía urbana del México colonial: 1604–1730," *Historia mexicana*, 29 (1979–1980), 562–601.

Asunción Lavrin, "El Convento de Santa Clara de Querétaro: La administración de sus propiedades en el siglo XVII," *Historia mexicana*, 25:1 (July–September 1975), 76–117.

Asunción Lavrin, "Ecclesiastical Reform of Nunneries in New Spain in the Eighteenth Century," *The Americas*, 22:1 (July 1965), 182–203.

Asunción Lavrin, "Female Religious," in Louisa S. Hoberman and Susan M. Socolow, eds., *Cities and Society in Colonial Latin America* (Albuquerque: University of New Mexico Press, 1986), 165–195.

Asunción Lavrin, "La riqueza de los conventos de monjas en Nueva España: estructura y evolución durante el siglo XVIII," *Cahiers des Amériques Latines*, 8 (1973), 91–122.

Asunción Lavrin, "Values and Meaning of Monastic Life for Nuns in Colonial

Mexico," *Catholic Historical Review*, 58 (October 1972), 367–387.

Asunción Lavrin, "La vida femenina como experiencia religiosa: biografía y hagiografía en Hispanoamérica colonial," *Colonial Latin American Review*, 2:1–2 (1993), 27–51.

Asunción Lavrin, "Women in Convents: The Economic and Social Role in Colonial Mexico," in Berenice Carroll, ed., *Liberating Women's History: Theoretical and Critical Essays* (Urbana: University of Illinois Press, 1976), 250–277.

Asunción Lavrin, "Women and Religion in Spanish America," in Rosemary Radford Ruether and Rosemary Skinner Keller, eds., *Women and Religion in America* (New York: Harper and Row, 1983), 2:42–75.

Rosalva Loreto López, "La fundación del convento de la Concepción: Identidad y familias en la sociedad poblana (1593–1643)," in Pilar Gonzalbo Aizpuru, ed., *Familias novohispanas: Siglos XVI al XIX* (Mexico: El Colegio de México, 1991), 163–177.

María Cristina Navarrete, "La mujer bruja en la sociedad colonial: el caso de Paula de Eguiluz," *Región*, 2 (July 1994), 37–47.

Octavio Paz, "Juana Ramírez (Sor Juana Inés de la Cruz)," *Signs*, 5:1 (Autumn 1979), 80–97.

Lucrecia Sáenz Quesada de Sáenz, *María Antonia de Paz y Figueroa* (Buenos Aires: SERVIAM, 1937).

Susan A. Soeiro, "Catarina de Monte Sinay: Nun and Entrepreneur," in David G. Sweet and Gary B. Nash, eds., *Struggle and Survival in Colonial America* (Berkeley: University of California Press, 1981), 257–273.

Susan A. Soeiro, "The Feminine Order in Colonial Bahia, Brazil: Economic, Social, and Demographic Implications, 1677–1800," in Asunción Lavrin, ed., *Latin American Women: Historical Perspectives* (Westport, Conn.: Greenwood Press, 1978), 173–197.

Susan A. Soeiro, "The Social and Economic Role of the Convent: Women and Nuns in Colonial Bahía, 1677–1800," *Hispanic American Historical Review*, 54:2 (1974), 209–232.

Nancy E. van Deusen, "Determing the Boundaries of Virtue: The Discourse of *Recogimiento* among Women in Seventeenth-Century Lima," *Journal of Family History*, 22:4 (October 1997), 373–389.

Nancy Elena Van Deusen, "*Recogimiento* for Women and Girls in Colonial Lima: An Institutional and Cultural Practice" (Ph.D. dissertation, University of Illinois, 1995).

WOMEN AND WORK

Arnold J. Bauer, "Millers and Grinders: Technology and Household Economy in Meso-America," *Agricultural History*, 64:1 (1990), 1–17.

Lolita Gutiérrez Brockington, *The Leverage of Labor: Managing the Cortés*

Haciendas in Tehuantepec, 1588–1688 (Durham, N.C.: Duke University Press, 1990).

Dora Estela Celton, *La población de la provincia de Córdoba a fines del siglo XVIII* (Buenos Aires: Academia Nacional de la Historia, 1993).

Edith Couturier, "Micaela Angela Carrillo: Widow and Pulque Dealer," in David G. Sweet and Gary B. Nash, eds., *Struggle and Survival in Colonial America* (Berkeley: University of California Press, 1981), 362–375.

Susan Deans-Smith, *Bureaucrats, Planters, and Workers: The Making of the Tobacco Monopoly in Bourbon Mexico* (Austin: University of Texas Press, 1992).

Catherine Doenges, "Sources and Speculations Concerning Women's Activity in Provincial Colonial Mexico," *Urban History Workshop Review*, 2 (Spring 1994), 17–24.

Judith Farberman, "Familia, ciclo de vida y economía doméstica: El caso de Salavina, Santiago del Estero, en 1819," *Boletín del Instituto de Historia Argentina y Americana Dr. Emilio Ravignani*, 12 (1995), 33–59.

Deborah Ellen Kanter, "Hijos del pueblo: Family, Community, and Gender in Rural Mexico; The Toluca Region, 1730–1830" (Ph.D. dissertation, University of Virginia, 1993).

Deborah Ellen Kanter, "Native Female Land Tenure and Its Decline in Mexico, 1750–1900," *Ethnohistory*, 42:4 (Fall 1995), 607–616.

John E. Kicza, "La mujer y la vida comercial en la ciudad de México a finales de la colonia," *Revista de Ciencias Sociales y Humanidades* (Mexico), 2:4 (September–December 1991), 39–59.

Elizabeth Kuznesof, "A History of Domestic Service in Spanish America, 1492–1980," in Elsa M. Chaney and Mary Garcia Castro, eds., *Muchachas No More: Household Workers in Latin America and the Caribbean* (Philadelphia: Temple University Press, 1989), 17–35.

John Tate Lanning, *The Royal Protomedicato: The Regulation of the Medical Profession in the Spanish Empire* (Durham, N.C.: Duke University Press, 1985).

Brooke Larson, *Colonialism and Agrarian Transformation in Bolivia: Cochabamba, 1550–1900* (Princeton: Princeton University Press, 1988).

Maria Luiza Marcílio, *A Cidade de São Paulo: Povoamento e Populaçao, 1750–1850* (São Paulo: Universidade de São Paulo, 1974).

Renée Levine Melammed, "A Sixteenth-Century Castilian Midwife and Her Encounter with the Inquisition," in Raymond B. Waddington and Arthur H. Williamson, eds., *The Expulsion of the Jews: 1492 and After* (New York: Garland Publishing, 1994), 53–72.

Paul Morgan, "The Working Women of Guadalajara, 1821: Class and Gender Issues on the Eve of Independence," *Urban History Workshop Review*, 3 (Spring 1996), 17–21.

Juan Javier Pescador, *De bautizados a fieles difuntos: Familia y mentalidades en una parroquia urbana: Santa Catarina de México, 1568–1820* (Mexico: El Colegio de México, 1992).

Juan Javier Pescador, "Vanishing Woman: Female Migration and Ethnic Identity in Late-Colonial Mexico City," *Ethnohistory*, 42:4 (Fall 1995), 617–626.

Susan M. Socolow, "Women of the Frontier: Buenos Aires, 1740–1810 (or The Gaucho Turned Upside Down)," in Donna J. Guy and Thomas E. Sheridan, eds., *Contested Ground: Comparative Frontiers in the Greater South West and the Río de la Plata* (Tucson: University of Arizona Press, 1998), 67–82.

Margaret A. Villanueva, "From Calpixqui to Corregidor: Appropriation of Women's Cotton Textile Production in Early Colonial Mexico," *Latin American Perspectives*, 12:1 (Winter 1985), 17–40.

CRIME, WITCHCRAFT, AND REBELLION

Solange Alberro, *Inquisición y sociedad en México, 1571–1701* (Mexico: Fondo de Cultura Económica, 1988).

Ruth Behar, "Sex and Sin: Witchcraft and the Devil in Late-Colonial Mexico," *American Ethnologist*, 14:1 (February, 1987), 34–54.

Ruth Behar, "Sexual Witchcraft, Colonialism, and Women's Power: Views from the Mexican Inquisition," in Asunción Lavrin, ed., *Sexuality and Marriage in Colonial Latin America* (Lincoln: University of Nebraska Press, 1989), 178–206.

Ruth Behar, "The Visions of a Guachichil Witch in 1599: A Window on the Subjugation of Mexico's Hunter-Gatherers," *Ethnohistory*, 34:2 (1987), 115–138.

Charles R. Boxer, *Women in Iberian Expansion Overseas, 1415–1815: Some Facts, Fancies and Personalities* (New York: Oxford University Press, 1975).

Dolores Bravo and Alejandra Herrera, *Ana Rodríguez de Castro y Aramburu, ilusa, afectadora de santos, falsos milagros y revelaciones divinas: proceso inquisitorial en el Nueva España* (Mexico: Universidad Autónoma Metropolitana, 1984).

Leon Campbell, "Women and the Great Rebellion in Peru, 1780–1783," *The Americas*, 42:2, (October 1985), 163–196.

Carmen Castañeda, "La memoria de las niñas violadas," *Encuentro* (Jalisco), 2:1 (October–December 1984), 41–56.

Martin A. Cohen, *The Martyr: The Story of a Secret Jew and the Mexican Inquisition in the Sixteenth Century* (Philadelphia: Jewish Publication Society of America, 1973).

Alvis E. Dunn, "A Cry at Daybreak: Death, Disease, and Defense of Community in a Highland Ixil-Mayan Village," *Ethnohistory*, 42:4 (Fall 1995), 595–606.

Carlos Garcés, *Brujas y adivinos en Tucumán (siglos XVII y XVIII)* (Jujuy, Argentina: Universidad Nacional de Jujuy, 1997).

François Giraud, "La reacción social ante la violación: Del discurso a la práctica (Nueva España, siglo XVIII)," in Seminario de Historia de las Mentalidades, *El placer de pecar y el afán de normar* (Mexico: Instituto Nacional de Antropología e Historia, 1987), 295–352.

Kevin Gosner, *Soldiers of the Virgin: The Moral Economy of a Colonial Maya Rebellion* (Tucson: University of Arizona Press, 1992).

Fernando Iwasaki Cauti, "Mujeres al borde de la perfección: Rosa de Santa María y las alumbradas de Lima," *Hispanic American Historical Review*, 73:4 (November 1993), 581–613.

Stephanie Merrim, "Catalina de Erauso: From Anomaly to Icon," in Francisco Javier Cevallos-Candau et al., eds., *Coded Encounters: Writing, Gender and Ethnicity in Colonial Latin America* (Amherst: University of Massachusetts Press, 1994), 177–205.

Noemí Quezada, "The Inquisition's Repression of Curanderos," in Mary Elizabeth Perry and Anne J. Cruz, eds., *Cultural Encounters: The Impact of the Inquisition in Spain and the New World* (Berkeley: University of California Press, 1991), 37–57.

Susan M. Socolow, "Women and Crime: Buenos Aires, 1757–1797," *Journal of Latin American Studies*, 12:1 (May 1980), 39–54.

Steve J. Stern, *The Secret History of Gender: Women, Men, and Power in Late Colonial Mexico* (Chapel Hill: University of North Carolina Press, 1995).

William B. Taylor, *Drinking, Homicide, and Rebellion in Colonial Mexican Villages* (Stanford: Stanford University Press, 1979).

Rima de Vallbona, ed., *Vida i sucesos de la monja alferez: Autobiografía atribuida a Doña Catalina de Erauso* (Tempe: ASU Center for Latin American Studies, 1992).

Women and Reform

Silvia M. Arrom, *La mujer mexicana ante el divorcio eclesiastico (1800–1857)* (Mexico: SepSetentas, 1976).

Alicia Bazarte, "El colegio de niñas de Nuestra Señora de la Caridad," in Pilar Gonzalbo Aizpuru, ed., *Imágenes de lo cotidiano* (Mexico: UNAM, 1989), 87–130.

Evelyn May Cherpak, "Devoted Wives and Determined Rebels," *The Americas*, 39:2 (March–April 1987), 32–37.

Evelyn May Cherpak, "The Participation of Women in the Independence Movement in Gran Colombia, 1780–1830," in Asunción Lavrin, ed., *Latin American Women: Historical Perspectives* (Westport, Conn.: Greenwood Press, 1978), 219–234.

Evelyn May Cherpak, "Women and the Independence of Gran Colombia, 1780–1830" (Ph.D. dissertation, University of North Carolina, Chapel Hill, 1973).

María Teresa García Schlegal, "Las mujeres de la Illustración," in Magdala Velásquez Toro, ed., *Las mujeres en la historia de Colombia*, vol. 1: *Mujeres, historia y política* (Bogotá, 1995), 60–82.

John Tate Lanning, *The Royal Protomedicato: The Regulation of the Medical Profession in the Spanish Empire* (Durham, N.C.: Duke University Press, 1985), chap. 13, "Government and Obstetrics."

Bernard Lavallé, "Amor, amores y desamor, en el sur peruano a finales del siglo XVIII," in Susana Menéndez and Barbara Potthast, eds., *Mujer y familia en América Latina, siglos XVIII–XX* (Malaga: AHILA, 1996), 27–56.

Asunción Lavrin, "Problems and Policies in the Administration of Nunneries in Mexico, 1800–1835," *The Americas*, 28:1 (July 1971), 57–77.

Johanna S. R. Mendelson, "The Feminine Press: The View of Women in the Colonial Journals of Spanish America, 1790–1810," in Asunción Lavrin, ed., *Latin American Women: Historical Perspectives* (Westport, Conn.: Greenwood Press, 1978), 198–218.

Gary Miller, "Bourbon Social Engineering: Women and Conditions of Marriage in Eighteenth-Century Venezuela," *The Americas*, 46:3 (January 1990), 261–290.

Raul A. Molina, *Historia de los divorcios en el período hispánico* (Buenos Aires: Fuentes Históricas y Genealógicas Argentinas, 1991).

Arij Ouwenell, "No hay más tortillas para Marcos Antonio (México 1780)," in Susana Menéndez and Barbara Potthast, eds., *Mujer y familia en América Latina, siglos XVIII–XX* (Malaga: AHILA, 1996), 57–68.

Matthew Restall, "'He wished it in vain': Subordination and Resistance among Maya Women in Post-Conquest Yucatan," *Ethnohistory*, 42:4 (Fall 1995), 577–594.

José G. Rigau-Pérez, "Surgery at the Service of Theology: Postmortem Cesarean Sections in Puerto Rico and the Royal Cedula of 1804," *Hispanic American Historical Review*, 75:3 (August 1995), 377–404.

Bernd Schröter, "Acerca de la posición de la mujer en el contexto del matrimonio en una región fronteriza de la América hispánica a fines del período colonial. Resultados y desiderata," in Susana Menéndez and Barbara Potthast, eds., *Mujer y familia en América Latina, siglos XVIII–XX* (Malaga: AHILA, 1996), 69–96.

Susan Migden Socolow, *The Bureaucrats of Buenos Aires, 1769–1819: Amor al real servicio* (Durham, N.C.: Duke University Press, 1987).

INDEX